Winning with Words

Winning with Words

Volume 2

How to Speak Effectively

Published by

World Book, Inc.
a Scott Fetzer company
Chicago

Acknowledgments

The publishers gratefully acknowledge the following for permission to use copyrighted material.

17 The story of the Christian and the lion is reprinted from *New Speaker's Handbook,* by permission of Sylvia Simmons Newmann.

21 The story about the man, the woman, and a dog is from *The Public Speaker's Treasure Chest,* fourth edition, by Herbert V. Prochnow and Herbert V. Prochnow, Jr. Copyright © 1942 by Harper and Row, Publishers, Inc. Copyright © 1964, 1977, 1986 by Herbert V. Prochnow and Herbert V. Prochnow, Jr. Reprinted by permission of Harper & Row, Publishers, Inc.

70 The story about the "audience of one" is from *Speakers on the Spot,* by Edgar Bernhard. Copyright © 1977 by Parker Publishing Company, Inc. Reprinted by permission of Parker Publishing Company, Inc.

75 The two speech openers are from *Speakers on the Spot* and are reprinted by permission of Parker Publishing Company, Inc.

119 Excerpt from *Jaws,* by Peter Benchley. Copyright © 1974 by Peter Benchley. Reprinted by permission of Doubleday & Company, Inc., and Andre Deutsch Ltd.

120 "Silence" reprinted with permission of Macmillan Publishing Company and Faber and Faber Ltd from *Collected Poems* by Marianne Moore, renewed 1963 by Marianne Moore and T.S. Eliot.
Excerpt from "The Road Not Taken" from *The Poetry of Robert Frost,* edited by Edward Connery Lathem. Copyright 1916, © 1969, 1979 by Holt, Rinehart and Winston. Copyright 1944, 1969 by Robert Frost. Reprinted by permission of Holt, Rinehart and Winston, Publishers, and Jonathan Cape Ltd.
"Dream Boogie" reprinted by permission of Harold Ober Associates, Incorporated. Copyright 1951 by Langston Hughes. Copyright renewed 1979 by George Houston Bass.

141 "Freedom, Our Most Precious Heritage" reprinted by permission of Scott Smalstig.

142 "Valedictory Speech" reprinted by permission of Lynn Bowen, Mary Campbell, Jenny Gill, Jill Hubbard, Joanne Hubbard, and Erin Miller.

149 Campaign speech reprinted by permission of Leslie Redman.

179 Excerpts from "Northwestern Endicott Report 1975," copyright 1975 by Northwestern University. Reprinted by permission of Victor R. Lindquist.

180 Excerpts from "Northwestern Endicott Report 1983," copyright 1982 by Northwestern University. Reprinted by permission of Victor R. Lindquist.

200 Plumber story from "How to Clear the Lines of Communication," by Dr. Edgar Dale and Dr. Jeanne Chall in *Educational Trend*, Jan., 1950. Copyright, Croft Educational Services. Used by permission.

255 Questions for parent/teacher conferences excerpted from *You Can Improve Your Child's School*, by William Rioux, copyright © 1980 by National Committee for Citizens in Education. Reprinted by permission of William Rioux.

The writers gratefully acknowledge the following for their assistance in compiling the manuscript: Henriette Kaplan, Father Justin Belitz, Geraldine Drexler, Deborah Simmons, Kathleen Oehler, Tamara Tudor, Alfred Rowe Edyvean, Martha Kelsey Eberts, John F. Barnes, Clem Butts, George Faeber, Gary F. Faust, Richard Graver, Merril Lappin, James Liebel, Thomas E. Meyers, Donald Caplinger, Lee Lonzo, Fred Chandler, Pat Delello, Rita Roesinger, Don Allen, Dr. James Dashiell, Dr. Robert Nelson, Judge Judy Profett, Judge Paul Johnson, Donald Bozic D.D.S., David Zoeller, Dottie Hancock, Pat Carey, John Pearce, Sam Robinson, DeWayne Akin, Nancylee Buckley, James A. McKinney, Michael J. Burchick, George Plaster, Peter Dehmel, Jane Gladden, Karen Nelson, Elizabeth Crosley, Jean Sauriol, June Correll, Evelyn Rockhold, Jane Brown, Lauryl Darnell, Judy Waugh, Bob Wise, Chris Little, Don Schroeder, Marcine Young, Peter Barry, and Pat Gilbert.

Photo Acknowledgments
All photography, unless otherwise noted below, is the property of World Book, Inc., photographed by Brent Jones.

68 AP/Wide World
72 Mimi Forsyth, Monkmeyer
78 Steve Leonard
93 Illinois State Historical Society
127 Joe Di Dio, National Education Association
129 Joe Di Dio, National Education Association
133 *World Book* photo
138 Historical Pictures Service
143 Rhoda Sidney, Monkmeyer
148 *World Book* photo by Steve Hale
154 Mimi Forsyth, Monkmeyer
160 Joe Di Dio, National Education Association
162 © Richard Gross, The Stock Market

171 CBS News
204 H. Armstrong Roberts
214 George Bellerose/Stock,Boston
218 Mimi Forsyth, Monkmeyer
225 *World Book* photo by Steve Hale
229 Sybil Shelton, Monkmeyer
232 © Joseph Schuyler/ Stock,Boston
238 © Hazel Hankin/Stock,Boston
251 *World Book* photo by Steve Hale
262 Rhoda Sidney, Monkmeyer
268 Steve Leonard
272 H. Armstrong Roberts
281 H. Armstrong Roberts
293 Bill Anderson, Monkmeyer
298 Steve Leonard

Staff

Publisher
William H. Nault

Editorial

Editor in chief
Robert O. Zeleny

Executive editor
Dominic J. Miccolis

Associate editor
Maureen M. Mostyn

Staff editor
Karen Zack Ingebretsen

Permissions editor
Janet T. Peterson

Writers
Marjorie Eberts
Margaret Gisler

Researchers
Karen Fleischer
Kathy Florio

Art

Executive art director
William Hammond

Art director
Roberta Dimmer

Assistant art director
Joe Gound

Photography director
John S. Marshall

Photographs editor
Carol Parden

Designers
Diane Beasley
Harry Voigt
Valerie Nelson

Illustrations
William Petersen
Nan Brooks

Product production

Executive director
Peter Mollman

Manufacturing
Joseph C. La Count, **director**

Research and development
Henry Koval, **manager**

Pre-press services
Jerry Stack, **director**

Production control
Lori Frankel
Randi Park

Adviser
Pamela Cooper, Ph.D.
Assistant Professor
Speech Education
Northwestern University
Evanston, Illinois

Contents

Introduction

No matter who you are or what you do, you spend part of
every day speaking. How effectively you speak determines
such important things in your life as whether you get
hired for a challenging job, get elected to the city council,
or communicate successfully with your family and
friends. This book is designed to help you speak effectively on special occasions and in all kinds of everyday
situations. It will help you say the right things as you interview for the job that you have always wanted as well as
when you go through a receiving line at a wedding.

No two people speak alike. No two people have the need
to learn the same things about speaking. This book pre-
sents a variety of material that allows you to select what
you need to learn to become an effective speaker in every
situation in which you need to speak. There are check-
lists that help you determine whether or not you have acquired specific speaking skills. The book also gives you
activities that allow you to develop these skills.

To get the most out of this book, the first thing that
you need to know is how it is organized. It has been set
up so that you can read the book straight through from
beginning to end or skip around, selecting sections as
you need them. It is suggested that everyone read the
first four sections, which are on the basics of effective
speaking. Then you may elect to read the sections on specific speech situations as you need them.

The book is divided into nine sections. Each section
helps you learn different speaking skills through a variety
of activities built right into the text. Familiarize yourself
now with what you can read about in each section.

Preparing and Delivering a Speech.   Find out what it takes to prepare and deliver a speech. Read about how to study an audience, choose an appropriate subject, gather materials, and organize your speech.

Using Speaking Tools.   Discover how to enhance what you say by learning the proper use of such speaking tools as the microphone, slide projector, overhead projector, charts, maps, and handouts. Learn all the things that you must do before making a speech to ensure that the setting will maximize the effect of your speech.

Stage Fright and the Unexpected.   Learn how to master stage fright, the number one fear of all speakers. Study how to cope with the unexpected problems that seem to appear in every speaking situation.

Improving Your Speaking Voice.   Learn how to get rid of common voice problems like speaking too loudly, softly, harshly, or rapidly. Find out how to avoid speech spoilers, like mispronouncing words and adding those unwelcome speech demons *and, uh, ur,* and *you know* to everything that you say. Learn all the basic facts about lisping and stuttering.

Speaking at School.   Read about the fundamentals of speaking in all kinds of school situations, from answering questions in class to making announcements over the P.A., giving oral reports and book reports, taking part in class discussions, trying out for a part in a play, talking to teachers and counselors, and making a valedictory speech. Be sure to check out whether you have mastered the basics of parliamentary procedure.

Speaking at Work. Read about what to say as well as what not to say in job interviews, evaluations, and reports. Find out how to talk to the people you work with. Learn about participating in and leading meetings that accomplish something. And finally, find out what the speaking secrets of successful salespersons are.

Speaking in the Community. Find out how to speak effectively with doctors, lawyers, accountants, salespersons, police officers, teachers, tradespersons, receptionists, and other people in your community. Discover what to say when you lead and participate in club meetings; raise funds; solicit votes; serve as a juror or witness; talk to your children's teachers, counselors, and principals; or publicize an event on radio or TV.

Speaking with People You Know. Learn the conversational secrets you need for talking with your family and friends. Discover how to handle introductions and small talk at parties. Find out how to say the right thing at weddings, funerals, and other social gatherings.

Speaking on the Telephone. Determine how to put a smile in your voice, make emergency calls, and sell on the telephone.

Everyone understands the need to speak effectively in his or her personal life, on the job, at school, and in the community. What people may not understand is that it is possible to improve their speech and to become effective speakers. Use this book to find out which of your speaking skills need to be improved. Then follow the book's suggestions to become an effective speaker. You can do it.

PREPARING AND DELIVERING A

Speech

You will find yourself in many different types of speaking situations in your lifetime. The speaking situation that calls for the most preparation and organization is that of delivering a speech. Whether your speech is a three-minute oral book report in school or an hour-long presentation to co-workers at your place of employment, all formal speaking situations call for a good deal of preparation beforehand.

Few people ever prepared for public speaking as the Greek orator Demosthenes. People are still talking about the way he taught himself to deliver a speech. As a young man in ancient Greece, Demosthenes was determined to be a lawyer-politician, despite his harsh and unpleasant voice, weak lungs, and awkward manner.

To overcome these difficulties, Demosthenes practiced speaking everywhere. At the seashore, he filled his mouth with pebbles and then shouted to hear himself over the noise of the wind and waves. He delivered speeches to himself while running up and down the hills. These efforts helped Demosthenes to become an outstanding speaker.

You probably don't need to prepare yourself for speaking as strenuously as Demosthenes did. Yet there are some elements of speech preparation and delivery that no one can ignore. In this section, you are going to explore preparing and delivering a speech.

Preparing Your Speech

A good speech is like a good trip. You begin by thinking about the purpose of your trip or speech. To plan a good trip, the traveler keeps in mind who is going, what he or she wants to do, and the amount of time available for the trip. To plan a good speech, the speaker thinks about the audience, what they want or are willing to hear, and how much time is available for the speech. Before taking a trip or delivering a speech, you gather information. This helps you plan the route you will take. A good speech is not a Sunday drive; it is a well-planned journey. Bon voyage!

Choosing Your Subject

Sometimes the subject of a speech is given to you. At other times, you have the task of choosing the subject. Don't just choose any subject for your speech. Consider the audience and the occasion of the speech.

Don't choose a subject that is so broad that it would take too long to cover. For example, if you are speaking to a garden club, the subject of flowers is too broad to cover in one

Giving a speech is like taking a trip: both call for lots of planning in advance.

speech. Even the subject of spring flowers is vast. However, the subject how to raise tulips is not too broad. You will be able to cover this subject in one speech.

Audience

Because you find a subject interesting is no reason that it will capture the attention of your audience. The only way to choose a good subject is to size up your audience and tailor your speech accordingly. You should know the average age, the sex, the nationality, the occupation, and the educational and social background of your audience. Along with this information, you should know the interests, values, and goals that the people in your audience share. It is also helpful to know how many people will be in the audience. There is a big difference between speaking to 10 persons and 200 persons. If you know that you are talking to a group of 100 middle-aged women who live in high-rise apartments, you will know that you should talk about raising houseplants instead of growing a beautiful lawn. If you are talking to a small group of pharmacists, it would probably be more appropriate to talk about the chemical compositions of different plants than about how to make floral arrangements for a church.

Occasion

You know what your audience is like. Besides fitting the audience, your speech must fit the occasion. Don't give a talk at a sports banquet on being a champion if the team has lost every game in the season. Instead, talk about the lasting advantages of team spirit.

Always find out if your speech is for a holiday, a special event, or a regular club meeting. Be sure to determine how long you will have to speak and at what time you will speak. An audience may be sleepy at eight o'clock in the morning and tired at five in the afternoon. They will always be bored if your speech is too long.

Knowing Where You Are Going

You can sometimes ramble on without a purpose when you are talking to a friend. But when you are making a speech, you need to know where you are going. You need to write down the specific purpose of your speech in one sentence. Study these examples:

My purpose is to convince an apartment dweller that a bird is an ideal pet.

My purpose is to explain how to insulate an attic.

My purpose is to tell humorous stories about being a detective in a department store.

Use your purpose sentence to keep you on the right track as you plan your speech.

Kinds of Speeches

Your purpose sentence will help you select the kind of speech that you are going to make. Most speeches are either to inform, to entertain, or to persuade. Each speech often contains elements of all three of these kinds of speeches.

To Inform

When giving a speech to inform, your purpose is to give information to the audience. This speech is to tell how, what, or why. The history teacher who explains to the class how the British Parliament works is giving a speech to inform. Coaches give speeches to inform when they tell their team members how to improve skills in a sport. Doctors give this kind of speech when they explain how to use the Heimlich maneuver to prevent a person from choking.

When you give a speech to inform, you must present the information in a way that will let your audience clearly understand it. Keep in mind as you are planning your speech that speaking tools are a great help. Use a chart to show muscles when you are telling people how to develop an exercise program. Show the equipment when you are talking to an audience about what they will need to scuba dive. Speaking tools are discussed in the next chapter.

To Entertain

Most speeches have parts that are designed to entertain the audience, but a speech to entertain must be humorous from beginning to end. The purpose of this speech is to get your audience to relax and enjoy themselves. You want them to laugh and clap. These speeches should have a definite purpose such as:

To describe what makeup will look like in the future.

To characterize how nervous an employee feels before starting a new job.

To tell how to give kittens, gerbils, or white mice away.

Speeches to entertain frequently begin with a humorous story like this:

Once upon a time, in the days of the Roman Empire, a mob was gathered in the Coliseum to watch as a Christian was thrown to a hungry lion. The spectators cheered as the wild beast went after its prey. But the Christian quickly whispered something in the lion's ear and the beast backed away with obvious terror on his face. No amount of calling and foot stomping by the audience could get the lion to approach the Christian again. Fearlessly, the Christian walked from the arena.

The Emperor was so amazed at what had happened that he sent for the Christian and offered him his freedom if he would say what he had done to make the ferocious beast cower in fear. The Christian bowed before the Emperor and said, "I merely whispered in the lion's ear: 'After dinner, you'll be required to say a few words.' "

It is always flattering to receive an invitation to address an audience as the after-dinner speaker. It is also somewhat unnerving to arrive at the moment of truth and wonder whether you have enough to say to keep a well-fed audience awake for another half hour.

To Persuade

The speech to persuade is probably the most difficult to make because you are trying to convince your audience to take action or to believe something. Politicians are faced with this task constantly. First, they have to persuade you to believe that they should be elected to an office; then they have to persuade you to actually vote for them.

To make a successful persuasion speech, you must know your audience. Decide whether statistics and facts or an emotional appeal will succeed best with them.

Gathering Materials

Briton Hadden, one of the founders of *Time* magazine, once said, "People talk too much about what they don't know." You don't want to be accused of this when you are giving a speech. Find out more about your subject than you will ever use in your speech. This lets you select the best materials on your subject. Most speakers begin their search for material by taking stock of what they know before going to other sources.

Your Knowledge

Begin by asking yourself, "What do I know about this subject?" Jot down these facts. You may find that you have made quite a list. Refine this list by next asking yourself, "What does my audience need to know about the subject?" You may wish to circle these items. Look at your list again and decide if there are any large gaps in it that need to be filled with information from other sources. At the same time, note the items that you want to check for accuracy. Now you are ready to scout out other sources.

Other People

Talk to people who have special knowledge of your subject. Test your own ideas by finding out whether other people agree or disagree with your thinking and why. Use interviews to find out what others think about a subject. Imagine what different viewpoints you could collect on gun control from a police officer, an avid hunter, and someone who was just shot by a burglar. If you want to find out what a fairly large number of persons think about several issues, conduct a survey. Be sure to write down all the ideas that you have gathered.

Reading

For many subjects, you will find much of your information through reading. Become well acquainted with the materials in your local library. Enlist the librarian's help when you cannot find a specific bit of information. Before you read anything, decide if you are reading it for general ideas, details, or definitions. Get in the habit of "talking" to the material as you read it. Ask questions about what is on each page. Take notes on the information that you wish to remember so that you won't have to go back and reread the material.

Organizing Materials

You cannot have an effective speech if you constantly jump from one idea to another. Your audience will feel like they are wandering in the desert, searching for an oasis as they try to identify the main points of your speech. You need to organize the information that you have gathered into an outline. It is the plan of your speech.

You are probably familiar with the mechanics of an out-line. Use the Roman numerals (I, II, etc.) to indicate the main points of your speech. These are the points that you hope your audience will remember. They must support the purpose of your speech. Develop each main point with two or more subpoints. Use capital letters to indicate these divisions. Each subpoint can have two or more subordinate points. Be careful not to subdivide your outline so far that

Researching the subject of your speech is one of the most important steps in your preparation.

you have written a speech, not an outline. Write the main points and subpoints as complete sentences to make you develop your points carefully. Your skeleton outline should look like this:

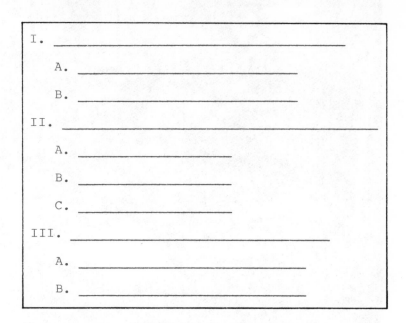

Putting Your Speech Together

In the fourth century B.C., Plato described the organization of a speech:

> Every speech ought to be put together like a living creature, with a body of its own, so as to be neither without head nor without feet, but to have both a middle and extremities, described proportionately to each other and to the whole.

Today, 22 centuries later, a speech is still organized in the same way. It should have an introduction, a body, and a conclusion.

Introduction

In the introduction, you are going to invite your audience to listen to the subject of your speech. To get the audience to accept your invitation, you have to win both their attention and support. You won't have much time to do so in a short speech. You can begin with standard remarks about the community, audience, weather, and the like. Or you can be more inventive and begin with a challenging question, drastic statement, startling statistic, interesting quotation, funny anecdote, or joke. Whatever your choice, make sure it leads into the subject of your speech. Look at these different openers for a speech about a dog as a faithful companion:

When Ulysses, the Greek hero, returned home after 20 years of adventure, the only creature to recognize him was his dog. (statement)

About *226 million* people live in the United States today, and they have about *50 million* dogs. (statement)

Who were the first animals to be tamed? (question)

The more I see of men, the better I like dogs. (quotation)
Madame Roland

For months he had been her devoted admirer. Now, at long last, he had collected up sufficient courage to ask her the most momentous of all questions.
"There are quite a lot of bachelors," he began, "but there comes a time when one longs for the companionship of another being—a being who will regard one as perfect, as an idol; whom one can treat as one's absolute property; who will be kind and faithful when times are hard; who will share one's joys and sorrows—"
To his delight he saw a sympathetic gleam in her eyes. Then she nodded in agreement.
"So you're thinking of buying a dog?" she said. "I think it's a fine idea. Do let me help you choose one!" (funny story)

Body

The heart of your speech is the body. Here you discuss the main points and subpoints of your speech. Limit the number of main points. Don't try to cover more than a few in any one speech. If you do, you won't do justice to each point, nor will the audience remember the points. Arrange the points in a logical order that your audience can understand. If you are using a time-order approach to tell how to change a tire, don't tell the audience to get out the jack after they have taken off the wheel. Be sure to identify the introduction of each new point by words such as *first, second, next, then, last,* or *finally.* Emphasize the key points by saying things like, "It is important to," "Don't forget," and "You need to know."

Conclusion

Your final chance to inform, entertain, or persuade your audience comes in the conclusion. Don't put new information in the conclusion. It is the time to review and summarize the main points of your speech. This isn't repeating but restating what you have said earlier. Don't use the same words in the conclusion that you used in the introduction and body of your speech. There are over 600,000 words in the English language. Put variety into your speech.

Wrap your speech up with a quotation, challenge, story, appeal, summary, or humor. Study the way these speeches ended:

Such are the measures which I advise, which I propose; adopt them, and even yet, I believe, our prosperity may be reestablished. If any man has better advice to offer, let him communicate it openly. Whatever you determine, I pray to all the gods for happy result.
  Demosthenes

And like the old soldier of that ballad, I now close my military career and just fade away, an old soldier who tried to do his duty as God gave him the light to see that duty. Good-bye.
  General Douglas MacArthur

As I now glance at the hour, I am reminded of a poem:
  "The coffee's cold, the sherbet wanes,
  The speech drones on and on . . .
  Oh Speaker, heed the ancient rule:
  Be brief. Be gay. Be gone!"
  Ross Smyth

How you put your speech together is your decision. Most people begin by planning the body of their speech, since you cannot really create the introduction until you know what you are going to say in the main part.

Speech Helpers

Decide now on whether you want to use a script, an outline, or note cards when delivering your speech. Using any one of these tools will prevent you from forgetting any important parts of your speech, getting away from the subject of your speech, or going blank about what to say next.

Card (1):

Pioneer Life in America.

The pioneers.
A. Conquering the wilderness.
B. Establishing the frontier.

Card (2):

Moving westward.
A. Crossing the Appalachians.
B. How the pioneers traveled.

Card (3):

A pioneer settlement.
A. A pioneer home (show model).
B. Education and religion.
C. Social activity.
D. Indian attacks.

Card (4):

Crossing the plains.
A. The wagon trains.
B. Life on the trail.

You prepared an outline when you organized your speech. You can expand this outline into the script for your speech. Since you don't talk like you write, be sure that your speech sounds more like a conversation than a composition. Keep your sentences short. Use informal language.

Many speakers prefer to reduce their outlines to a key-word or phrase outline or to reduce them further to notes. Write the outline or notes on 3"-by-5" cards. Then you can refer to the cards as you talk to your audience instead of reading a script. Helpful hints for using an outline or note cards include:

Write on only one side of a card.
Number the order of the cards.
Don't clutter your cards with writing.
Write your words large enough to read.
Underline key points with a different color.
Write out quotes and statistics.

Many speakers like to use note cards to help them remember what they want to say.

Practicing Your Speech

Practice does make perfect. You don't have a speech until you know what you are going to say and how you are going to say it. Practice lets you iron the bugs out of your speech. It gives you a smooth speech with a steady flow of ideas.

Before you begin to practice your speech, you must choose how you are going to give it. You have three choices. You can memorize your speech, read it, or speak extemporaneously. There are advantages and disadvantages to each choice:

Memory. Giving a long speech from memory is a dying art. Today most memorized speeches are for ceremonial occasions like graduations, toasts, and eulogies. They are a good choice when it is important for a speaker to know exactly what should be said. They have the flaw of sounding canned. They are dangerous if a memory block occurs. They can require a considerable effort. Memorizing a 15-minute speech is roughly equivalent to memorizing one-half of this chapter.

Reading. Politicians and businesspersons often read their speeches because they do not wish to be misquoted or misunderstood. Others like this type of speech because there is no way that they can fumble a word. It is a good choice when words are important. But it is a poor choice if you forget to look at your audience and stop communicating with them. Beware: few people are skilled enough to read a complete speech successfully.

Extemporization. The speech of choice for most people is an extemporaneous speech. It is a speech that is prepared in advance. It is delivered from an outline or note cards. It frees the speaker to adjust the speech to the changing reactions of the audience.

Not having the speech memorized or written out may make the insecure speaker feel nervous. The secret for giving a successful extemporaneous speech is to know the order in which you will present the main points of the speech. Fix this order in your mind before you begin practicing what you are going to say. As you practice, avoid starting over if you forget a point. It disrupts the flow of the entire speech and will give you a speech with an over-rehearsed introduction.

Practice is your rehearsal for the actual speech. Make it as much like the speaking occasion as you possibly can. If

Practice your speech in front of a mirror in order to evaluate your movements and gestures.

you are using a speaker's stand, make one for practice by putting a box on a table. If you are using notes, script, slides, charts, models, or other speaking tools, practice with them. During practice, refine your delivery. Make eye contact with the chairs, gesture to the lamps, smile at the plants. They are your audience; don't ignore them.

You can check that you are on target during your practice sessions in several ways. Time your speeches. Add or subtract material until your time is within 10 per cent of the allotted time. For a 10-minute speech, you should talk between 9 and 11 minutes. Evaluate how effective your eye contact, facial expressions, movements, and gestures are by giving your speech in front of a mirror. To know how you really sound, record your speech. If you have a video recorder, you can use it to check how you look and sound. To find out what an audience thinks of your speech, present it to your family and friends. When you discover an area of your speech that needs to be improved, work on it. Practice your speech until you feel comfortable with it. Few people ever practice too much.

Checklist for Preparing Your Speech

Successful speakers follow the Boy Scout's motto. They are prepared. Not only do they create and practice their speeches, they also tend to the other details that are a part of an effective speech. Some of these details must be taken care of several days before the speech:

Find out the exact time and place of your speech.

Learn the best route to the location.

Know what the occasion of your speech is.

Determine the makeup and size of your audience.

Find out who will introduce you. Provide a written introduction for this person.

Determine if anyone should be acknowledged in your speech.

Check out the setting.

Get your speaking tools in order.

Select your clothing for the speech.

Give yourself plenty of time on your speech day to tend to the things you have to do as well as to handle the unexpected things that may occur. Don't forget to:

Pack your speaking tools.

Rehearse your speech for the last time.

Get dressed early.

Arrive where you are going to speak one-half hour to an hour early.

Check out the setting and the equipment to make sure that they are as you arranged.

Find a quiet place to sit down and relax before beginning your speech.

You can get into trouble if you neglect even a tiny detail in your preparation. A speaker, during the height of the Cold War, was scheduled to appear after the meal at a banquet closing a business convention in Milwaukee. To make his speech more realistic, he had dressed as a Soviet naval officer for the occasion. He arrived at the hotel in good time, but as he entered the corridor leading to the banquet hall, a guard stopped him. Did he have a ticket? Although long experience had made him mindful of the details of preparing for a speech, this time he had neglected one. No one had mentioned tickets, and he had not asked. The guard marked the speaker as a gate-crasher, and, considering his attire, a rather peculiar one. The speaker finally found a police officer who would admit him. But after that day, even before he discussed time, place, or even fees, this speaker always asked, "Do I need a ticket to get in?"

How Much Time to Prepare?

How long will it take you to prepare your speech? Mark Twain once said it took him three weeks to develop an impromptu speech. It took President Johnson and 24 speech writers six weeks to write his 40-minute State of the Union message for 1964. How long it takes you will depend in part on how important the speech is to you. Make sure that you start your speech in time to gather and organize the materials that you will need. Few people ever start early enough to totally avoid a last-minute rush. Don't forget to include time to practice your speech.

Delivering Your Speech

The moment of truth is at hand. You have just been introduced. Move confidently to the speaker's stand. Arrange your notes with care. Take the time to adjust or clip on the microphone if you are using one. Then stand up straight on both feet. Don't rush immediately into your speech. Give your audience time to shift in their chairs to see you. Look over the audience. Let your eyes rest on several individuals. Take two deep breaths. Smile. Begin your speech with the opening lines that you memorized.

What Is Delivery?

Actions speak as loudly as words in a speech. Each speech is really two speeches. There is what you say and how you say it. Your delivery is how you say the content of your speech to the audience. Delivery has two aspects. It is what the audience sees. It is what the audience hears.

Your appearance, gestures, and movements are important factors in your communication with the audience.

Body Actions

From the minute you walk to the speaker's stand, you are communicating with the audience. People know at once whether you are interested or bored with your subject. They can see whether you are nervous or confident. The way you appear, stand, move, gesture, look, and react to the audience should give them the same message that they are hearing.

Appearance

You expect to see lawyers dressed differently in court-rooms and at football games. Your audience expects you to be appropriately dressed for the occasion. Avoid any extremes in style that can steal attention from your speech. Be neatly groomed. You will be more effective if your clothing is pressed and your hair is brushed. Don't let your appearance alienate your audience.

Posture

Stand or sit in a comfortable position so that you are relaxed when you are speaking. The audience does not want to see a rigid tin soldier or a rag doll. Avoid slouching because it limits the air supply to your lungs and doesn't let you use your best voice.

Movement

It is unnecessary to stand perfectly still when you are speaking. A little movement can be used effectively to emphasize a point, to call attention to a new topic, or to move to a chair or the chalkboard. However, beware of excessive movement, for it detracts from your speech. Don't pace the stage like an expectant father or shift your feet back and forth like a dancer.

Facial expressions help add variety and meaning to what you are saying.

Gestures

When you talk to your family and friends, you automatically use your fingers, hands, and arms to add meaning to your words. Don't change when you talk to your audience. Use the same gestures for a speech. Do try to avoid distracting habits like jingling coins, tugging at your belt, or playing with your glasses.

Eye Contact

If you continually look out the window during your speech, your audience will be distracted and wonder what is happening outside. Look at the people as you speak, not just the people in the front row but everywhere. Eye contact lets the people know that you are talking personally to them. It also lets you know if they are receiving your message. You can see if they are enthused, bored, or restless and make necessary adjustments in your speech.

Facial Expression

The furrowed brow, the jutting chin, the wide smile, and the raised eyebrows give additional meaning to what you are saying. Avoid giving your speech with a deadpan expression; share your feelings with your audience.

It is important to maintain eye contact with your audience.

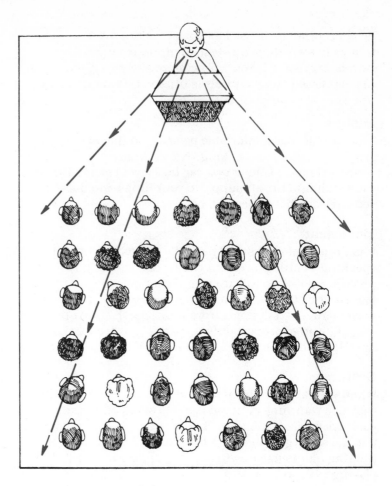

Voice Elements

People frequently say, "It's not what you say, but how you say it." From the minute you open your mouth to begin your speech, the pitch, intensity (volume), rate, and quality of your voice play a large role in determining how the audience reacts.

Pitch

If you deliver your speech in a monotone or the same up-and-down pitch pattern, your voice will bore your listeners. Problems with pitch should be corrected in practice sessions before you reach the speaker's stand.

Intensity

Audiences do not enjoy hearing voices that are too loud or soft. Intensity refers to the volume of your voice. Adjust the intensity of your voice by observing whether people in the back of the room can hear comfortably or not.

It is <u>important</u>, of course, to <u>recognize</u> that the average citizen today is <u>better</u> educated and <u>more</u> knowledgeable than the average citizen of a <u>generation</u> ago-/-more <u>literate</u>, and exposed to more <u>mathematics</u>, <u>literature</u>, and <u>science</u>.// The <u>positive</u> impact of this fact on the

It's a good idea to mark words for emphasis and places for pauses in your speech. It helps add variety to your voice.

Rate

Professional speakers have a wide range of speaking rates. Speeches are usually given at a slower rate than everyday conversation. Vary your rate to meet the occasion. At a eulogy, don't speak like a racetrack announcer.

Quality

If your voice has too much nasality, denasality, hoarseness, harshness, or breathiness, these undesirable characteristics may cause your audience to tune out what you are saying. The sound of your voice irritates them.

It is not just the way your voice sounds that is important in a speech, it is the way the words sound. They need to be articulated clearly and pronounced correctly. The important words need to be stressed. Raise or lower the intensity of your voice to call attention to a word or a point in your speech. Tips on adjusting your voice appear in the chapter titled "Improving Your Speaking Voice."

Speaking with Sincerity

The first step to becoming a good speaker is being well prepared. The next step is to deliver the speech in such a way that your body and voice accurately communicate your message to your listeners. Finally, to be a good speaker, you must convince the audience that you are honest and sincere in what you are saying. Abraham Lincoln had this ability. President Harry Truman also had this ability. If you choose a subject that you believe in, you can too.

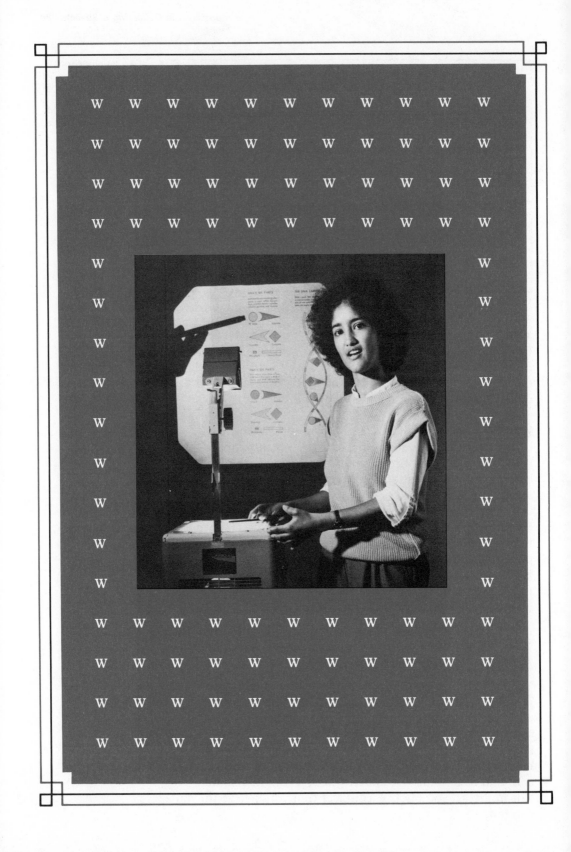

USING SPEAKING Tools

I magine that you are listening to a speech about birdcalling. Even with the best description, would you really know what a bobwhite quail looks or sounds like? Speakers who rely on words alone may find it difficult to convey that this kind of quail is a plump bird that looks like it is wearing a speckled jacket and that it has a whistling call that sounds like *ah bob WHITE*. No audience should ever have to wonder about descriptions like this. They should be shown a picture or model of the bird and hear a tape recording of its whistle.

Speakers have a duty to use a variety of tools to enhance communication. A speaking tool is anything other than words that a speaker uses to make the major points of a speech clearer and more interesting. It is such a device as a picture, a model, a chart, or a movie projector.

Whether addressing a small group or a large audience, an effective speaker knows that a speech is far more than saying the words. It is knowing what speaking tools to use. It is knowing how to use and operate them. It is making appropriate gestures during a speech. It may also include using a microphone effectively. It is even arranging chairs for the audience correctly. This section of the book discusses the different kinds of speaking tools and the part the physical setting plays in a speech.

All About Speaking Tools

Speaking tools reinforce a speaker's message. They give a speech an extra dimension. They are helpful in speeches that persuade and sometimes in speeches that entertain. They are almost essential in speeches that inform. When airline employees tell you how to fasten your seat belt or how to use an oxygen mask, they always show a belt and a mask. It is difficult to understand how a food processor works, how to make a quilt, or how to change an oil filter without looking at the actual objects or pictures of them.

Many tools are available to help the speaker. The problem is to select the right tool or tools for each topic and audience. You may want to use charts or graphs if your speech is full of statistics. If you are talking about political boundaries in the Middle East, either maps or slides are a good choice. Before you select any tool, make sure you really need this tool. After all, Abraham Lincoln gave the Gettysburg Address without using any tools.

Don't use speaking tools that you don't need. Too many speaking tools can detract from your message.

There are certain practical guidelines for using speaking tools:

1. Don't let speaking tools overshadow your message.

2. Make sure that you and your speaking tools are sending the same message. You don't want to display a picture of a tropical storm while you are telling about the good weather in Hawaii.

3. Plan when and how you are going to use the tool or tools, including your use and arrangement of the setting.

4. Know where in your speech you are using the tools. If you are speaking from notes, mark the places in the notes.

5. Rehearse with the tools.

6. Display or use a speaking tool only when it is needed. If people are looking at a model or chart before it is used, they are not giving you their full attention.

7. Always have your speaking tools handy and ready to use. This will let you avoid unpleasant surprises like not being able to find a model or a piece of chalk while you are speaking.

8. Learn how to operate any audio, visual, or audio-visual machinery before the day you speak.

Visual Tools

Don't waste words and your listeners' time by trying to describe something that would be better explained through a visual tool. Keep in mind that if you select the correct visual tool, it will be worth a thousand words. Using such a tool will also help an audience remember what you say.

Certain hard-and-fast rules must be followed to ensure the effective use of visual tools:

1. Make sure the audience can see what you are showing. Check this out in a trial run before you speak.

2. Don't talk to your tools. Look at your audience.

3. Stand out of the way so that your audience can see what you are talking about.

4. Don't pass speaking tools around. This will distract your listeners.

Charts

Charts are used in textbooks and encyclopedias. Large commercial charts are also used in schools and businesses. If you cannot find a printed chart to fit your needs, make your own chart. Make sure the size of your chart is suitable for your material, the size of the room, and your audience. Use different colors to show distinctions on the chart. Make all the lines heavy and broad. Print large letters on a chart. Don't write. You won't always need to show a title. Be sure to limit the number of words on the chart. People cannot read and follow a speaker's thoughts at the same time.

Remember when selecting or making a chart that it should have only one main idea. Make sure that the idea is clearly presented. A cluttered chart will only confuse and distract your audience. If you have more than one idea to present, use several charts or a flip chart. When an audience sees more than one idea on a chart, they begin thinking ahead of what the speaker is saying. The best way to present a chart to your audience is by using a pointer.

There are several different kinds of charts. You must choose the one that will best display your information.

Organization Charts.   This type of chart shows the chain of command of an organization. It can be used to show how the executive branch of the government or your local school board is organized.

Classification Charts.   Similar objects are grouped together under general headings in a classification chart. Use these charts to group the flowers that grow in your community under the headings *annual* and *perennial.*

Time Lines.   A series of events can be easily shown on a time line. You can use this type of chart to show the dates of major events that have occurred in your community.

Tables.   Number information is often shown in tables. You probably can still see in your mind the table of elements hanging on the wall in your chemistry classroom.

Flow Charts.   This chart shows how different things are joined together into one final product. You may want to use a flow chart to show how a car or a crepe is made.

Special Charts.   Airline pilots use aeronautical charts. Soldiers use topographical charts. You see weather charts on television and in the newspaper. You may wish to use special charts like these in your speech.

A clearly drawn chart can be a very effective speaking tool.

Flip Charts

A flip chart is an excellent way to show the order in which things happen. It is a series of charts that are clipped together at the top. This keeps the charts in the right order. It is easier to use a flip chart than individual charts.

Flip charts are not difficult to make. Begin by making the individual charts. Then make a summary chart so that you won't have to waste time flipping back through the charts when you are wrapping up your speech. Next, place a plain cover over the front of all the charts and then follow these steps:

Stack the charts in the correct order.

Lay the charts on top of a slightly larger piece of plywood or heavy cardboard.

Staple or use rings to attach the charts to the backing.

Preconstructed blank flip charts are probably available at your local stationery store.

Chalkboards

One visual tool that is available in most settings is the chalkboard. Come prepared with chalk and eraser if you are going to use this tool. Draw graphs, charts, and cartoons on the chalkboard. Use it to write key points that you want your audience to remember.

Chalkboards are especially effective when you need to explain something step by step. You draw and explain each step as you speak. The listener's attention is not distracted by other steps in the process as it might be on a single, complete chart.

Keep the board erased or covered when you are not using it. Any writing on the board will distract your audience. You can use a blank flip chart in the same way as a chalkboard. In that case, bring your marking pens.

Maps

Maps are good speaking tools when you are discussing the geographic location of something.

A map is an essential speaking tool if you are talking about the location of something, whether it's a star or Timbuktu. There are many different kinds of maps, like

transportation maps, population maps, and physical maps. Yet all maps can be classified as general reference maps or special maps.

General Reference Maps.   These maps give general information about continents, countries, rivers, cities, and other geographical features. Use these maps to show information about a certain area or about the world as a whole. They will let you show whether a place is inland or on the coast. They will let you compare the size of China and Japan. Make sure that you select the map that best illustrates your speech. Avoid using a world map if you are talking about the location of historical buildings in London. Even a large map of England would not meet your needs. The best selection would be a large city map of London. This map would let you point out to your audience the location of each historical building.

Special Maps.   When you want to talk about the rainfall, different crops, or population distribution, use a special map that emphasizes the feature. Be sure to explain the special symbols used on each map to your audience.

Globes.   Don't forget that the globe is also a map. A terrestrial globe shows the continents and oceans, while a celestial globe shows the stars and planets. As a globe has limited viewing power, it will only be a good tool for a very small group.

Graphs

Graphs give an audience a clearer understanding of numerical information. They present this data in a picture form. The simpler the graph, the better it illustrates your purpose. There are four major types of graphs. Notice how these graphs show four different ways of presenting the same facts.

Line Graphs.   These graphs use lines and points to show how things change over a period of time. Use these graphs for statistics about income, taxes, and population.

Bar Graphs.   Horizontal or vertical bars are used on these graphs to show increases or decreases over a period of time. They let you see right away if a quantity is changing.

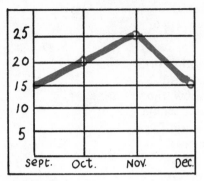

Line graph

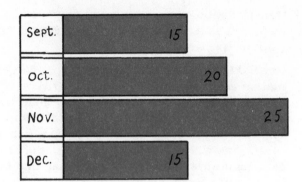

Horizontal bar graph

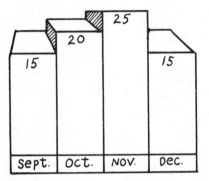

Vertical bar graph

Picture graph

These five graphs show the same
numerical information in five
different ways.

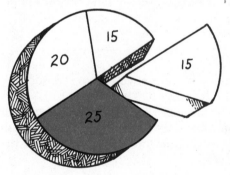

Circle graph

Picture Graphs.   Picture writing was one of the earliest
forms of communication. A picture graph uses pictures or
symbols instead of bars or lines to make its point. This
type of graph appeals to a wide audience because it is visu-
ally interesting and easy to read.

Circle Graphs.   Often called a pie chart, this type of graph
divides a circle or pie into parts. It shows the relation of
the parts to the whole.

Real Objects

Using objects like telephones, computers, and flowering plants lets the audience see the actual objects that you are speaking about. It is a concrete experience for the audience. Real objects are the thing to use when you are doing a demonstration. The golden rule about using objects is never to pass them around. Let the audience touch them afterward.

Models

When you cannot bring in a real object, or the object is too small or large to show an audience, use a model. Not only is a model a three-dimensional representation of a real object, it can also be larger or smaller than the actual object it represents. A model lets you show your audience such varied things as a volcano, an atom, a motor, or a tooth.

A model can help you show what may be otherwise difficult to see.

Pictures, Drawings, and Sketches

When it is impossible or impractical to show your audience an object or a model, a picture, drawing, or sketch is a good substitute. Drawings and sketches have another advantage. They let you blow up details. As you are drawing or sketching, don't ever interrupt the flow of your speech by saying, "I'm not really an artist." Instead, keep your audience's attention on what you are saying rather than on your artwork. It is your responsibility to make sure the artwork is clear and legible. If necessary, arrange to have someone help you.

Handouts

Speakers use handouts to summarize what they have said or to give their audience additional facts about a subject. Handouts are frequently used in workshops and classes. The problem with handouts is that the only good time to distribute them is at the end of a session. If you distribute them beforehand, your audience will read them as you speak. If you distribute them during the session, the flow is disrupted. Another drawback to handouts is that they may be expensive to produce for large groups. Still, they are very effective reminders for your audience to remember what you said.

Projected Visuals

As the size of your audience increases, the effectiveness of holding up visual tools like charts, graphs, and pictures decreases. A large audience will be able to see your visuals better if you project them on a screen. Place the screen where everyone can see it. The general rule is that no member of your audience should be farther than six screen widths from the screen or closer than two screen widths to it. Don't place the screen in a position that gives it more attention than you. Two problems that you will meet when you project visual materials are how to darken the room and how to operate the machine while you are speaking. Solve these problems before the day you speak. Here are three special guidelines that you should follow when using projected visual tools like the opaque, overhead, or slide projector:

1. Never make people strain to see the image projected on the screen.
2. Keep an image on the screen at all times. Never show a white screen; it will blind your audience.
3. Always have a spare bulb for the projector.

Opaque Projectors

If you want to show your audience what a coin, a leaf, a picture in a book, a postcard, or a fabric looks like, use an opaque projector. It enlarges two-dimensional objects that are too small to be seen by the audience and lets you show some three-dimensional objects. Most machines will project as large as a 10-inch × 10-inch- (250-mm × 250-mm) object. The opaque projector works by sending light onto an opaque image (one that light cannot pass through), like a coin. The light is reflected onto mirrors, then through a series of lenses and onto a screen.

The disadvantages of using an opaque projector usually outweigh the advantages. It is a very awkward and heavy machine to move. It must be used in a room that is completely dark because reflected light gives a dimmer image on the screen. This means that if you need to read notes, you will have to use a flashlight to see them. The opaque

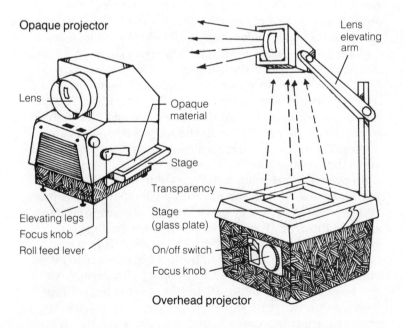

Opaque projector

Lens

Opaque material

Stage

Elevating legs
Focus knob
Roll feed lever

Transparency

Stage (glass plate)

On/off switch

Focus knob

Overhead projector

Lens elevating arm

Opaque and overhead projectors enlarge and project images onto screens.

projector's lamp becomes so hot that it can make parts of the projector too hot to touch, and it can even damage what you are projecting. In addition, only groups of standard classroom size can really see the image projected by this machine.

The major advantage of using an opaque projector is that this is the best way to project three-dimensional objects. It is also the quickest way to show maps, illustrations, and other material from books without having to make a transparency or slide.

Overhead Projectors

The overhead projector is fast becoming the most popular projector for speakers to use. It has certain advantages over other projectors. It puts so much light on the screen that it can be used in normal lighting; there is no need to darken the room. The speaker can operate the projector without using a helper. However, the biggest advantage of the machine is that it allows the speaker to face the audience. You can talk and maintain direct eye contact with the audience.

The overhead projector passes light through a transparency and projects the image into a lens and mirror system and then back over the shoulder of the operator onto a nearby screen. The transparency itself is a clear plastic sheet that can be imprinted with an image. You can buy transparencies or make them yourself. The easiest way to make a transparency is simply to write or draw on a plastic sheet with special marking pens. You can use color. Another easy way to make a transparency is to run a frosted sheet of acetate through a ditto machine. You can also use an office copier and specially treated film to make transparencies. Finally, as in the illustration, you can make color lift transparencies by following a process similar to the one used with decoupage.

An overhead projector can be used in a variety of ways. You can draw, sketch, or write on a transparency. You can add details to previously made transparencies, highlight special points on them, or write on them during your speech. You can simplify complex topics by laying one transparency over another to build a complete picture. You can even show silhouettes of opaque materials. You can be creative and make attractive designs by swirling food color in water on top of a transparency. Place cellophane over a transparency, and you can make the image on the screen shimmer.

Color lift transparencies. Make your own transparencies by following the step-by-step instructions below. You will need a picture from a magazine, a sheet of laminating acetate, a pan of soapy water, a ruler (or other hard, smooth object), a sponge, plastic spray, and a sheet of clear acetate.

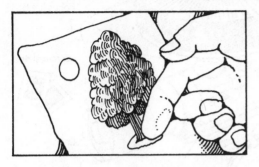

1. Make sure the picture is printed on clay-coated paper. Check by wetting your finger and rubbing it on a white area of the page. If your finger picks up a whitish residue, it is suitable for lifting.

2. Cut out the picture. Remove the backing from the laminating acetate. Bend the acetate into a U-shape, and press it down onto the picture from the center outward.

3. Rub the back of the picture with a ruler or a similar hard, smooth object. This ensures full adhesion and removes any air bubbles.

4. Place the picture and acetate in a pan of soapy water. Let it soak for a few minutes. Peel the soaked paper from the acetate.

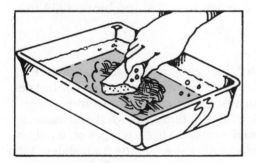

5. After the paper is peeled off, rub the transparency with a sponge to remove excess residue. Hang the transparency up to dry.

6. Once dry, spray the dull side with a clear plastic spray and cover the vulnerable side (or both sides) with a sheet of clear acetate.

A slide projector is an effective visual tool that is simple to operate.

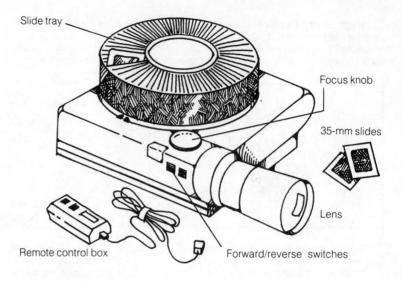

Slide tray

Focus knob

35-mm slides

Lens

Remote control box

Forward/reverse switches

Slide Projectors

For large audiences, a slide projector is a more effective tool than an opaque or overhead projector. You can use your own slides or purchased slides. Your slides should be of professional quality. If you don't use a remote control device, you will have to have an operator for the projector, since you want to remain in the front of the room to keep eye contact with your audience.

Take the time to arrange your slides in sequence. Put a black or gray slide at the beginning, ending, and where pauses occur so that your audience will never have to look at a white screen. Make sure the slides are all facing the right way. You don't want to distract your audience with upside down or backward slides. You can put a mark on each slide to show the correct way to put it in the projector. Before beginning, make sure that you have a light to read your notes.

Filmstrips

The filmstrip projector, like some of the other projectors, must be used in a darkened room. If there is no control device, you will need an assistant to run the machine. The projector pulls a roll of 35-mm film through it one frame at a time. There are usually from 20 to 60 images on a roll. You can buy filmstrips or have them made from slides. The greatest disadvantage of a filmstrip is that you cannot change the sequence of the images. The filmstrip projector has the advantage of being easy to operate.

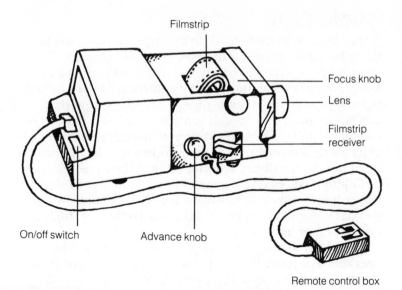

Filmstrip

Focus knob

Lens

Filmstrip receiver

On/off switch   Advance knob

Remote control box

Filmstrip projectors allow you to show a roll of 35-mm film one frame at a time.

Reminders

When you are projecting visual materials, you must place the screen and projector so that the image is not distorted. They need to be at right angles to each other. If you don't place them in this position, you will get what is known as the *keystone effect*. As in the illustration, your picture will be wider on one side than the other. This happens most often with the overhead projector.

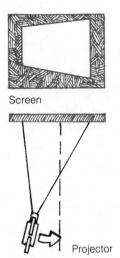

Screen

Projector

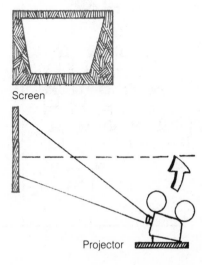

Screen

Projector

The keystone effect occurs when the projector is not at a right angle to the screen. The dashed lines show the correct placement of the projector.

Audio Tools

It may be even more difficult to describe sounds than to describe sights to your audience. Fortunately, many sounds are recorded or can be recorded so that you can bring a variety of sounds to your audience. The sound that is most used in speeches is music. Another sound that can add interest to a speech is a different voice. Instead of reading a quote, a comedy sketch, or a story yourself, consider using a recording. Let your audience listen to Robert Frost or Carl Sandburg reading some of their poems. Just as different voices give a quartet variety, different voices can enhance a speech. Choose a voice that complements yours. Decide whether you want a male or female, high or low, or soft or loud voice.

Remember as you are placing an electric speaker or speakers in a room that sound waves travel straight from their source to the listener. Don't distort sound by hiding a speaker behind a plant or a desk. Make sure that the speaker or speakers or portable equipment are facing the audience. If you are using more than one speaker, make sure that the speakers are placed far enough apart to balance the sound. To avoid feedback, place the speaker or speakers in front of where you are speaking.

Left: A single speaker should be placed near the screen, and it should be aimed toward the audience. *Right:* Stereo speaker placement should be such that the distance between speakers equals the distance from the front of the room to the middle of the audience.

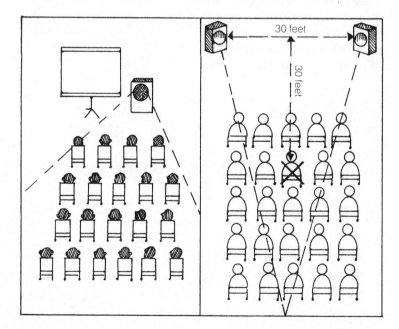

The real challenge in using sound equipment is to find a volume that is not too loud for the people close to the equipment and not too soft for those in the back of the room. It is also hard to achieve adequate volume from speakers built into portable tape recorders or record players. To get sufficient volume from these units, you should plug them into auxiliary speakers.

Sound quality depends on the quality of both the equipment and the recorded materials. The better the quality of both, the better the sound will be. Often, you won't be able to do much about the quality of the equipment that is provided for you. However, you can sometimes improve the sound of your voice by adjusting the tone control.

Tape Recorders

Today most tape recorders are cassette recorders. You will want to operate a tape recorder yourself because timing is critical in inserting recorded material into your presentation. The recorder should be right next to you on a table or stand for ease and smoothness of operation. The sound can be sent out through your microphone or any amplified sound system. Practice using the tape recorder until there

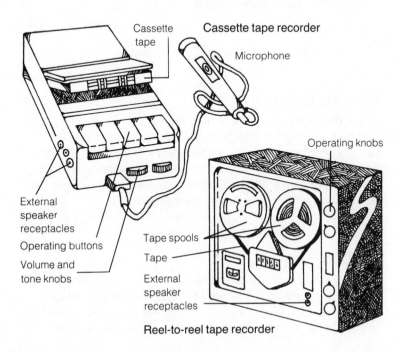

Cassette tape

Cassette tape recorder

Microphone

Operating knobs

External speaker receptacles

Operating buttons

Volume and tone knobs

Tape spools

Tape

External speaker receptacles

Reel-to-reel tape recorder

Cassette and reel-to-reel tape recorders are good tools for playing recorded sounds to your audience.

is no break in the flow from you to the recorded material. To ensure that you play and record the best possible sound from a machine, keep the record/playback head clean. Debris constantly builds up on this head and reduces the quality of the sound. Check the operating manual for the tape recorder to find out how to clean the head.

A record player is another audio tool that can be used to bring recorded material into your presentation.

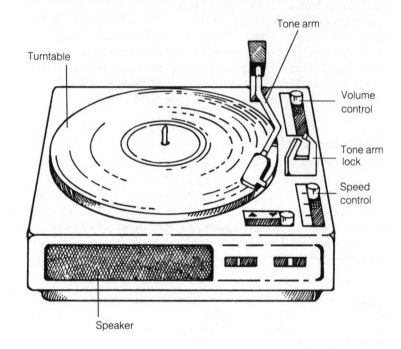

Tone arm

Turntable

Volume control

Tone arm lock

Speed control

Speaker

Record Players

A record player is not as versatile as a tape recorder. A tape recorder is a better choice as an audio support tool because there is no way to pinpoint an exact spot on a record. If the selection you play is not the first one on a record, the audience will be distracted by what they hear as you search for the right spot on a record.

Audio-Visual Tools

When you use a filmstrip, motion picture, videotape, or a television show accompanied by sound, you are using both audio and visual media. The tools that you are using in presenting this combination are appropriately named audio-visual tools. You may wish to use these tools at the beginning or ending of the session to avoid interrupting the flow of your presentation.

Motion Picture Projectors

Showing a motion picture to your audience lets them move out of the room to another time or place. Movies have an advantage over most other speaking tools because they show motion. They are exceptionally helpful in speaking situations that are intended to inform. To show a movie effectively, a certain amount of mastery is required. The sound level and focus should be adjusted before the movie begins. Have the movie ready to start on the title. Don't show the part with numbers on it. Make fine adjustments on the volume and focus at the start of the movie. Stop the movie immediately at the end of the film. Don't rewind it until after your audience leaves.

There are drawbacks to showing movies. They are expensive. You must select one early to ensure that it will be available. You have to rely on a company or organization to send the movie to you on time.

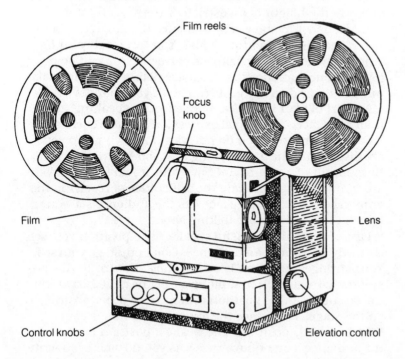

Film reels

Focus knob

Film

Lens

Control knobs

Elevation control

Motion picture projectors allow you to bring live action and sounds into the room where you are speaking.

Sound Filmstrip Projectors

You should use a sound filmstrip instead of a movie when you want to control the viewing of individual frames. The sound track for a filmstrip is either on a cassette built into the filmstrip projector or on a separate machine. On modern equipment, a silent signal on the sound track advances the filmstrip. On older equipment, you may have to advance the filmstrip manually.

Reminders

It is more difficult to use audio-visual equipment than just visual or audio equipment. You must coordinate the placement of the screen and the speakers. Because people associate sound with its source, the speakers should be located close to the screen.

Your Body as a Speaking Tool

Don't ever forget that one of the most effective speaking tools that you can use is your body. Let it help your listeners understand your ideas. You can use your body to demonstrate the height of an ostrich or the size of a statue. You can use it to show your audience the difference between the rumba and the samba. You can teach your listeners how to carry a backpack correctly. You can step toward your audience to emphasize points. You can make numbers stand out by gesturing with your hands.

No part of your body is a more effective speaking tool than your face. Your facial expression should reflect the mood of your topic. You do not want to frown when you are discussing the great feeling that you had on reaching the summit of a mountain. Save your frown for when you are trying to communicate the difficulties of resolving the arms race. An expressive face lets the audience see your interest in what you are talking about.

Part of being a successful speaker is to position yourself correctly in front of an audience. Don't outstage yourself. Your strongest position is center stage. Return to this position after using charts, pictures, or the chalkboard. Note the strength of this position compared to other positions on the stage. Try to face the audience, as this is your strongest body position. The weakest position is to give the audience a one-quarter view as you do when you write on a chalkboard.

The four body positions, from strongest to weakest. *Upper left:* full; *upper right:* three quarters; *lower left:* one-half; *lower right:* one-quarter.

The Setting

When the United States Tennis Association moved the U.S. Open Tennis Tournament from Forest Hills, New York, to Flushing Meadows, they forgot one detail. It is difficult to play tennis matches when jet airplanes are taking off every few minutes over the courts. Just as tennis players are bothered by not having the best setting for a match, speakers are bothered by not having the best possible setting for their presentation. The setting plays a large role in your success. It can lessen the effectiveness

The relative positions of your speaking tools and your body are important. *Left:* speaker is dominant. *Below left:* speaker and tool are equal. *Below:* tool is dominant.

of, or even ruin, the best presentation if it interferes with the message the speaker is trying to send to the audience. Unlike the tennis player who cannot make changes in the setting before a match, you, as a speaker, have the opportunity to make changes in the setting you will have.

Checking Out the Setting

You need to visit the setting beforehand because it determines the kinds of speaking tools that you can use as well as the type of presentation you should make. This visit gives you the opportunity to tell the people who will be setting up the room how you would like it arranged and what equipment you will need. Don't rely on someone else to do this job for you. No one else knows all the details that are important to you. Use this visit to find out the following information:

> The size of the room.
>
> What the acoustics of the room are like.
>
> The level and type of lighting in the room.
>
> The normal internal and external noise level of the room.
>
> Where you will stand or sit.
>
> The quality of the equipment available to you.
>
> The availability of people to operate equipment and help you in other ways.
>
> The name of the person responsible for setting up the room and any equipment that you will use.
>
> The location of the electrical outlets.

The Room

Begin your visit to the setting by studying the room. Decide if the room temperature will be comfortable when the audience is there. Consider the acoustics of the room along with the size of the group you will be speaking to, and decide whether you will need a sound system. Take a minute to listen to the sounds of the room. You want to find out if there are any distracting noises. Ask yourself, "Can I hear the ventilation system? Are any carpenters or repairpersons working inside the building today? Will they be working on the day of my speech? Can I hear street noise? Is the room by a fire station or a hospital?" You don't want to have any noise surprises on the day you speak.

The Lighting

Stand on the spot where you will speak. Look at where the audience will be seated. Will you be able to see your listeners? Will they be able to see you? You must be able to see each other for effective communication to take place. Now is the time to decide on the light level. Try to avoid shadows. Don't forget to notice if there are curtains on the windows. The curtains may need to be adjusted. Remember that the amount of available light will vary with the time of day and the weather.

The Seating

You want to get as close to your audience as possible, but people tend to choose any seat except the front seats. Solve the problem by limiting the number of chairs or the seating area. You can bring a small audience closer to you by having them sit in a semicircle or by sitting with them in a circle. Don't forget to consider the comfort of your listeners. The seating arrangement should give them room to stretch their legs.

The Speaker's Stand

If Napoleon Bonaparte and Charles de Gaulle were both using a standard speaker's stand, Napoleon would be peering over the top and De Gaulle would have to bend down to read his notes. Check out the height of the speaker's stand if you plan to use it. Make adjustments so that you will be comfortable on your speaking day. Investigate the interior of the stand to see if there is sufficient space to hold any speaking tools you wish to use.

The Microphone

All microphones do not operate in the same way. Some are so simple to use that they even turn themselves on when you say anything. Be sure to find out if you will be using a stationary microphone or one that allows you to move around as you talk. If the microphone is stationary, the audience will lose your voice every time you step away from it.

You will want to find out about the sound equipment on your visit. Modern systems will give you good sound without the whistles, squawks, and feedback of older systems. Try to meet the person who will be setting up the sound system to find out about its quality. Ask this person to help you check out the microphone on the day you speak.

Other Details

Don't forget to check details. Make arrangements for projectors, tables, easels, and chalkboards to be in the room if you will need them. If you require help in operating equipment, arrange for this help now..You should even request a pitcher of water if you will want one.

The Day You Speak

The first rule is to arrive early. Give yourself at least half an hour to set up your speaking tools and to check that the setting is as you expected. Check out details: seating arrangement, lights, temperature, curtains, speaker's stand. Make sure that the room is neat and clean. You may find it necessary to empty ashtrays, erase chalkboards, and throw away used coffee cups. The more complicated the presentation is, the greater the amount of time you should allow to check the arrangements.

If you are going to use a microphone, allow at least 15 minutes extra time to check it out. It is best if the person who set it up will help you. Begin by making sure you can turn the microphone on and off as well as raise or lower it. Next, ask how close you should be to the microphone and whether you need to speak directly into it. Then try speaking a few lines of your speech into the microphone at different distances to discover how far away it will pick up your voice. Finally, one word of caution—never test whether a microphone is working or not by tapping it. You could damage the microphone.

The last thing you should do is check out your path to the speaker's stand or wherever you will speak. Practice walking to this spot. This will let you see if there are any obstacles in your way. Once you have done so, your setting is ready.

Tools Are Only Helpers

Beautiful slides, fantastic charts, exciting music, and unusual models can greatly improve your speaking. But what makes it successful is your message to the audience. The right tools add variety and help make points. Use them with such proficiency that they are an integral part of your presentations. Don't ever let tools compete with you for the attention of your audience. Remember, they are only helpers.

STAGE FRIGHT AND THE Unexpected

Most people talk successfully all day long. They communicate clearly with teachers, clerks, baby sitters, secretaries, bosses, co-workers, children, friends, neighbors, and strangers. Yet, put these same people in front of a formal audience and guess what happens! Their ability to communicate vanishes. They cannot handle simple things like a broken fingernail or hiccups, and they feel an absolute panic about saying anything to a (usually) friendly group of people. This section is designed to help you avoid those feelings. It will show you how to handle yourself in front of an audience when stage fright hits or the unexpected happens.

Stage Fright

Many people have a fear of speaking in public. It bothers some people so much that they cannot even share their ideas in office discussions or at club meetings. It may be worse for beginning speakers, but it bothers all speakers, from U.S. Presidents at press conferences to experienced professional actors. Think of how the sweat would pour down Nixon's face and Carter would clasp his hands together so tightly that his knuckles turned white when these Presidents spoke to the press. Take comfort from

Carol Burnett's confession that making a speech does more than make her a nervous wreck; it terrifies her. Or Yul Brynner's admission that he was just as tense before the 557th performance of *The King and I* as he was before his first performance.

This problem of fear of public speaking, or stage fright, as it is often called, is not new. More than two thousand years ago, the famous Roman orator Cicero wrote: "I turn pale at the outset of a speech, and quake in every limb and in all my soul." So if you get butterflies in your stomach whenever you even think about speaking, you are not alone. It can happen to anyone who is concerned about how a presentation will turn out.

Strange as it may seem, some nervousness is helpful. It gives your body more energy and makes your mind more alert. Many actors claim that stage fright actually stimulates them to give superior performances. Dinah Shore once said, "You've got to be a little nervous." However, if your stage fright is so great that you cannot communicate effectively while speaking publicly, you will need to learn ways to control it. You begin by learning more about the symptoms and causes of stage fright.

Stage Fright Symptoms

Jacqueline Bisset, the actress, appeared calm before she went onstage to present an Oscar for best foreign picture. Yet, as she took her place, her copresenter, Jack Valenti, noticed that her left hand, which was resting on the speaker's stand, was trembling. Nat King Cole was so nervous when he once accepted an award that he told the audience that he had five sons when he meant five daughters. Reactions to stage fright occur in your body as in Jacqueline Bisset's, and in your mind as in Nat King Cole's, or in both your body and mind. These reactions can vary from a mild one, like trembling knees, to a reaction so severe that you faint.

Bodily Reactions

Whenever you find yourself in a stress situation, your body reacts. You may find that your heart pounds, you gasp for breath, your mouth becomes dry, your voice sounds higher, or your hands and underarms perspire more than usual. You may not be able to help blushing, swallowing repeatedly, or licking your lips. Because fear brings your body extra energy, your hands, knees, and voice may trem-

Nearly everyone experiences stage fright at some time.

ble. The paper you are holding may rattle. You may find yourself using up some of this energy by jingling coins in your pocket, swaying back and forth on your feet, or pacing around.

Mental Reactions

Your mind can become so overloaded with fear that it does not function at its usual level. Your ideas may appear unrelated as you speak. You may make slips of the tongue. You may mispronounce familiar words. You may find yourself adding *uh*'s and *ur*'s as you search for what you want to say next. If you think of how nervous you were during other speaking situations or of how nervous you are during this one, you may upset yourself more. You may become so upset that your mind even goes temporarily blank.

The Final Reaction

Because you are aware of how your body and mind are acting, you may begin to feel a strong desire to withdraw or escape from a speaking situation. You think that your listeners are aware of your discomfort and are beginning to judge you unfavorably. Actually, you probably appear more confident than you feel. Still, you may begin to withdraw in some way. Most people try to escape by looking anywhere but at the audience. They may look out the window, at the floor, or toward the ceiling. Some people begin to speak faster in hopes of getting through the ordeal sooner.

Stage Fright Causes

Study after study has been made of stage fright. The results are always the same. They show that most people experience some form of stage fright every time they speak publicly. They also show that even experienced speakers are found to be nervous or tense before speaking. The question is: Why do people have stage fright?

The physical symptoms of stage fright are close to those that are triggered by a dangerous situation. When people must avoid a runaway car, flee a burning building, or save someone from drowning, their hearts beat faster, they begin to perspire, and their mouths become dry. It seems likely that people who suffer from stage fright see their situations as dangerous because they feel that they must succeed and are not sure that they can. This is true for athletes, actors, musicians, politicians, and those who must speak publicly.

The Need to Succeed

Many people who believe that successful speaking is vital to their welfare view speaking as a dangerous situation. Perhaps they have a boss whom they need to impress. Maybe they need to speak well to sell merchandise, promote an organization, or sway a group to their candidate's viewpoints. Or they may simply need to win personal approval. In many cases, the greater the need a speaker has to succeed, the greater the chance the speaker will suffer from stage fright.

Feelings of Inadequacy

Many speakers are not confident of their ability to handle a speaking situation. Inexperienced speakers often think that they will not be able to remember, have a smooth delivery, or keep the attention of their listeners. Experienced speakers worry that they will not give as convincing a message as their audience expects. All speakers have feelings of inadequacy when they are not well prepared. Stage fright is the end result of these feelings of inadequacy.

Controlling Stage Fright

What can you do about stage fright? Can you ever get rid of it? Should you try to eliminate it? The answer to these questions is: learn to control your stage fright. This will reduce its harmful effects and let you use the energy it gives you to speak better. Besides specific suggestions to overcome stage fright, two things are of major importance in controlling it: confidence and preparation.

Confidence

The first jump a parachutist makes is the hardest. So is the first dive from a high board, the first solo drive in a car, and the first time you speak publicly. Yet each succeeding jump, dive, drive, or speaking situation becomes easier for people, who gain confidence through knowing that they can cope successfully. You don't have to jump right into formal speechmaking. You may never want to. But everyone must prepare to speak effectively in public at some level, sometime.

Raise your confidence by involving yourself in relatively unthreatening speaking situations at first. You can make a motion at a meeting, contribute an idea in a class discussion, or volunteer to make telephone calls for an organization. Take the time right now to make a list of the types of speaking situations in which you can gain confidence and experience. Use this list until you feel ready to give a short talk. Then use every opportunity you can get to gain experience in speaking for longer intervals. Watch other speakers, too. You can learn much from their successes and mistakes.

Preparation

To become champions, Jack Nicklaus and Chris Evert Lloyd spent years preparing their games. They still prepare for each tournament they play. You have taken the first step in becoming a winner as a speaker by studying this book and learning how to improve your speaking. The next step is to prepare so well for each speaking opportunity that you won't have to worry. Most experienced speakers agree that being well prepared is the best way to avoid severe stage fright. Just imagine how nervous you would be while talking to the town council about lowering local taxes, if you had not studied the existing rate structure and then found out that 500 persons instead of 50 were at the meeting.

Specific Suggestions

Since even experienced speakers who are well prepared admit to stage fright, let's look at some of the methods they use to lessen it.

Understanding Stage Fright.   An important step in controlling stage fright is to understand that stage fright is normal. This book has already shown you that. When you begin to feel stage fright, think of the symptoms as your body's way to prepare you for speaking.

Thinking Positively.   Some people talk themselves into a severe case of stage fright. They destroy their confidence by saying negative things to themselves like, "I don't really know enough about this subject," or "No one in the audience will like what I say." If you are in the habit of doing this, use a notebook to write down positive thoughts like these before speaking:

> I know my subject matter.
> Many people are interested in this subject.
> I am well prepared.
> I have selected good examples to support my point.

Make sure that you write down only those thoughts that are accurate. Don't lie to yourself, for example, by saying you know a subject if you only have read one article about it. Memorize your positive thoughts and repeat them to yourself until they replace the negative thoughts that tear down your confidence. Begin now to build your speaking confidence by writing down some positive thoughts about what you have learned about speaking, such as:

> I know how to organize a speech.
> I can choose intriguing subjects for my audience.

Evaluating the Situation.   Learn to be reasonable about what is expected from you as a speaker. Most audiences, for example, will not demand that any speaker have the evangelical zeal of Billy Graham, the dramatic expression of Laurence Olivier, or the humor of Johnny Carson. If you do, that's great. What your listeners want to hear is organized remarks that will amuse them, give them helpful information, or stimulate them with new ideas. They want you to succeed, not fail.

Being Realistic. Since stage fright is tied to the danger you see in a speaking situation, be realistic about how important a speaking opportunity is to you. Failure to speak well in a given instance will rarely change your life. It will not usually embarrass you forever, cause you to lose friends, or hurt your career.

Beginning to Speak. As you prepare to speak, review the positive thoughts that you have written down earlier to encourage yourself. Start slowly. Be sure to memorize your first few sentences so you can get off to a smooth start. It is often helpful to direct these lines to an encouraging listener who will give you positive reinforcement to continue. Take two deep breaths before you start. They will help you relax and give you a sufficient air supply to start speaking. Just as most athletes forget their nervousness after they begin to play, most speakers forget their nervousness after they begin to speak.

Moving to Relax. If you move as you speak, you will use up some of the extra nervous energy stage fright gives you. Use gestures. Step forward to emphasize a point if you are standing. If appropriate, write on an available chalkboard. Point to parts of a model or a chart. Change your position from time to time. Drink water if it is provided. Press your thumb and index finger together tightly. Curl up your toes. Use these movements in practicing so that they become natural to do.

Emphasizing Communication. Put your mind on the message you are communicating to your listeners rather than on yourself or your nervousness. Constantly monitor if your listeners are understanding what you are saying. Many speakers feel that the secret to overcoming stage fright is to concentrate on communicating the message.

The Last Suggestion

Even if you follow all the preceding suggestions to lessen your stage fright, tension usually builds up before you begin to speak. You need to find an outlet for this tension. Some formal speakers meditate before they speak. Many find exercises helpful in reducing tension to a manageable

Gestures and motions may help
to ease some of your tension.
Top: Gesture with your hands.
Left: Step forward when making
a point.

level. Practice these relaxation exercises now. Find a quiet place, and do them a few minutes in preparation for your speaking situation.

Breathe deeply four or five times. Hold each breath for a count of 5.

Drop your head forward. Move it slowly in a circle— first from left to right, then right to left. Repeat 5 to 10 times.

Hold your arms out from your sides as far as you can. Then slowly rotate your arms in larger and larger circles. Continue for 10 times.

Keep your lips closed as you drop your jaw. Then open your mouth and yawn.

Open your mouth wide as you say the following sounds, using different rhythms and volumes:
bah–bah–bah–bah–bah
fah–fah–fah–fah–fah
hah–hah–hah–hah–hah
mah–mah–mah–mah–mah

Right before being called on to speak, many speakers yawn several times to relax the muscles of their faces. Just don't let your listeners catch you yawning.

Freezing While Speaking

Most experienced speakers admit that they have occasionally drawn a blank and forgotten what they planned to say next. Even such talk-show pros like Johnny Carson and Merv Griffin have told about freezing on camera. If this should happen to you, don't panic. Your listeners will not immediately notice that anything is wrong. You have time to do several things to get yourself back on track.

The first thing to do is to take a deep breath. This should help reduce your tension. If your mind remains blank and you are standing, take a step toward your listeners. More than likely you will make eye contact with a sympathetic person who will make you feel more confident and relaxed. If you still cannot remember what you want to say, check any notes you have made. This should lead you to your next idea. Finally, if these steps don't help, say something like this to your listeners: "My mind has gone blank. Can you tell me what I just said?" Such a confession should generate feelings of sympathy from the audi-

Johnny Carson is just one of many celebrities who have experienced freezing while speaking.

ence and will also enable you to know where you are in your comments. Then you will be able to continue your talk. You may or may not recall exactly what you had planned to say, but you should be able to complete your remarks with poise and confidence.

Stage Fright Checklist

You must try to overcome stage fright long before you start to speak. You begin with careful preparation, sufficient practice, and relaxation exercises. As stage fright affects people in different ways, take the time now to inventory how it affects you.

Bodily Reactions

_____	rapid heartbeat	_____	feeling faint
_____	perspiring	_____	shaky voice
_____	trembling hands	_____	dry mouth
_____	knocking knees	_____	blushing
_____	stomach butterflies	_____	diarrhea
		_____	nausea
_____	tearing eyes	_____	other
_____	tense muscles		

Nervous Habits

_____ jingling coins	_____ pacing
_____ playing with jewelry,	_____ rubbing or
glasses, pens	wringing hands
_____ licking lips	_____ clearing throat
_____ frowning	_____ scratching
_____ shifting feet	_____ other

Mental Reactions

_____ excessive worry	_____ unrelated ideas
_____ slips of the tongue	_____ going blank
_____ long, complicated	_____ mispronunciations
sentences	_____ other
_____ *uh*'s, *ur*'s and *and*'s	

Once you have determined how stage fright affects you, work out your own personal plan to cope with it.

Unexpected Speech Problems

Even if a speaker is as well prepared as an Olympic athlete, something can still go wrong. You can never predict what will happen when you are speaking. Only 10 people may show up when you expected an audience of 50. You may have spilled coffee on your clothes two minutes before you are to begin. The projectionist may have disappeared when it is time to run your movie. Whatever happens, you must be able to cope with the unexpected. Problems can arise from the audience, yourself, or the setting and the equipment. You can try to eliminate a problem or even make it work to your advantage.

Audience Problems

Each audience is different. You can never completely anticipate what barriers may arise to interfere with your communication with one. As you are speaking, continually study your audience. It is much easier to cope with a problem as it is developing than after you lose your audience completely to the problem.

Smaller or Larger Audiences

Icy roads have stopped most of the expected audience from coming to hear you speak at the community center. Chairs have been set up for 200 persons; only 30 persons

There is no way to predict the number of things that might go wrong while you are speaking.

are scattered throughout the auditorium. You cannot ignore this situation. The following story is a good one to keep in mind as you think about how to resolve the problem:

> A speaker arrived to give his speech and, much to the speaker's amazement, only one person had shown up to hear the speech. The speaker went up to this person and said, "I came here to make a speech. What do you think I should do now?" The person replied, "Well, being a farmer, I know if I went down to feed the chickens and only one showed up, I would feed that chick." So the speaker gave his full speech to the audience of one. After the speech, the speaker asked, "How did you like my speech?" The farmer said, "Great, but if I were feeding one chick, I would not give that chick the whole bucket of grain."

Just as the chick wanted to eat, your small audience really wants to hear you speak. Don't disappoint them.

First, devise a way to bring them closer to you before beginning. Ask the people to sit in the first few rows, rearrange the chairs in a less formal arrangement, such as a circle or semicircle, or stand or sit closer to them. Next, be more informal for the smaller audience.

If an audience is larger than anticipated and it is too late to find a larger room, help the people find chairs or invite them to sit on the floor wherever space is available. Be more formal with the larger audience.

Not-the-Expected Audience

They told you that you were talking to the scouts, but when you arrived, you found out that their parents were also part of the audience. Instead of delivering your original speech, telling the scouts what *Be prepared* means, include comments now for their parents about how they can help their children learn to be prepared. If you were scheduled to speak to the Jaycees about the draft, and you find that the audience is made up of both Jaycees and Jayncees, don't ignore the Jayncees. Adjust your speech to include information about women and the draft. This is the time that all the research you did in preparing your speech pays off. Whenever your audience changes, you need to change your speech to communicate with that audience.

Hostile Audiences

Sometimes an audience may be hostile to your viewpoint. A group of dog lovers may not be receptive to you if you are asking for stronger leash laws. If you've identified hostility in an audience in advance, you should find areas of agreement to explore in your speech before you push your own views. Plan to begin by commenting on your love of animals, their role as companions, and your concern for animal safety. If you establish a common ground that you and your audience share, they will be more receptive to your viewpoint. Remember this technique and play it by ear if you encounter unexpected hostility on the day of your speech.

If your audience is there because their attendance is required, they may be a hostile or indifferent group. Then it is your job to find out beforehand what they would like to know about your subject and get them actively involved in your speech.

Emotional Audiences

If you ask people what they were doing when President Kennedy was shot in Dallas, most will be able to answer. If you had been speaking at that moment, the mood of your audience would have changed to one of shock and disbelief. When an event occurs that changes the mood of your audience, you cannot ignore it. You must talk about what has affected them. Events like assassinations, the death of someone the audience knows, earthquakes, or a sports championship must be mentioned. You need to be sensitive to the feelings that your audience is experiencing.

Troublemakers

Comedians like Don Rickles and Johnny Carson handle hecklers with great skill. Few speakers ever need this skill. However, if someone is yelling, "Baloney," or is loudly disputing what you are saying, you are going to need to si-

Try to ignore any troublemakers or hecklers that may be in your audience.

lence the troublemaker. Don't fight fire with fire. Don't risk offending the rest of the audience with sarcasm or a lengthy debate with the offender. Instead, try keeping your cool by ignoring the first few comments. If this fails, inject a humorous remark in your speech. If all your efforts fail, you will have to ask the chairperson to have the trouble-maker removed from the audience.

Distractions

People talk, cough, whisper, rummage for things; children fight; and babies cry while you are speaking. The sky is the limit for the number of distractions that can draw your audience's attention away from what you are saying. There can be an emergency telephone call for a member of the audience, someone can faint, or people can enter or leave the room. Whatever the distraction is, you will have to meet it face on, deal with it, and then continue. This is where your preparation shows. If you are well prepared, you will be able to handle a distraction and then get right back to the material where you were interrupted. Study your audience carefully. If they are restless, give them a break, change the pace of your speech, introduce new material or a story, use audio or visual tools, or conclude your speech.

Test Yourself

Large or small, most audiences want to hear what you are saying. Make it as easy as possible for them to do so. Give yourself armchair experience now before you meet the un-expected in an actual speech. Put yourself in the following situations. See how quickly you can resolve them. There are no right answers.

1. You have planned a formal speech about the quality of local television programs for children. Only 10 inter-ested parents have shown up. The room has been set up for 100 persons.

2. You thought that you were speaking to science fair participants about how to set up their experiments. Instead, you are speaking to their teachers.

3. You have prepared a speech to convince your audience that smoking should be banned from all public build-ings. As you begin your speech, you observe that more than half of your audience is smoking.

4. You are speaking to a meeting about providing help for hungry children in Asia. Suddenly, the caterer breaks into your speech and announces that dinner will be served in 15 minutes.

5. You are in the middle of your speech on the effects of stress on the body, when someone faints.

Speaker Problems

Since a variety of unexpected things can happen to you as you are speaking, you will need to keep a calm air and overlook or adjust to the problems that may confront you. While you read about the following types of unexpected happenings that speakers must endure, think about how you would cope with each one.

Physical Problems

Most physical problems that occur during a speech can be handled without completely interrupting your speech. For example, if you have a sudden attack of the hiccups or begin to cough, you can try sipping a glass of water or taking a lozenge. If you belch or burp noticeably, simply say, "Excuse me," and continue. Some physical problems will interrupt your speech. You will have to pause for nosebleeds, nausea, or diarrhea. If you think that you can return, leave as calmly as possible. It can be done. Just say, "Excuse me, I will be back in a minute." If you leave calmly, the audience will be sitting there when you return.

Saying the Wrong Thing

You may watch programs on television about bloopers. At some time, you will probably make a blooper during a speech. Perhaps you will talk of the "Awful" Tower instead of the "Eiffel" or say "stage flight" for "stage fright." You may have the President trying to prevent "peace" instead of "war." Saying the wrong thing can send your audience into gales of laughter or completely confuse them. If they laugh, join in. If they are confused, repeat the word or sentence correctly. Handle saying the wrong thing with humor. Take the time now to develop some one-liners like these in case you ever make a blooper:

> "Let me untie my tongue."
> "George Washington isn't the only person with wooden teeth."
> "Who said I couldn't speak Greek?"

Assorted Mishaps

A hundred years from now, no one will remember if you tripped as you walked to the speaker's stand, had tomato soup on your clothes, or dropped your note cards. The audience will not still be talking about how your wig fell off or how you knocked the pitcher of water off the speaker's stand. Ignore most mishaps or comment humorously on them. For example, if you are introduced by the wrong name, you can correct the error by saying:

> "This introduction reminds me of a letter that my mother received from my high school counselor. It told of my scholastic achievements and my outstanding record in sports. My mother answered by saying that she was delighted to hear about Fred's success, but she still wondered how her child (your name) was doing. My name is (your name) not (the name mentioned in the introduction)."

Another mishap that you may experience is to hear the speaker ahead of you give almost the same speech that you had planned. In this case, you may want to do what Adlai Stevenson did when this happened to him. When he got up to speak, he said:

> "Ladies and gentlemen, I was very pleased to see how enthusiastically you received [Mr. X's] speech. At first I was surprised to hear [Mr. X] saying what I was prepared to say this evening, but I soon realized what had happened—[Mr. X] picked up my speech and left me his. I assure you that his speech, which I have before me, is not nearly as good as mine, and I'm not going to give it. Instead, let me just emphasize some of the things in that beautiful address of mine which you have already heard."

Solve These Problems

As you read the following situations, pretend that they have just happened to you. Decide how you would handle each one:

1. You have a fever and are perspiring profusely. Perspiration is rolling down your face and dripping on your note cards.

2. You look like a drowned rat because a sudden rainstorm drenched you as you walked from the parking lot to the auditorium.

3. Your heel broke off as you were walking to the speaker's stand, and you are going to have to walk around the stage to use charts and models in your speech.

Setting and Equipment

You can check out the setting and equipment just before you are ready to speak and still have unexpected problems with them. It is impossible to anticipate when low-flying planes will be overhead, sirens will roar, or cars will backfire. Nor do you know when bathing beauties will walk by the windows or waiters will begin to set or clear tables. You cannot stop filmstrips from breaking or microphones from going dead.

Don't compete with visual or audio distractions. Try to eliminate a distraction, stop until it disappears, or work out a way to outperform it. If you must refer to the distraction, use humor. When you cannot get equipment to function, continue without it. Consider now how you would stop these distractions from ruining your speech:

1. You are giving a speech on office manners when the sound system begins to play music.

2. You have just started a speech when the microphone goes dead.

3. You are in the middle of a speech when a hailstorm drowns out what you are saying.

Think on Your Feet

When you are talking to a friend and the telephone rings, a child cries, or you mispronounce a word, you handle the situation easily. When you are speaking to an audience and an unexpected problem arises, handle it with the same spontaneity. Keep your cool. Learn to think quickly when you are speaking to an audience.

Adapt and Speak On

Whatever happens, adapt and speak on. If a thunderstorm comes up, a tape recorder won't work, or your knees begin to knock, adapt and speak on. When your charts fall down, your voice begins to quiver, and your nose starts to run, adapt and speak on. Ignore the hecklers, crying babies, and the yawners; adapt and speak on. Whatever goes wrong, don't apologize—adapt and speak on. Keep speaking because your listeners are there to hear you speak. They will survive and so will you if you can remain calm and confident.

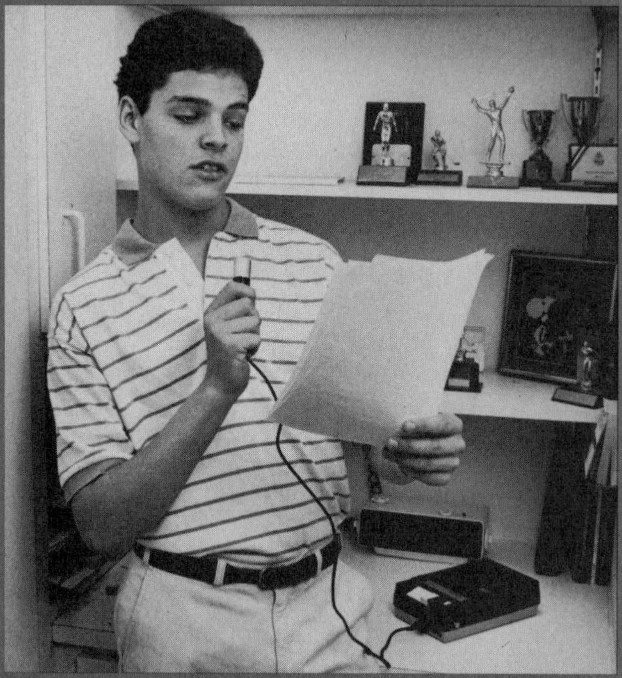

IMPROVING YOUR
Speaking Voice

P eople spend a lot of time improving their appearance. They style their hair. They buy new clothes. They bathe. They shave. They try to correct any flaws in their appearance before they step out to meet other people. Yet, appearance is not the only thing that people notice about each other. They notice the way others sound. They notice whether people speak too loudly, slowly, shrilly, harshly, or indistinctly. And they don't understand what others are trying to communicate to them if voice flaws interfere. This section will tell you ways to improve your speaking voice. It will give you exercises and activities to help you correct flaws in your voice.

How Your Voice Works

Do you know that your voice is like a yardstick? People use it to measure and judge your capabilities. That is why it is important for you to understand how your voice works. The more you know about how your speech is produced, the more you will know about developing a pleasing and effective speaking voice. Not knowing how the voice works is like driving a car without knowing anything about how it works. You can still drive the car, but not half as effectively as you would if you knew something about its inner

Like a car, your voice is a complicated mechanism of interconnected parts.

workings. Learning about how your voice works is like learning about how your car starts, runs, and stops.

An amazing fact that most people don't know is that all the organs that are used to produce your voice have other major functions in your body. For example, your lungs are used to bring oxygen to your body. They are also used to produce the air necessary for you to create a sound. Your tongue, lips, and teeth, which help you take in and chew your food, also let you produce speech sounds.

Just as there are different steps in driving a car, there are different steps in producing sounds. The steps in speaking are closely related. It is hard to tell where one step ends and another begins. Like a car, your voice is a complicated mechanism. It takes four steps to get your voice in gear and produce speech: breathing, vibration, resonance, and articulation.

Breathing

Breathing is an automatic body function. Good speaking depends on good breathing. To ensure that you have good breathing, check your posture. Are you slouching? Is your middle drooping? Take a minute now to check your posture. When you sit or stand carelessly, you could be cutting off vital air support that your speaking organs need. Improve your posture now before you read on. Remember that good posture is a vital part of good speaking. Your ability to produce sounds depends on the airflow through your lungs.

The diaphragm is the main organ you use when you breathe. It is attached to the lower ribs and separates the chest from the abdomen. The diaphragm pumps air in and out of the lungs. It begins the airflow by pulling the chest down, increasing the chest space. Then through inspiration (breathing air in), air rushes into this space. Next, the diaphragm pushes up, and the chest space is reduced. This action is called expiration (breathing air out). It forces the air out of the lungs. The illustration below gives you a clearer picture of how this works. Notice the size of the chest when air is taken in. You can see how the space becomes smaller as air is released. Sound is pro-

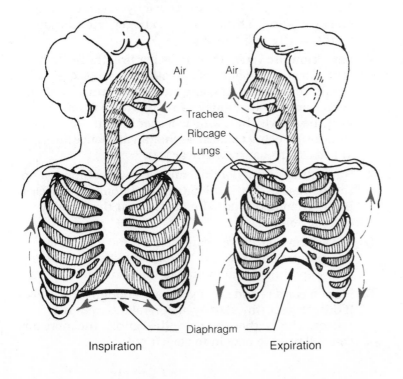

Air

Air

Trachea

Ribcage

Lungs

Diaphragm

Inspiration

Expiration

The parts of your body that help you breathe are your diaphragm, lungs, ribcage, and trachea.

duced when you breathe out. Just for fun, see if you can produce a word as you inhale.

Do you know that you breathe differently at times? When you are not speaking, you use fewer muscles to breathe, and the rate of air going in and out of your body is equal. When you speak, air is taken into the lungs, and this air is released at a much slower rate as you produce sounds.

You need to learn how to control the airflow through your lungs in order to speak your best at all times. Use the following breathing exercises. You should practice these exercises in different positions. Begin by doing the exercises lying down. Place a small towel or pillow under your head. Then repeat the same exercises during the day in sitting and standing positions. Before doing the following exercises in any position, make sure your posture is correct. This will enable your lungs to fill freely with air.

1. Place your hands on your abdominal area. It is located between the navel and lower ribs. Take air in slowly through your mouth and feel this area expand. Try the same activity again, only this time breathe through your nose. What happens to your abdominal area?

2. Take a deep breath and see how far you can count on one exhalation. This activity can be repeated as you count by 10's or 5's to 100.

3. Say, "How are you?" four times per breath. Begin by taking a small amount of air into your lungs. As you speak, control the air going out of your lungs so that people on the other side of a room will hear you. Repeat the activity by taking a deeper breath. Now control the air being exhaled so that an audience sitting at least 20 feet away will hear you.

4. Strengthen the abdominal muscles by pushing out on these muscles. This will make the abdominal muscles tight. Then take a deep breath. Repeat this activity several times.

5. Try seeing how far you can walk around a room on one exhalation. You can also do this activity climbing stairs or while you are taking a walk outside.

6. Light a candle, and see if you have enough air to blow it out. Repeat this activity at several different distances. The further you place the candle, the more air you will need to take in to blow it out.

7. Count as you inhale. Begin by counting to 10 and then increase to 20 and 30. As you exhale, see how many letters of the alphabet you can say. Try to work up to saying the complete alphabet on one breath.

8. Read two lines of the following poem in one breath. Keep adding lines until you can read three or four lines in one breath.

Windy Nights

Whenever the moon and stars are set,
   Whenever the wind is high,
All night long in the dark and wet,
   A man goes riding by.
Late in the night when the fires are out,
Why does he gallop and gallop about?

Whenever the trees are crying aloud,
   And ships are tossed at sea,
By, on the highway, low and loud,
   By at the gallop goes he.
By at the gallop he goes, and then
By he comes back at the gallop again.
     Robert Louis Stevenson

Vibration

Remember that sound is produced when you exhale. As air leaves your lungs, it is pushed through the trachea (windpipe) and then into the larynx (voice box), setting up the second step in the production of speech: vibration. This step takes place inside your larynx, which is the

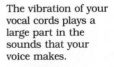

The vibration of your vocal cords plays a large part in the sounds that your voice makes.

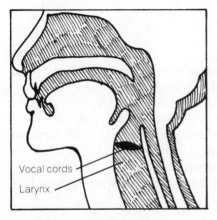

Vocal cords
Larynx

Vibrating vocal cords produce sound

Nonvibrating vocal cords do not produce sound

bump in the front of your neck that is commonly called the Adam's apple. Sound is produced when the outgoing air makes the vocal cords at the top of the larynx vibrate. While you are breathing normally, the vocal cords open wide to let air pass in and out freely. When you speak, they come together and vibrate. The illustration on page 83 shows the different positions of the vocal cords. The air vibrates the vocal cords just as clarinet players vibrate their lips on a mouthpiece. The sound that is produced at this stage of speech is weak and has little volume.

Practice the following exercises to achieve the muscle tone that you need during this step in the speaking process. You want to relax your throat and jaw.

1. Begin by twitching your nose like a bunny. Then move your lower jaw in a circle. Repeat this activity, only this time put both your lips together. Next, pretend you are exhausted. Make several large yawns. Finally, move your neck in circles. Go slowly from left to right first and then from right to left.

2. Once your muscles are relaxed, read the following poem softly:

Who Has Seen the Wind?

Who has seen the wind?
   Neither I nor you:
But when the leaves hang trembling,
   The wind is passing through.
Who has seen the wind?
   Neither you nor I:
But when the trees bow down their heads,
   The wind is passing by.
                    Christina Rossetti

Resonance

The circus ringmaster's voice cannot be heard by the audience without a microphone to amplify it. Your voice cannot be heard without its own built-in microphone to amplify the sound produced at the vibration stage. Your body's microphone is the series of organs that act as resonators. The resonating organs are the larynx, pharynx (back part of the throat), mouth, and nasal passages. These organs reinforce and build up the weak sounds pro-

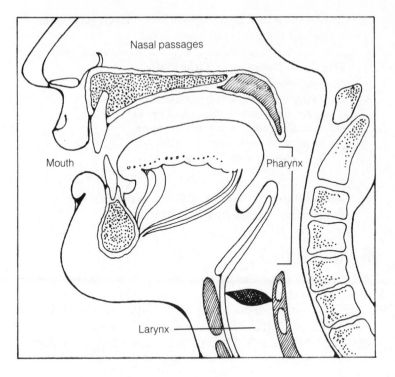

Nasal passages

Mouth

Pharynx

Larynx

Your resonators help amplify the sound of your voice.

duced by the larynx. The size of each resonator determines the loudness that it produces. The air that passes through the resonators is vibrating in time with the vibrations in the vocal cords. The hollow cavity inside a resonator creates the needed space for the sound to resonate and reverberate. Take time now to look at the illustration above and to locate your resonators.

It is interesting to note that if the size or shape of any resonator is changed, the characteristics of your voice change. The nasal passages vary only slightly in size, but the larynx, mouth, and pharynx are more flexible and can change their size and shape.

People who are good speakers use their resonators effectively. In order to improve the use of your resonators, try doing the following exercises. Make a tape of yourself doing the exercises. Then wait a week or two and record yourself again. Listen carefully to the tapes and note how much richer your voice sounds.

1. Look in a mirror as you yawn. Notice the position of your tongue. The tongue should be flat to enable the

sound being produced to exit freely. Keep your tongue flat as you read this passage aloud:

The Tide Rises, the Tide Falls

The tide rises, the tide falls,
The twilight darkens, the curlew calls;
Along the sea—sands damp and brown
The traveller hastens toward the town,
  And the tide rises, the tide falls.
      Henry Wadsworth Longfellow

---

2. Now read the passage again. Try to prolong the sound of the vowel in each stressed syllable.

Articulation

Articulation is the final step in the speech process. It is during this step that sounds produced in the earlier steps are turned into words. As a sculptor shapes clay into statues, the articulators shape the sounds you make into understandable speech. The organs in your body that work as articulators are the tongue, lips, teeth, and hard and

Your articulators help you shape sounds into understandable speech.

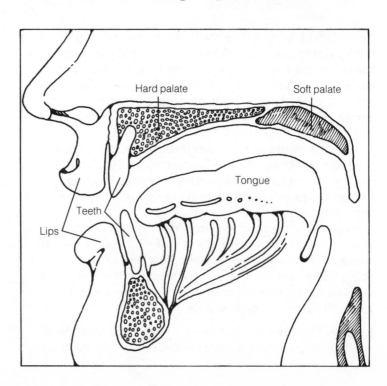

soft palates. These organs shape and separate your sounds into words. The articulators also select and change the path of the air. They can send the air through the nose or mouth.

Take a minute and study the illustration on page 86. Next, look in a mirror and locate all of the articulators. Then explore your articulators. First, place the tip of your tongue against the back of your teeth. Now slide your tongue up until it feels the hard ridge that joins your gums and teeth together. Let your tongue travel back into the vast space in your mouth. The roof of this area is known as the hard palate. Do you ever wonder what that soft piece of flesh hanging in the back of your mouth is? Open your mouth and take a look at it. It is called the uvula, and it is part of the soft palate.

While you are speaking, all of your articulators are in action. The soft palate is continually rising and lowering. Its job is to direct the airflow between the mouth and nasal cavities. When the soft palate presses down, it prevents the mouth cavity from receiving any air. When it rises up, it sends air into the mouth cavity.

Let's look at the jobs of the other articulator organs. The hard palate separates the mouth and nasal cavities. The tongue hits against this surface to make some sounds. The lips play a critical part in helping you to form your words. To help you realize just how important your lips are, watch the news or a favorite television show with the volume off. Look at the actors' or newscasters' lips. They never stop moving. Notice the different shapes that are formed.

Your teeth are another surface that the tongue and lips touch against in order to make sounds. Do you realize that without teeth it is impossible to make the *s* sound? Listen to a little child who is missing front teeth speak. Even a slight space between the front teeth can cause the *s* sound to become *th*. The tongue is very agile. It is constantly changing its shape and position. It has so many complicated movements that incorrect movement of the tongue is frequently the cause of speech problems.

Practice doing the following exercises to improve your articulation flexibility. Remember that when you do these exercises, you will need to overenunciate. Do so only when you practice these exercises. When you are speaking at any other time, remember to be yourself and to speak naturally.

1. Warm up your tongue by repeating as fast as you can:

   tah–tah–tah–tah–tah–dah–dah–dah–dah–dah
   bah–bah–bah–bah–bah–pah–pah–pah–pah–pah
   mee–mee–mee–mee–mee–nee–nee–nee–nee–nee
   fee–fee–fee–fee–fee–vee–vee–vee–vee–vee

2. Exercise your tongue by opening your mouth wide and running your tongue around the edges of your lips as fast as you can. Go clockwise and then counterclockwise with your tongue. Now, just for fun, stick out your tongue as far as it will go. See if you are one of the few people that can touch their nose with their tongue.

3. Exercise your lips by saying the following words three times. Be sure to exaggerate your lip movements.

   sal-a-man-der
   pol-y-un-sat-u-rat-ed
   be-wil-der-ment
   rec-tan-gu-lar
   nav-i-ga-tion
   su-per-in-ten-dent

   Complete the exercises by saying these two blockbusters clearly and distinctly:

   antidisestablishmentarianism
   supercalifragilisticexpialidocious

4. To exercise your mouth, lips, and tongue, say the following tongue twisters slowly. Then repeat them a little faster. Finally, tape yourself saying them at full speed:

   The crow flew over the river with a lump of raw liver.
   She sells sea shells by the seashore.
   Thirty-three tigers tramp through the thicket.
   Forty-four fireflies fly fast for fun.

5. Complete your exercise session by singing a lively song like "Yankee Doodle" or "Jingle Bells," which require the vigorous action of your articulators.

You can talk without thinking about how words are formed. But now that you know how the different organs work together to produce speech, you can improve the way you speak. You have taken the first step in becoming the speaker you want to be.

Voice Characteristics

Your voice carries your ideas to your listeners. It also tells them what you are like and what you feel. When your voice has no expression, your listeners may think that you are an uninteresting person. When your voice trembles, they imagine that you are nervous. The characteristics of your voice give people an impression of what they think your personality might be like.

An inadequate or inappropriate voice is a major handicap for anyone. Think of how ineffective a person who speaks slowly would be as an auctioneer. How successful would an umpire with a soft, whispery voice be? How many sales would a salesperson with a harsh, grating voice make?

There is no need for anyone to live with a minor speech problem. Let's get started now examining the characteristics of your voice. Now you are going to learn how you can improve the pitch, intensity, rate, and quality of your voice to make it sound like the interesting person you are. You will find out if you need professional help in a specific area or if you just need to pick up a few pointers to make your voice pleasant and effective.

Pitch

Pitch tells your listeners how you feel about what you are saying. Pitch is the highness and lowness of the sounds in your voice. Your voice has its own natural pitch range. If you are curious, you can find this range by using a piano. Strike middle C on the piano. Then sing the scale to find the highest and lowest notes you can reach comfortably. Your pitch range is the distance between these notes. It is determined by the size of your vocal cords. Most men have a lower range than women.

Too High. Speaking at too high a pitch makes the voice sound piercing and metallic. It irritates the listener's ears just as running a piece of chalk across a board will. A 40-year-old businessman with a high-pitched voice will sound like a 10-year-old boy instead of a high-powered executive.

Generally, the faster you speak, the higher the pitch of your voice is. Slow down your speech, and you will lower your pitch. Keep in mind that anger, worry, and tension tighten your vocal cords and thus raise the pitch. Try the following relaxation exercises to help lower your pitch:

1. Yawn several times to relax your throat muscles. Then open your mouth wide and say, *"ah, ah, ah,"* 10 times.

2. Say the vowel sounds several times to relax your jaw muscles.

3. Rotate your head from side to side several times to help relax your neck muscles.

4. Turn on your tape recorder. Read a paragraph from a book. Then put the book on the floor. Bend at your waist, relax your shoulders, and read the passage. This will automatically lower your pitch. Play the tape back and hear the differences in pitch.

Too Low. Few people have too low a pitch, which gives their voices a harsh, hollow sound. Most people have to try to keep their pitch low.

Monotone. Some people use the same pitch or a limited pitch pattern when they speak, perhaps due to tone deafness or a hearing loss. Most monotone speakers, however, sound this way because they are disinterested and unenthusiastic about what they are saying. You have probably tuned out, even become drowsy, sometime because you were listening to someone drone on in a dull, colorless tone. If you want to hold your listeners' attention, use a pitch pattern that goes up and down the musical scale. The next two exercises will help you vary your pitch patterns. Pitch patterns are closely related to music. Begin by saying this familiar tune. Make your pitch move up and down the scale.

little

twinkle   star

how I

wonder

what you

Twinkle   are.

Use melody in your voice as you read the following famous quotes:

"Nothing so needs reforming as other people's bad habits."
Mark Twain

"Men seldom make passes at girls who wear glasses."
Dorothy Parker

"Speak in French when you can't think of the English for a thing."
Lewis Carroll

Speaking with a singing melody in your voice pattern will give you greater flexibility in your pitch. It will make your voice more interesting.

Keep in mind that appropriate pitch is not the same for everyone, nor is it the same at all times. Actors often vary their pitch for greater dramatic effect. The right pitch for a boxer is not right for a soprano. The pitch of your voice at a funeral will not be suitable for a wedding.

Intensity

Intensity is the voice characteristic that refers to the loudness or softness of your voice. Intensity is a result of the energy, or air, behind your voice, and it is controlled by your diaphragm. If you wish to speak loudly, you must increase the amount of air released when you speak. On the other hand, if you release too little air, your voice will be too soft.

Most beginning speakers speak too softly and do not project, or make their voices carry over distance. To be an effective speaker, you will need to control the intensity and projection of your voice, just as you control the volume knob on your radio. Adjust your projection according to the size of the room, the number of persons listening, and the background noise. Vary your intensity to emphasize certain words and sentences.

Controlling your intensity and projection means controlling your breath. Practice reading these ever-longer lines smoothly in one breath:

1. Fire! Fire! Burn stick! Stick won't beat dog.
2. Fire! Fire! Burn stick! Stick won't beat dog, dog won't bite pig.

3. Fire! Fire! Burn stick! Stick won't beat dog, dog won't bite pig, pig won't jump over the stile.

4. Fire! Fire! Burn stick! Stick won't beat dog, dog won't bite pig, pig won't jump over the stile, and I can't get home tonight.

If you are unable to achieve proper intensity or control, the problem may be a breathing or a hearing problem.

Rate

Rate is the speed at which you talk. Just as most drivers go at different speeds, most speakers speak at different rates. Abraham Lincoln made his speeches at about 100 words a minute. John F. Kennedy raced through his. The average rate at which most people speak is somewhere between 140 and 180 words per minute. If you would like to know how many words you say in a minute, see how much of the following speech you can read aloud in that time. A speech is usually given at a slower rate than an ordinary conversation. The italicized numbers in parentheses refer to the number of words at various points in the speech.

Lincoln's Gettysburg Address

Four score and seven years ago, our fathers brought forth on this continent, a new nation, conceived in Liberty, and dedicated to the proposition that all men are created equal.

Now we are engaged in a great civil war, testing whether that nation, or any nation so conceived and so dedicated, can long endure. We are met on a great battlefield of that war. We have come to dedicate a portion of that field, as a final resting place for those who here gave their lives that that nation might live. It is altogether fitting and proper that we should *(100)* do this.

But, in a larger sense, we can not *(110)* dedicate—we can not consecrate—we can not hallow—this ground. The brave men, living and dead, who struggled here, have consecrated it, far above our poor power to add *(140)* or detract. The world will little note, nor long remember what we say here, but it can never forget what *(160)* they did here. It is for us the living, rather, to be dedicated here to the unfinished work which they *(180)* who fought here have thus far so nobly advanced. It is rather for us to be here dedicated to the *(200)* great task remaining before us—that from these honored dead we take increased

Abraham Lincoln
delivering the
Gettysburg Address.

devotion to that cause for which they *(220)* gave the last
full measure of devotion—that we here highly resolve that
these dead shall not have died in *(240)* vain—that this
nation, under God, shall have a new birth of freedom—
and that government of the people, by the people, for the
people, shall not perish from the earth. *(271)*

Your speech speed depends on the speed with which you
move your articulators (lips, tongue, teeth) and the pauses
you make between groups of sounds. It also depends on
how fast you are able to gather your thoughts. The ideal
rate is slow enough to be understood by your listeners and
fast enough to hold their attention. You make no uninten-
tional pauses or hesitations. It is a good idea to vary your
rate to emphasize certain words and parts of your
speeches.

Nervousness often makes people increase their speed.
You can lower your speaking rate by drawing out vowel
sounds and lingering over periods and commas. Reread
the Gettysburg Address. Try to lower your rate.

Quality

Quality is one of the most important characteristics of
your speaking voice; tone and sound make your voice different from anyone else's. Just as fingerprints are unique,
no two persons have identical voice quality. It is voice

quality that lets you pick up the telephone and know to whom you are talking. In fact, legal experts are investigating the use of "voice prints" to identify people.

Your voice quality is determined by the sound waves that you produce. It is made up of noise and musical elements. The more musical elements in your voice, the better the quality you will have. It is quality that makes listeners decide whether your voice is pleasant or not. It is quality that lets you show your feelings.

There are five common causes of poor voice quality. You need to know what these are to avoid having an unpleasant voice.

Nasality

Whining children, auctioneers, and carnival barkers have one thing in common. They talk through their noses. People often describe this type of speech as a nasal twang. Technically, it is called nasality.

Only three sounds in the English language need to be said through the nose: *m, n,* and *ng.* When people pronounce other sounds—especially vowels—in this way, most listeners find the voices unpleasant.

It's easy to find out if you talk through your nose when you shouldn't. Pinch your nostrils shut and read one of the words below. Then say the word again after releasing your nostrils. The vowels should sound the same both times if you don't talk through your nose. Have a friend judge how you sound.

> hall
> boat
> set
> fix
> cut

A self-test is to say the same words holding a mirror under your nostrils. If the mirror clouds, you probably have a nasal twang.

Sometimes professional help is required to eliminate excessive nasality; however, exercise can be effective. First, identify what the vibration of nasal sounds feels like by playing Santa Claus. Lay your finger on the side of your nose as you say, "Mom sang seven songs." Then keep your forefinger on your nose as you say the five words that you read aloud earlier to check for nasality. Try to reduce or eliminate the nasal vibration by lowering the pitch of your voice, speaking louder, and opening your mouth wider.

Denasality

Denasality is almost the opposite of nasality. It is stuffy, cold-in-the-head speech, as if you need to blow your nose or have a clothespin clamped over it. There is a lack of nasal vibration on the sounds for *m, n,* and *ng.* In extreme cases, a sentence like "Nothing matters now" sounds like "Dothig batters dow."

For denasality, you should consult your doctor. One or both of your nostrils may be blocked, causing this kind of speech. Vocal exercises will not improve this physical problem.

If you have fallen into the habit of speaking without nasal vibration because of a lengthy cold, a bout with allergies, or because of imitating the way someone else talks, vocal exercises can help you restore the correct sounds to *m, n,* and *ng.* You might begin by holding a plate right under your nostrils and trying to blow a cotton ball slowly across the plate as you hum.

For your next exercise, put your forefinger along your nose again. Say the following word pairs. There should be no vibration when you say the first word. Try to have vibration when you say the second word.

bag-bang	tap-tan	hug-hum
bet-met	wig-wing	cat-can
deck-neck	bad-mad	pig-ping

Harshness

A harsh or strident voice is caused by overtension in the throat and neck muscles. Many people refer to harshness as a pinched throat. A voice may be harsh because a person tries to speak louder than normal, for example, trying to talk at a convention without a microphone. Harshness may also be caused by an emotional condition that makes the throat tighten up. To improve harshness, you need to do relaxation exercises. Review the breathing, throat, and jaw exercises described at the beginning of this section.

Hoarseness

A voice that sounds both husky and coarse is a good description of hoarseness. You usually hear some hoarseness in the voices of boys between 7 and 14 years old. When you suffer from hoarseness, you can hear it in your own voice. You hear hoarseness when a person has laryngitis. With laryngitis, the larynx becomes sore and swollen, restricting the movements of the vocal cords. Hoarseness is also caused by smoke and dust in the air. It can also be caused by a sinus infection or a growth on your vocal cords. For these reasons, you should have persistent hoarseness checked out by a doctor. To improve hoarseness, you need to do some of the exercises to vary your pitch and relax your throat.

Breathiness

Do you sound like you have just completed the Boston Marathon when you talk? Are you unable to project your voice? People with these problems are said to have breathiness. They talk using as much air as voice. Breathiness comes from failure of the vocal cords to completely close. Thus, air is allowed to escape with the voice. This condition could be caused by a health problem, so you should have it checked by a doctor.

Rating Your Voice

Remember that your voice carries your ideas to your listeners. In order to have a pleasing and effective voice, you want to have appropriate pitch, intensity, rate, and quality at all times. Your voice is your own unique blend of these characteristics. Complete the following rating chart to evaluate the characteristics of your voice. You may find it interesting to let someone else rate your voice. Then compare the results.

Recruit the help of family members or friends to help you rate and evaluate your speaking voice.

Voice Characteristics

pitch	too high	satisfactory	too low
intensity	too loud	satisfactory	too soft
rate	too fast	satisfactory	too slow
quality	pleasant	satisfactory	unpleasant

Speech Spoilers

So far, this section of the book has talked about how to develop a pleasing and effective speaking voice. However, having a beautiful, melodious speaking voice isn't enough if your listeners are baffled by what you say. Is your speech so full of carelessly pronounced words, *uh*'s, *ur*'s, and other speech spoilers that your listeners keep asking, "What was that you said?"

If all of your speech organs function properly, there are several reasons why you may not speak as well as you could.

Habit.   You learned to speak in childhood by imitating others. If some of the people around you then did not say certain words correctly, you may still be saying these words incorrectly. Habits, like saying *pitcher* for *picture* or *libary* for *library*, are hard to break.

Carelessness.   Good speech requires considerable effort and attention. It's easy to slip into careless speech patterns. *Give me* can easily become *gimme*, and *did you* become *didya*.

Rapid Speech.   Most adults say between 140 and 180 words a minute, and the average word has four or five sounds. This means you could be producing 900 sound units in a minute. No wonder people fumble a sound occasionally.

Personality.   The type of person you are plays an important part in how you speak. The nervous person often talks too fast, while the low-keyed individual may draw each word out forever. And then there are shy people who are afraid to talk at all.

It is interesting to know why you speak as you do. However, to improve your speech, you need to identify what is stopping you from speaking as well as you could. Let's find out what your own personal speech spoilers are.

Articulation Problems

Articulation is the process of producing vowel and consonant sounds and joining them to form words. Consonants are more important than vowels in making your speech understandable. Notice how the phrase, *where in the world,* would sound with just consonants, *whr n th wrld.* It might be understood. It would not be understood with vowels alone: *ee i e o.* You have articulation problems when you do not say sounds distinctly and every word is not easily recognized. Almost everyone has them. Articulation problems that are caused by physical defects or inability to make a sound require professional help. Most problems can be blamed on habit or carelessness. To improve your articulation, you need to avoid omitting, adding, substituting, and reversing sounds in words. Once you become aware of these problems, you can often correct them by working conscientiously.

Omissions

One of the most common articulation problems is leaving out sounds. Two sounds frequently omitted in speech are the final *t* and *d*. Have you ever forgotten these sounds in words like kep*(t)* or thousan*(d)*? To say these letters, the tip of the tongue is placed against the upper teeth ridge. Explore this position with your tongue. Then say the following paired words clearly and distinctly so that your listeners can distinguish one word from another:

nod-not	send-sent	toad-tote
feed-feet	pod-pot	fried-fright
mold-molt	cold-colt	hard-heart
fad-fat	wad-watt	seed-seat

Continue increasing your awareness of the final *t* and *d* sounds by saying these tricky tongue twisters:

(d) A tree toa*d* love*d* a she toa*d*.
   That live*d* up in a tree.
   He was a two-toe*d* tree toa*d*.
   While a three-toe*d* toa*d* was she.

(t) You've no need to ligh*t* a nigh*t* ligh*t*
   On a ligh*t* nigh*t* like tonigh*t*.

People don't just omit final sounds like the *t* and *d*. They also jangle others' ears by leaving out sounds in the beginning and middle of words. You have probably heard people talk about the *Merican govment, plitical canidates,* and the *worl.* Try saying the following list. People frequently leave out one or more sounds in these common words. Be sure to say the underlined letters, as they are the ones that are often omitted.

as<u>k</u>	lib<u>r</u>ary	privi<u>l</u>ege
po<u>l</u>ice	pum<u>p</u>kin	gove<u>r</u>nor
<u>h</u>er	prob<u>ab</u>ly	lab<u>o</u>ratory
bal<u>l</u>oons	int<u>e</u>resting	temper<u>a</u>ture
gift<u>s</u>	erro<u>r</u>s	di<u>a</u>mond
<u>a</u>cross	p<u>e</u>rhaps	vi<u>o</u>lent
<u>th</u>em	batt<u>e</u>ry	poinsett<u>i</u>a
eighth<u>s</u>	Feb<u>r</u>uary	cemet<u>er</u>y
<u>th</u>at	c<u>o</u>rrect	particu<u>l</u>ar

Additions

Just as some people drop sounds when they speak, others add sounds. Are you a person who says *ath-a-lete* for *athlete?* Do you put up your *umber-ella* to avoid an *Apeer-il* shower? If you carelessly add sounds to words, you will need to get in the habit of using a dictionary to find out how to say words correctly. Can you find the extra sounds in the following words? You may find it helpful to use a dictionary to complete this exercise.

acrosst	ekscape	idear
filum	electorial	statikstics
reminant	drownded	attackted

Substitutions

Another articulation error that causes confusion is substitution. This means saying an incorrect sound for the correct one—for example, *jist* for *just.* Children often make this error. Study the list of common substitutions below:

dat for *that*	*wus* for *was*
liddle for *little*	*yur* for *your*
agin for *again*	*git* for *get*
becuz for *because*	*tuhday* for *today*

One of the most common sound substitutions is changing the final *-ing* sound to *-in'.* If you say the words *working* and *workin',* you will see how the sound is changed. Practice saying the following words carefully:

coming (not *comin'*)	*morning* (not *mornin'*)
going (not *goin'*)	*evening* (not *evenin'*)
dying (not *dyin'*)	*nothing* (not *nothin'*)

Now make a list of 10 words that end in *-ing* that you use all the time. Most of these words will be verbs like *eating, playing,* and *talking.* Practice your list until you automatically say *-ing* in every word.

Reversals

Some people mix up sounds when they are talking. They use the right sounds, but they invert the order in which two sounds are said, saying the second sound first. They say *occifer* for *officer.* They also speak of the *calvery* instead of the *cavalry.* People making this type of error may know how to say these words correctly, but they tend to keep on saying the words in the same old way.

Many reversal errors are made with words that are spelled with an *er* or *re*. Look at the words below. Which word is spelled correctly in each group?

> *children* or *childern*
> *prespiration* or *perspiration*
> *prescription* or *perscription*
> *modren* or *modern*

Pronunciation Problems

Pronunciation refers to the way a word should be said. Articulation, the process of forming the word, requires skill. Pronunciation requires knowledge. To have good pronunciation, people must know how to say each sound in a word, which part of a word is stressed, and what is acceptable speech for where they live.

Good English pronunciation is challenging because the English language is difficult to pronounce. Many letters and letter combinations can be said more than one way. Notice, for example, the different ways *ou* sounds in the words *thousand, thought, could, through,* and *rough.* People mispronounce a word because they are not familiar with the word or are imitating the incorrect pronunciation of others. Let's look at two of the more common pronunciation problems.

Misplaced Stress

One problem in pronouncing words correctly is knowing which part of a word is stressed. Say ho*tel,* not *ho*tel, and cigar*ette,* not *ci*garette. To find out which part of a word is stressed, it is often necessary to look the word up in a dictionary. Be sure to read the dictionary's explanation on pronunciation. All dictionaries do not follow the same system to show stress. If a dictionary gives you more than one choice, say the word each way. Then decide which way is more common in your area. The words below are problem words. People often stress the wrong part in these words. Decide which part you think should be stressed in each word before checking your choice in a dictionary.

in-fa-mous	pro-nun-ci-a-tion
gon-do-la	re-cess
clan-des-tine	com-pa-ra-ble
A-rab	su-per-flu-ous

Dialect

When you pronounce a word, how it sounds may depend on where you learned to speak. Think of how Jimmy Carter, John F. Kennedy, and Ronald Reagan sounded in their inaugural addresses. It is obvious that people in the United States pronounce words differently. The way most people in an area pronounce words is called a standard dialect. There are three major American dialects: Eastern Standard, Southern Standard, and General American.

Eastern Standard Dialect. This is the English that is spoken in the New England states. The eastern part of New York state is also included in this area. Here people often drop their r's and make a sound like *ah*. You will hear *wah* for *war* and *fahm* for *farm*.

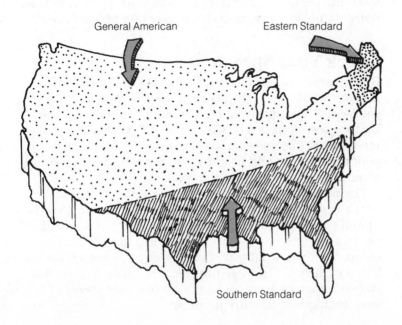

General American   Eastern Standard

Southern Standard

The three major American dialect regions.

Southern Standard Dialect.   This is the language spoken in the Southern states. You will hear it from the Middle Atlantic states south to Florida and west to Texas. *R*'s are dropped in this dialect, as in the Eastern Standard dialect, and *I* sounds like *ah. I work* becomes *Ah wuk.*

General American Dialect.   The vast majority of the people in the United States speak this dialect. This is the pronunciation you hear in all but the Southern and New England states. It is also the pronunciation you usually hear on television.

Local Dialect.   Within each dialect, there are variations in pronunciation. People who live in Manhattan do not sound exactly as those who live in Boston, even though both speak Eastern Standard dialect. Nor do people who live in New Hampshire sound exactly like those who live in Rhode Island. Some small communities, like Brooklyn, have a dialect that is quite different from the standard dialect of the area.

Foreign Dialect.   For many people, English is a second language. These people frequently pronounce words as they sound in the first language. These speakers may also have great difficulty pronouncing sounds that are not found in their language. You may wonder if a native of Hong Kong means *fly* or *fry.* Perhaps a German puzzles you by saying *vest* for *west.* Then there are the Spanish-speaking people who do not pronounce the letter *h* in their native language. For them, it's a *'orse of a different color.*

Check Your Speech

Good speech can be learned. One of the first steps is to find out what others think about the way you talk. Ask yourself: "Do people frequently want me to repeat a word? Do they seem puzzled by what I mean? Do they like to listen to me?" The answers to these questions will tell you if poor articulation and pronunciation are hampering your communication with other people.

The next step is to learn how to analyze your speech to find any problems that you may have. One way to do so is to make a tape recording of a short newspaper article that doesn't take you more than two or three minutes to read aloud. Listen to what you read. Better yet, have a friend listen with you. Then use the checklist below to pinpoint the areas in which you need to improve your speech. Answer each question with *yes* or *no.*

Speech Checklist

Are there errors of: omission? _____

addition? _____

substitution? _____

reversal of sounds? _____

misplaced stress? _____

Does your pronunciation sound like
the dialect of your community? _____

If you answer *yes* to any of the first five questions, the first
thing you need to do is to start listening carefully to the
speech of others. Notice the different sounds in each word.
Observe what part of each word is stressed. Next, get in
the habit of looking up words in the dictionary to find out
how to say them correctly. Begin now by looking up these
words, which are frequently said incorrectly:

admirable	ensemble	subtle
crochet	comparable	chiropractor
hypocrisy	garage	exponent

Study the pronunciation symbols in the dictionary before
you try to say the words. Then say each word several
times. Keep practicing until good articulation and pronunciation of these words become a habit. Start making
flashcards for words that you find difficult to say. Put the
word on the front of the card and its pronunciation on the
back. Use these cards frequently.

To determine if your pronunciation sounds like the
standard dialect of your community, compare it to how
the local newscasters sound when they read the news. Use
these people as your models. You want to use a dialect that
is most commonly used in your community. If you move
from one dialect area to another, you should keep your
own standard dialect. It is silly for someone from Chicago
or New York to move to New Orleans and immediately begin lacing their speech with *y'all.* As time passes, your
speech will change to fit your new environment.

Speech Tics

Articulation and pronunciation problems aren't the only
speech spoilers. What about the person who says:

"It was a scary movie *you know.* The special effects
you know were unbelievable. There was a demon computer *you know* that hurt people. It shocked anyone
who pushed the escape key *you know.*"

Perhaps this conversation exaggerates the use of *you know*. However, there are people who fill their conversations with speech tics like *you know, I mean, I believe, that's a fact,* and *they say.* An annoying habit like this can drive your listeners up a wall. The way to eliminate speech tics is to become aware of them. Make a tape recording of several of your telephone conversations. Play them back to discover if you have a speech tic. If you do, make a conscious effort to eliminate it from your speaking habits.

Conversation Fillers

Some people seem to be afraid to have a natural pause in a conversation or a speech. Whenever they stop to think about what they are going to say next, they compulsively fill the break with an *and, ur, um, uh,* or *ah.* Check to make sure that you don't have this speech spoiler by listening again to the telephone conversations that you taped earlier. If you find that you have this habit, you will need to start putting your mind in gear before you speak. Be sure to plan your formal speeches so carefully that you don't have to think about what topic is next. Remember this advice from Oliver Wendell Holmes:

> And, when you stick on conversation's burrs,
> Don't strew your pathway with those dreadful *urs.*

Serious Speech Problems

Few people speak so well that their speech cannot be improved. You have learned how to correct minor speech problems. There are, however, serious speech problems that require professional help for improvement. This type of problem interferes with communication, calls attention to itself, and frustrates both speaker and listener. It sets a person apart from other people.

Some serious speech problems result from a physical condition such as cleft palate, brain damage from seizures and strokes, cancer of the larynx, or partial or complete hearing loss. Other serious speech problems may be caused by a person's environment. Think about the child who does not receive encouragement at home to talk. This child may not develop normal speech skills. Severe emotional problems can also lead to speech problems.

The method of treatment of serious speech problems varies from case to case, depending on the age of the person and what the problem is. In every case, the motivation of the individual is crucial in determining the success of the treatment.

Stuttering

One serious speech problem is stuttering. In stuttering, the normal flow of speech is broken. The stutterer may repeat sounds and say things like *c-c-c-car* or *st-st-st-street*. You have probably heard sentences that sound like this: *M-m-m-my f-f-f-friend has g-g-g-gone.* Sometimes a stutterer draws a sound out (usually a vowel), as in *I seeeeeeeee you.* In stuttering, there may also be a spasm of the speech muscles that stops, or almost stops, speech. The effort to speak is frequently so great that a stutterer makes unusual facial and body movements.

Stutterers usually have problems when they have to speak in public or in any situation in which they feel uncomfortable. Almost all stutterers can speak smoothly at times. They can sing, read aloud, and talk to themselves without stuttering.

There are many theories about what causes stuttering. It has been blamed on the environment, the way people hear, and the way the brain works. We know that from four to six times more males than females stutter. But the exact cause of stuttering remains unknown.

Stuttering is most common in young children. It usually begins when a child is between 3 and 5 years old. Sometimes it appears in a school-age child. It rarely appears for the first time in an adult.

Caution.   Parents need to be extremely careful about mistakenly labeling their child a stutterer. Between the ages of 2 and 6, almost all children will at times lose some fluency in speech. They begin to repeat sounds and even whole words when they try to speak too rapidly or if they are upset or excited. They may make these repetitions for a period of weeks or months. Sometimes they may stop repeating and then start again. This is not stuttering. This is a normal step in speech development. During this time, parents should take great care not to call their child's attention to repetitions in speech. They should never tell their child to slow down or relax. The repetition becomes worse if the child is made aware of it. What parents should do is provide a warm, loving atmosphere and listen to what their child is saying rather than to how it is being said. If parents think their child is really beginning to stutter, they should look for professional help so the problem can be treated.

Over the years, many different treatments have been used to stop stuttering. You have probably heard about how Demosthenes, a famous Greek orator from the 300's B.C., put pebbles in his mouth to improve his speech. Impressive progress has been made in the treatment of stuttering in recent years. New treatment programs have shown a high rate of success in treating stutterers.

Lisping

The sounds *s* and *z* are hissing sounds. Snakes and angry cats hiss. So do tires that are going flat. People who lisp have trouble making hissing sounds. Sometimes they substitute other sounds, like *th*. Instead of saying, *My sister went to the zoo,* a person who lisps may say, *My thithter went to the thoo.* Another may just leave out the hissing sounds entirely and say, *My -i-ter went to the -oo.* And still another may change the hissing sounds into whistling sounds.

When children first begin to talk, many lisp. Most will learn to make the hissing sounds of *s* and *z* long before they start school. Almost all children will lisp again when they lose their front teeth. Lisping is probably the most common speech problem for school-age children. This is because the *s* sound is a very difficult sound to produce correctly. It is the sound in the English language with the highest frequency, and it is very noticeable when mispronounced.

People lisp for a variety of reasons. Some have a hearing loss and cannot hear hissing sounds to imitate them. A few people still use *baby talk.* Others have problems with their teeth or tongue that stop them from making these sounds correctly. Environmental and psychological problems also play a role in causing some people to lisp.

Fortunately, lisping is usually correctable with professional help. Adults do need serious commitment for treatment to be successful. People who have mouth or teeth defects will need to have these defects corrected before completely normal speech will result from treatment.

Getting Professional Help

Serious speech problems require professional help. You can actually damage your voice and even jeopardize your health if you try to improve some problems by yourself. For example, persistent hoarseness may be a sign of cancer, not a speech problem. The first step in improving a serious speech problem is to find someone who is qualified to advise you. Your family doctor should be able to help you find the right person.

The doctor may send you to a speech-language pathologist, the correct name for a speech therapist. Most speech-language pathologists hold a state license as well as a Certificate of Clinical Competence (CCC) from the American Speech-Language-Hearing Association. In order to hold a CCC certificate, a person must have a graduate degree, serve a period of internship, and pass a national test. Holders of this certificate are able to evaluate speech problems and help children and adults improve their speech.

For school-age children, help with speech problems is often available at their own schools. Today, many school systems have speech-language pathologists who screen every child for speech problems. If you have any questions about your child's speech, you can always ask them to evaluate it. They will either help children with problems or refer them to people who can.

If you have a question about a speech problem or need to find a speech-language pathologist, you can call the National Association for Hearing and Speech Action (NAHSA). Their number is in the phone book or available through directory assistance. The association is happy to answer your questions. It also has brochures about speech problems as well as about the normal speech and language development of children.

Helping Yourself

Just as exercising once a month will not let you keep a trim body, doing voice exercises occasionally will not let you develop or keep your best voice. You now have the facts to improve your voice. It's up to you whether or not you continue practicing the exercises that will give you a pleasant and effective speaking voice.

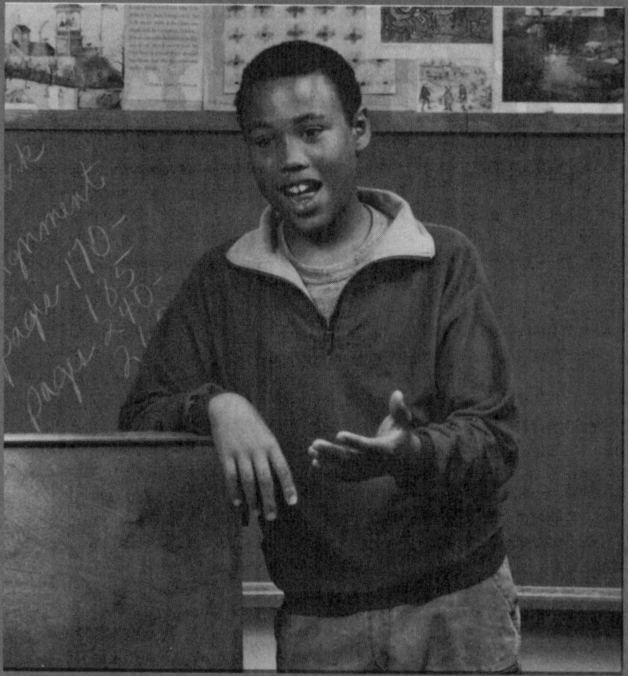

SPEAKING AT School

ou don't learn at school just by studying books. You learn through asking and answering questions, listening to others, and participating in discussions and debates. All of this involves communication. Communication is a two-way process. It involves sending messages and receiving messages. In reading this section, you will find out how to send effective messages by studying speaking in the classroom and at club meetings. You will find out how to make announcements and formal speeches, as well as certain speeches of courtesy. You will discover how to really talk with your teachers and counselors. As you learn to speak at school, don't forget that successful communication also means you must learn to listen.

Talking in Class

Have you ever stopped to think about how much you speak every day in school? There is hardly a class that you don't speak in. You speak to the teachers and to the other students. You speak to answer as well as to ask questions. You participate in class discussions. Classroom speech is different from the slang you use in the halls and the cafeteria. It is more formal. You say, "Hey, sport, what's the general's orders for tomorrow?" to your friends. You say,

Speaking in the classroom is more formal than the conversations that you have with fellow students.

"Could I have the assignment for tomorrow?" to your teachers.

You spend many hours in the classroom. The way you speak often affects your grades. This section will show you how to check your classroom speaking performance and will give you ideas on ways to improve your classroom speech.

Answering Questions

A day does not pass without your having to answer a question in some class. Even though classes and teachers are different, there are things that you can do to help improve your skill in answering questions. The first step is to learn to listen to questions. Don't jump in and answer a question before the teacher has finished asking it. Besides being rude, you may not be answering the question that the teacher was going to ask. Watch for question words like *who*, *what*, *when*, *where*, *how*, and *why*. They give you a clue to the information that a teacher or classmate is looking for. Study these examples:

1. When did Marco Polo arrive in China? (date)
2. Where was the Mayflower going to land originally? (place)
3. What is a symposium? (definition)

Now, just for fun, write down the answers to the following questions:

1. Is there a speech class in your school?
2. Have you ever taken a speech class?
3. Do you like to give speeches?

Notice that all the questions were answered with either *yes* or *no.* Look at the first word in each question. Then use these words to write some questions of your own. Have a friend answer your questions; look at the answers.

As you listen to a question, make a mental note of the words that are emphasized. These words will tell you what the question is really asking. Read the following questions and emphasize the word that is in italics:

1. Which country is the *largest* in Asia?
2. Which country is the *smallest* in Asia?

Be careful when you answer a question like "Where is the game, what time does it start, and are you going?" How many questions are you really being asked? When you are asked more than one question, you should repeat each question as you answer that segment. Your answer to the three-part question could sound like this: "First, you asked where the game is. It is at Northwest High School. Next, you wanted to know when the game starts. It starts at 8 o'clock. Finally, you wanted to know if I am going to the game. Yes, I'll be attending the game."

Always answer questions clearly. Don't overload your answers with trivia that will confuse the listeners. If asked for your opinion, support it with facts. Finally, if you are asked a question and you don't know the answer, the best solution is just to admit you don't know.

Asking Questions

Did you miss an assignment, do you want to know when a test is, or would you like additional information about a lesson? In order to solve these problems, you will need to ask questions. Just as there are different ways to answer questions, there are different ways to ask questions. Many people don't realize that it takes a certain skill to be able to ask a good question. You must know what kind of answer you are looking for in order to ask a question correctly. There are different styles of questions that can be used. Ask a general question if you want to give people the freedom to answer it in their own way. These questions let people ramble on forever as they give their answers. For example:

> "Why are we studying this lesson on climate?"
> "What can I learn from reading this book?"

Ask a limiting question if you want to have more control over how people answer. Their responses will be shorter and should give the information that you are looking for. Think of how your teacher would answer these questions:

> "What page does this lesson begin on?"
> "When will we have a test on this section?"

Ask a series of probing questions when you want to get all the information you need about a subject. To find out about a play, you might ask:

> "Who wrote the play?"
> "What is the setting?"
> "Why did you like it?"

You can practice asking questions by doing the following activity with a friend. Have your friend make a statement. Then ask a question using a word in the statement. This activity continues with statement, question, statement, question, and so on. Read the following example, and then see how far you can continue in this activity and in one of your own:

"I have a *pet*."

"What kind of a *pet*?"

"A *dog*."

"What kind of a *dog*?"

"My *dog* is a St. *Bernard*."

"Where did you find your St. *Bernard*?"

"I found him on a *farm*."

"How far away is the *farm*?"

Oral Exams

Maybe you have not had an oral exam yet, but someday before you finish your education you will experience one. They are more frequently used in college. However, some junior high school and high school teachers use oral exams. They may give them to students who have missed an earlier test or to find out how much students know about a book or experiment.

On a written exam, you can reread a question as often as you want. On an oral exam, you hear a question only once. Listen carefully to each question on an oral exam. After you have heard the question, it is a good idea to repeat the question. Then pause and get a mental picture of your answer before you open your mouth to give it. Remember, there is no eraser in an oral exam.

Speaking Up

Class participation is important. It lets the teachers see what you know and shows your interest in learning. Many teachers give a grade for class participation. Don't be afraid to take part. Ask questions. Give answers.

Give yourself practice in asking and answering questions by reading aloud the questions at the end of a chapter in any one of your books and then answering them. Begin practicing right now by answering the following questions:

1. What two words are usually used to answer questions beginning with the words *do, is,* or *have*?

2. What one question did you ask in school today, how was it answered, and in what class did you ask the question?

Speaking up and participating in class discussions is an important part of learning.

Reading in Class

Your teachers frequently ask you to read aloud in class. Sometimes you have the opportunity to prepare if you are going to read a poem, a story, or a part in a play. Usually, you are just told, "Read the next paragraph or problem."

Because you can read well silently does not mean that you read well aloud. Does your reading sound smooth, or do you fumble words and sentences? Is the class interested in what you read, or do they find your reading dull? Most important of all—do you get the message across when you read aloud in class?

Ordinary Classroom Reading

When you read parts of a textbook to a class, you are really acting as a reporter. You are reporting to them what the author says. Your approach should usually be unemotional. However, you do need to show interest in what you are reading, or your listeners will be bored.

To improve your reading, begin by slowing down, unless you normally read quite slowly. Most students race through textbook material and fail to make meaningful pauses. Pause for every punctuation mark. Come to a complete stop for periods, colons, and semicolons. Be sure to raise the pitch of your voice to identify questions for your listeners. Pause to emphasize certain words or phrases. When a word is underscored or written in italics, the author wants the reader to notice it. When you read one of these words aloud, increase the volume or change the pitch of your voice so your listeners will notice the word. Before you begin to read, check your posture. Make sure that you are sitting up straight and holding the book properly. As you read, think. It will help you make sense of the material for yourself and your listeners.

The best way to improve your ability to read aloud is to practice. Read the following textbook selections aloud several times. Record your first and last readings of the selections. Pay close attention to the words that are special vocabulary for each subject. Remember to follow the suggestions given for improving your reading.

Mathematics. The top of a flagpole is 50m above the level of the ground. The angle of depression from the top of the flagpole to a picnic table is 27°. How far from the base of the flagpole is the picnic table?

English. Some words or phrases in sentences interrupt or break the flow of a sentence. These words are often called *interrupters.* Interrupters are set off from the rest of the sentence with commas or parentheses to show that you should pause before and after them.

Social Studies. President Truman had declared that the United States would help other nations of the world fight the spread of communism. Under President Eisenhower, an idea about the spread of communism called the *domino theory* became accepted by many American leaders. This theory held that countries touch each other like dominoes. If one country fell to communism, then the countries touching its borders would soon fall also.

Science. The gravity of the earth pulls the moon toward earth to hold it in orbit around the earth. The gravity of the moon pulls our ocean waters to make tides. Magnetic force can also pull objects from far away. So can electrically charged objects. Scientists believe that the protons inside an atom exert a force on the neighboring electrons.

Now play back your recordings. Notice how your reading improved. You will continue to improve if you read paragraphs from your textbooks aloud every day. Practice really does make perfect.

Interpretive Reading

When you read a poem, story, or part in a play, you are not acting as a reporter but as an interpreter. You are trying to communicate the author's meaning to your listeners. Singers communicate a lyricist's meaning as they sing the words of a song. Musicians communicate a composer's meaning as they play the notes.

Analyzing What You Read

In order to communicate what an author means, you need to analyze a selection. Begin your analysis by finding out what the main idea or ideas of a selection are. You may have to read a selection several times to do this. Then try to catch the mood of the selection. Ask yourself if it is happy, sad, or humorous. Note how the author has used such devices as repetition, rhythm, or rhyme to show the mood. It may be easier to analyze a selection if you know something about the author. For example, knowing about all the tragedy in Edgar Allan Poe's short life helps you understand the melancholy mood of his poems. Remember that authors choose their words with care; make sure that you know what each word in a selection means. Look up any word that you don't know in a dictionary. Search for figures of speech. Authors use them to show their ideas and feelings.

Analyze the following excerpt from a speech by Martin Luther King. Can you find the main idea? Can you catch its mood? Do you see how he used repetition to show the mood? Would it help to know about his role in the civil rights movement in understanding the speech? Are there any words you should look up in a dictionary? Can you find any figures of speech?

I Have a Dream

I say to you today, my friends, that in spite of the difficulties and frustrations of the moment, I still have a dream. It is a dream deeply rooted in the American dream.

I have a dream that one day this nation will rise up and live out the true meaning of its creed: "We hold these truths to be self-evident; that all men are created equal."

I have a dream that one day on the red hills of Georgia the sons of former slaves and the sons of former slave owners will be able to sit down together at the table of brotherhood.

I have a dream that one day even the state of Mississippi, a desert state sweltering with the heat of injustice and oppression, will be transformed into an oasis of freedom and justice.

I have a dream that my four little children will one day live in a nation where they will not be judged by the color of their skin but by the content of their character.

I have a dream today.

I have a dream that one day the state of Alabama . . . will be transformed into a situation where little black boys and black girls will be able to join hands with little white boys and white girls and walk together as sisters and brothers.

I have a dream today.

Marking Your Copy

Once you have analyzed a selection, you are ready to begin preparation to read it aloud. Whether you are reading poetry or prose, it is helpful to copy the selection so you can mark the places where you want to pause or stress a word or phrase. You can show pauses by drawing vertical lines or slashes. Many readers use one line or slash for a brief pause and two for a full stop. Underline the word or words that you wish to stress. You will want to vary the loudness of your voice to show stress.

One of the most dramatic speeches ever made was Winston Churchill's address to the House of Commons on June 4, 1940, after the English army had escaped from Hitler by crossing the English Channel in all kinds of boats. Churchill felt that the following passage from his speech was important in the decision of the United States to enter World War II the following year. Perhaps he marked his copy like this:

Even though large tracts of Europe / and many old and famous States / have fallen or may fall into the grip of the Gestapo and all the odious apparatus of Nazi rule, / we shall not flag or fail. / / We shall go on to the end, we shall fight in France, / we shall fight in the seas and oceans, / we shall fight with growing confidence / and growing strength in the air, / we shall defend our island whatever the cost may be, / we shall fight on the beaches, we shall fight on the landing-grounds, / we shall fight in the fields and in the streets, / we shall fight in the hills; / / we shall never <u>never</u> surrender, / and even if, / which I do not for a moment believe, / <u>this island</u> or a large part of it were subjugated and starving, / then our <u>Empire</u> beyond the seas, / <u>armed</u> and <u>guarded</u> by the <u>British Fleet</u>, / would carry on the struggle, / until, / in <u>God's</u> good time, / the New World, / with all its power and <u>might</u>, / steps forth to the <u>rescue</u> and the <u>liberation</u> of <u>the Old</u>."

Analyze Churchill's speech. Then try to communicate his feelings as you read it aloud. You can use the copy markings or create your own.

Building to a Peak

Many short stories, poems, and plays build to a climax. It is the dramatic point of the selection. Keep this in mind as you are preparing to read. Build steadily toward the climax. Let your audience know when you have reached it.

Jaws by Peter Benchley is a dramatic story. As you may know, in this story a woman is attacked by a shark. The following excerpt begins just after the shark has sensed the presence of the woman in the water. Practice building up to the peak of interest when the shark attacks the woman.

Good interpretive reading will capture and hold the interest of your fellow students.

The fish closed in on the woman and hurtled past, a dozen feet to the side and six feet below the surface. The woman felt only a wave of pressure that seemed to lift her up in the water and ease her down again. She stopped swimming and held her breath. Feeling nothing further, she resumed her lurching stroke.

The fish smelled her now, and the vibrations—erratic and sharp—signaled distress. The fish began to circle close to the surface. Its dorsal fin broke water, and its tail, thrashing back and forth, cut the glassy surface with a hiss. A series of tremors shook its body.

For the first time, the woman felt fear, though she did not know why. Adrenaline shot through her trunk and her limbs, generating a tingling heat and urging in her to swim faster. She guessed that she was fifty yards from shore. She could see the line of white foam where the waves broke on the beach. She saw the lights in the house, and for a comforting moment she thought she saw someone pass by one of the windows.

The fish was about forty feet from the woman, off to the side, when it turned suddenly to the left, dropped below the surface, and with two quick thrusts of its tail, was upon her.

Making Poetry Musical

Poetry is language handled in a special way. It is musical. You have to think about how the poet meant the poem to sound when you read it aloud. Each poem has its own rhythm. For some poems, it is a fairly regular beat like de-*dumm* de-*dumm* de-*dumm* de-*dumm* de-*dumm* de-*dumm*. For others, there is no regular pattern. Read a few lines of the first stanzas of the poems below aloud, and you should be able to detect the rhythms.

The Raven

Once upon a midnight dreary, while I pondered, weak
   and weary,
Over many a quaint and curious volume of forgotten
   lore—
While I nodded, nearly napping, suddenly there came
   a tapping,
As of some one gently rapping, rapping at my chamber
   door
" 'Tis some visitor," I muttered, "tapping at my chamber
   door—
Only this and nothing more."
                Edgar Allan Poe

Silence

My father used to say,
"Superior people never make long visits,
Have to be shown Longfellow's grave
Or the glass flowers at Harvard.
Self-reliant like the cat—
that takes its prey to privacy,
the mouse's limp tail hanging like a shoelace from its
      mouth—
they sometimes enjoy solitude,
and can be robbed of speech
by speech which has delighted them.
The deepest feeling always shows itself in silence;
not in silence, but restraint."
Nor was he insincere in saying, "Make my house your inn."
Inns are not residences.

                                Marianne Moore

Two Cautions.   Don't forget that the meaning and mood of a poem are more important than the rhythm. Never read a poem in a singsong fashion. Remember too that poets decide where lines end. Be sure to pause at the end of each line. But do not make a long pause unless the thought is complete. Study the first stanza of this poem by Robert Frost. Decide on where and how long you will pause before you practice reading the poem aloud.

The Road Not Taken

Two roads diverged in a yellow wood,
And sorry I could not travel both
And be one traveler, long I stood
And looked down one as far as I could
To where it bent in the undergrowth;

Hear the Music.   Learn to feel the rhythm of a poem. Communicate what you feel to your listeners. Imagine that you are dancing the boogie-woogie as you read aloud this poem by Langston Hughes:

Dream Boogie

Good morning, daddy!
Ain't you heard
The boogie-woogie rumble
Of a dream deferred?

Listen closely:
You'll hear their feet
Beating out and beating out a—

> *You think*
> *It's a happy beat?*

Listen to it closely:
Ain't you heard
like a—

> *What did I say?*

Sure,
I'm happy!
Take it away!

> *Hey, pop!*
> *Re-bop!*
> *Mop!*
>
> *Yeah!*

Becoming a Better Reader

Whether you have to read at a minute's notice or have days
to prepare a selection, there are several things that you
can do now to prepare for reading aloud in class. Spend
some time listening to others read aloud. Study how re-
porters read the news on radio and television. Find out
how actors communicate the main ideas and emotions of
a selection to their listeners by listening to recordings of
speeches, plays, and stories. Most important of all—learn
to enjoy reading aloud. A good way to do this is to read stories and nursery rhymes to children. Most children's liter-
ature is meant to be read aloud. Let yourself go as you become the voice of such characters as the big, bad wolf and
Snow White. The children will show you how much they
enjoy your reading, and it will give you confidence to read
aloud in the classroom.

Making Oral Reports

The most common kind of speech that you give in school
is the report. It may be a report on a U.S. President for social studies, a report on the results of an experiment for a
science class, or a book report for English. Most reports
that you make are really speeches to inform. The members
of your class and the teacher will expect to hear facts, not

Be sure to appeal to your audience when you are giving an oral report.

opinions. You will need to avoid saying such things as, "I think," or "I believe." Just stick to the facts. Don't describe Monticello as an interesting home filled with the golden memories of a fascinating part of our history. Language like *interesting, golden memories,* and *fascinating past* is not objective. In a report, Monticello should be described as the home of President Thomas Jefferson that was built in the classical European style of architecture and completed in the year 1809. You may add that Jefferson said that he hoped to end his days at Monticello. Your listeners should be able to find everything that you say in a report in the references that you used.

Plan your report just the same as you would plan a speech to inform. Research the subject that the teacher has assigned, or choose one that is so narrow you can become an expert on it. Often the hardest part of organizing a report is to select the most important facts. As you prepare your report, keep these suggestions in mind:

1. Start with an outline.
2. Use information that is new to your listeners.

3. Tie your information to what the class knows.
4. Begin your report with an attention-getting opener.
5. Repeat the main ideas of your report in the conclusion.

Most students use note cards when presenting an oral report to a class. If you are to read your report, you must write it in an oral style. Imagine that you are saying the report as you write it. Be sure to mark your copy so you will know where to pause and where to stress words and phrases when you read it.

Appealing to Your Audience

An audience will accept what you are saying in a report if they think that you know what you are talking about. For example, if you were going to hear reports on boxing by Muhammad Ali and the psychologist Joyce Brothers, which speaker would you expect to be the expert on the subject? You are probably familiar with Ali's accomplishments in the ring and will accept him as an expert on boxing. You may not know that Joyce Brothers won thousands of dollars on a television quiz show due to her knowledge of boxing. Joyce Brothers would probably have to tell you about her background for you to accept her as an expert on boxing. Ali would not need to tell you of his background. Sometimes it may be necessary for you, like Joyce Brothers, to tell your audience why you are an expert on a subject. You can do this by telling them about how you learned about your subject through experience or research. Don't overdo your sales job, though. Make it brief but convincing.

Studying a Sample Report

Read this report that was given in a high school science class. Observe how the speaker established herself as an expert on the subject.

Carbohydrate Loading

I am a tournament tennis player. Do you know what I have in common with the New York Jets football team? We both follow a special diet called carbohydrate loading to improve our performances in athletic events. Carbohydrate loading is more than stuffing yourself with spaghetti, macaroni, potatoes, rice, pancakes, and waffles right before going out to compete in an athletic contest. It means following a special diet procedure for at least four days before an athletic competition.

There are three major carbohydrate-loading procedures. The original procedure, which was developed by Scandinavian sports scientists, involves both exercise and diet. Seven days before an athletic competition, an athlete exercises to exhaustion. Then for the next four days, the athlete eats a low carbohydrate diet. During the three days before the competition, the athlete stops exercising and eats a high carbohydrate diet. On the day of the competition, the athlete can eat anything he or she wants.

Many athletes follow a shortened four-day version of the original procedure. On the first day, they exercise to exhaustion. Then on the next three days before the competition, they eat high carbohydrate diets and do not exercise.

In the third diet procedure, which I follow, you don't exercise to exhaustion to start the diet. You just stay on a high carbohydrate diet for four days before an athletic competition.

Athletes used to consume protein before athletic events. In fact, Babe Ruth once ate 20 hot dogs before a game. Recent research has shown, however, that the energy used in sports like long distance running, distance swimming, basketball, football, tennis, and other long duration sports comes from carbohydrates rather than protein.

Carbohydrates are stored in the muscles. As an athlete exercises, these stores of carbohydrates are reduced. When they are nearly empty, the muscles will fail to contract and the athlete will be exhausted. Marathon runners call this *hitting the wall.*

Research studies in the Scandinavian countries and at Purdue University have shown that there is a direct relationship between the amount of carbohydrates stored and the length of time in which exercise can be performed. They have also found out that following any one of the different carbohydrate diets does increase the amount of carbohydrates stored in the muscles. The longer diets have been found to be more effective than the shorter ones.

Athletes who take part in endurance events need a good supply of energy to perform their best. Carbohydrates give them the fuel they need for prolonged, vigorous exercise. The greater the amount of carbohydrates they are able to store in their muscles, the greater their endurance will be. Following one of the carbohydrate-loading diets lets athletes store more carbohydrates in their muscles. Carbohydrate loading does work. I know that it has given me extra energy in some tough tennis matches.

Make a tape of yourself reading this report on carbohydrate loading. Then listen to your recording. Finally, ask yourself the following questions:

1. Did the speaker begin with an attention-getting opener?
2. Did the speaker stick to the facts?
3. Were the main ideas repeated in the conclusion?

Book Reports

During your school years you will probably give more book reports than any other kind of report. Book reports are slightly different from other reports because they let you give your opinions as well as the facts about a book. If your teacher does not tell you what to include in a book report, you may find it helpful to follow these ideas:

1. Begin by telling the name of the book and the author.
2. Identify the book as a member of the mystery, biography, science fiction, romance, or other category.
3. Describe the most interesting character or characters, the setting, and the plot.
4. Include actual quotes from the book to make the setting and characters come alive.
5. Point out what the theme of the book was.
6. Tell your audience what you think of the book. Back your opinion with reasons.

There are two basic reasons for giving a book report: to convince your teacher that you read the book and to help your audience determine whether they want to read the book. Read the following book report. Then decide if the speaker satisfied both reasons.

Gulliver's Travels

I would like to introduce you to Lemuel Gulliver, a surgeon, sea captain, and traveler, who is the main character in the book *Gulliver's Travels* by Jonathan Swift.

Gulliver is a good and honest middle-class Englishman. He is never content to remain at home with his wife and children. Instead, he spends his life traveling to strange lands. Gulliver gets himself into adventures because he is gullible. He writes about his travels in this book.

One of the lands that Gulliver tells about is Lilliput. In Lilliput, the people are so tiny that he could put five of them in his pocket. The tallest trees are seven feet tall. The tallest horses are four and five inches tall. A sheep is the size of a sparrow. A lark is not as large as a fly. Another place that Gulliver visits is Brobdingnag. This is a land of giants. A little girl of 9 is already 40 feet tall. A dwarf is 30 feet tall. A rat is as big as a dog. The other lands that Gulliver visits are also quite different.

Wherever Gulliver goes he has adventures. The Lilliputians tie him down with thread. In Brobdingnag, he fights rats the size of dogs with a hanger. In another place, he talks to Brutus and sees Caesar and Pompey. Gulliver survives a shipwreck, piracy, and a mutiny. He is picked up in his house by an eagle and dropped in the ocean.

Gulliver's Travels is a fantastic adventure story. Even though this book was published in 1726, Gulliver met as many interesting and unusual characters in his travels as Luke Skywalker did in *Star Wars*. Read this book if you like adventure stories. Read this book if you like satire. The author makes fun of people in high office, and he makes fun of all the people who take themselves too seriously.

If you had listened to this book report, would you have wanted to read *Gulliver's Travels*? If so, think about what the speaker said that made you want to read the book. If not, think about how the speaker could have convinced you to read the book.

Making a Good Report

Like a good speech, a good report is well prepared. If you are going to read your report, practice reading it aloud until the copy is no longer a barrier between you and the audience. As a general rule, a good report is brief and factual. Avoid too much detail; it can drown your listeners. Use speaking tools when it is appropriate to explain the subject of your report. To have a good report, you must communicate your enthusiasm for a subject to your audience as well as establish yourself as someone who knows the subject.

Group Discussion

A good way to encourage group discussion in the classroom is to arrange the seating in a round-table fashion.

> No man is an Island, entire of itself; every man is a piece of the Continent.
>
> John Donne

You are not just a student at school. You are also part of classes, clubs, and informal social groups. As a member of these groups, you participate in discussions. Discussions are a way of talking things over. In group discussions, you solve problems, make plans, and provide and acquire information. In a discussion, you share your ideas with others. They share their ideas with you. Some of your discussions are formal. Most are informal. You have discussions in the classroom, the school auditorium, gym, on the bus, and in the halls. Some of your discussion groups may be quite large—over 100 people. Others may be quite small—perhaps only two people. The people in your discussion groups may be friendly, unfriendly, or even hostile.

Group discussions are often concerned with solving problems. Even though discussions have been going on ever since Adam met Eve, it was not until 1933 that John Dewey, the American philosopher, laid down the essential steps to solving a problem in his book *How We Think.* Dewey wrote his steps for individuals, but through the years these steps have been used effectively by discussion groups. Take the time now to familiarize yourself with them so you will be able to use these steps the next time you are taking part in a discussion to solve a problem.

1. Identifying the problem.
2. Analyzing the problem.
3. Bringing up possible solutions.
4. Evaluating different solutions for the problem.
5. Deciding on the best solution.
6. Verifying the solution by observation or practice.

You can participate in different kinds of group discussions. There are classroom discussions, panel discussions, symposiums, forums, conferences, brainstorming sessions, role-playing dramas, and many more.

In each kind of discussion, there is usually a leader and members. To make communication effective, certain rules should be followed by everyone:

1. Come prepared. Know what you are going to say.
2. Listen carefully when others are speaking.
3. Take your turn in speaking.
4. Look at the group as you listen or speak.
5. Speak so that you can be heard.
6. Limit your own speaking time.
7. Stick to the subject.
8. Be courteous at all times. Disagree politely.
9. Control your emotions.
10. Accept the decision of the majority.

When a discussion group has a definite leader, that person bears most of the responsibility for making the discussion successful. To do this, a leader needs to do the following:

1. Arrange the setting for the meeting.
2. Plan the meeting.
3. Help the group become acquainted.
4. Start the discussion.

5. Keep the discussion moving toward its goal.
6. Relate to the members and the audience.
7. Encourage each member to participate.
8. Give credit for all suggestions.
9. Stay in the background.
10. Close the meeting with a summary.

Classroom Discussion

Each day you may take part in discussions in many of
your classes. Your teachers usually lead these discussions.
They will probably begin a discussion with a question and
then ask a series of probing questions to keep the discussion moving. They use the discussion to stimulate the
thinking of the class. Take the time now to evaluate your
contribution to a recent classroom discussion. Look back
over the rules for participating in a discussion; see how
many you followed.

Panel Discussion

An informal conversation about a subject or a problem
that takes place in front of an audience is called a panel
discussion. It is designed to stimulate and inform an audi-

A panel discussion is
an informal
conversation between
two or more students
that takes place in
front of the class.

ence. Most panels have from two to eight members. These people should sit so that they can see and be seen by the audience. A panel discussion usually has a leader who begins by introducing the panel and stating the subject or problem. The members ask questions, make statements, and talk about what the others have said. The panel tries to cover the subject or problem in an organized way.

Read the following panel discussion in which class officers discuss adding new subjects to the curriculum. Notice the roles played by the different members of the panel. The leader of the panel is the class president.

President: Our school only offers college preparatory courses. Today, the officers of our class are going to discuss what other subjects should be taught. Let's begin by finding out what subject each panel member thinks should be added to the course offerings.

Vice President: I talked to the members of the Honor Society who suggested a class in using computers. Many of them already have home computers.

Secretary: I'd like a computer class too.

Treasurer: We need business classes. No one even knows how to type. So how could they use computers?

Secretary: Business classes would be great. If I knew shorthand, I could take better notes for my classes and meetings like this.

Vice President: How about starting a business club? Maybe we could also have a computer club.

President: That's an interesting idea. But today we are talking about new classes, not clubs.

Treasurer: What about a basic cooking class? We all need to know how to cook.

Secretary: Great idea! Super!

Vice President: That's fine, but I really think that we would benefit more from a computer class than a cooking class.

Secretary: We should have all these classes. The students in our school have different needs.

President: Thank you for your excellent suggestions. It would seem that the school needs to have computer, business, and cooking classes.

Now evaluate the roles each member played in the discussion. Decide who advanced the discussion and who sidetracked it. Study the rules for being a leader again. Did the president follow them?

Symposium

A symposium is more formal than a panel discussion. Several participants give speeches in a symposium. Each speech represents a different viewpoint on a subject or problem. The participants do not usually interact unless a question-and-answer session follows the individual speeches. The leader makes an opening statement, introduces the speakers, and winds up the symposium with a short summary of the speeches. If the preceding panel discussion had been presented as a symposium, the vice president would have spoken about a computer class, the treasurer would have spoken about either business or cooking classes, and the secretary would have had to select a subject.

Forum

A forum is a discussion in which the audience has a chance to participate. A forum lets an audience ask questions of speakers and panel members or make comments about what has been said in a presentation. A forum is usually held at the end of a panel discussion or a symposium. Forums are also held at the end of debates, lectures, and films. Sometimes members of the audience can ask questions or comment during a presentation. No matter when a forum is held, the members of the audience should follow the rules for participating in a discussion.

Other Group Discussions

Any time you talk things over with other people, you are participating in a group discussion. Brainstorming is a stimulating form of group discussion. A leader sets a time limit in which the participants are to give as many ideas as they can about a subject or problem. For example, the ninth-grade class president might have given the other class officers five minutes to name the new subjects that should be added to the course offerings. Even wild ideas are appreciated in a brainstorming session, so suggesting classes in karate, French cooking, and ice fishing would have been acceptable.

Role playing is another form of group discussion. It can be used to explore personal relationships. You can play the role of a teacher, a team member, or a member of your family. Role playing helps you understand the feelings of others.

Your Role in Group Discussion

A class committee meets to decide when and where the junior prom will be held. The Spanish Club officers meet to decide how to spend the money from the candy sale. The football team meets to discuss how they can win the big game. Many decisions that affect your life are arrived at through discussions. Learn to participate in and lead discussions so that you can take part in those decisions.

Your participation in group discussions will not end when you leave school. Adults participate in club meetings, office meetings, homeowner meetings, political meetings, and many other meetings.

Debate

People take part in debates throughout their lives. You may have debated the merits of an assignment with a teacher, the advantages of an after-school job with your parents, or the dangers of smoking with your family or friends. A debate is a clash of ideas. It is a series of oral arguments for and against a definite proposal. When you debate, you are trying to convince others of the value of your argument.

Debates can be either formal or informal. Most debates that you participate in are informal. Informal debates do not have clear-cut rules, definite time limits, or the same number of people on each side. Formal debates are conducted according to definite rules of procedure. High school debates are considered formal debates. The Lincoln-Douglas debates and the more recent presidential debates are formal debates. This part of the book will introduce you to formal debates. Once you have mastered the skills of formal debating, you will also be able to use them in your informal debates.

Formal Debate

A formal debate has a subject. The subject is written as a carefully worded statement called a proposition. The statement, usually formed as a resolution, makes clear both the position of the side in favor of the statement and that of those against the statement. Here are several examples of debate subjects:

Resolved, that contact sports in high schools should be abolished.

Resolved, that a course in typing should be required for high school graduation.

Resolved, that Saturday morning cartoons should be limited to two hours.

Resolved, that the United States and Canada should establish joint citizenship for their citizens.

Resolved, that the federal government should pay for a college education for everyone.

Debate teaches you to organize your arguments and support them with evidence.

There are two sides in a debate. The side that agrees with the proposition is called the *affirmative side.* The side opposed to the proposition is called the *negative side.* This side does not agree with the statement. Look at the statements above again. Choose which side you would defend in each statement. Before making your choice, think about how well you know the subject and how strongly you feel about each side.

Preparation for a Debate

If you have a debate partner or partners, you must work together closely to prepare your arguments. You have completed the first step in preparing for a debate when you choose, or are assigned, which side you will argue. The next steps are analyzing the statement, finding your evidence, and building your case. You will probably find yourself doing parts of these steps at the same time. You may not always do the steps exactly in this order. Sometimes you will have to find your evidence before you can analyze the statement, especially if you are not familiar with the subject. Your preparation will always take time.

Analyzing the Statement

Both sides in a debate have to analyze the statement. Begin your analysis by trying to get a broad understanding of it. You have to know as much about the opponents' arguments as you do about your own. Then define the terms of the statement. The first speaker for the affirmative side will define these terms in opening the debate so that both sides know they mean the same thing when the terms are used in the debate. For example, if you are debating the subject of abolishing contact sports in high school, you will have to spell out exactly which sports will be considered contact sports and what grade levels are meant by the term *high school*. Study all of the sample statements again. Decide which words you would have to define in each statement.

The most important part of analyzing the statement is to find the issues. The issues are the major points on which the affirmative side says *yes* and the negative side says *no*. These are the points that you will argue in the debate. They are usually written as questions. For the subject of abolishing contact sports in high school, you might choose these issues:

1. Are high school students too young to participate in contact sports?
2. Do contact sports encourage violence?
3. Would abolishing contact sports save lives?

Study all the statements again. Find one issue for each statement. For a debate, you would need to find at least three or four issues for each one.

Finding the Evidence

Once you know what the issues are, you need to find the evidence to prove your side of the issues. Your best evidence will be facts. Include the opinions of experts. Write your evidence on note cards as you gather it. The more evidence your side collects, the better the chance you have to win the debate.

Building Your Case

When lawyers prepare a case, they write a brief. It is an outline of how they are going to present their arguments. You need to do the same thing for a debate. Your brief should include all the arguments your side will make, along with the evidence that supports them. You can put your brief on note cards to use during the debate. When your opponents bring up an argument during the debate, your answer will be ready.

The following outline shows how a debate brief is usually arranged. As you study it, think about how you would complete the outline for the statement above it. This statement was actually debated by high school students across the country in 1983 and 1984.

> Resolved, that the United States government should establish uniform rules governing the procedure of all criminal courts in the nation.

A Sample Outline

I. Introduction
    A. The importance of the statement
    B. Brief history of the statement
    C. Definition of terms in the statement
    D. Listing of the issues of the debate
II. Body
    A. One issue of your case
        1. evidence for your side of the issue
        2. more evidence and so on
    B. Same as A
    C. Same as A and B
III. Conclusion

The Actual Debate

During the debate, the two sides take turns giving their arguments. The affirmative side always begins and ends the debate because it has the harder job of proving the statement. In a formal debate, each side usually has two speakers. Both speakers give two speeches during the debate. First, they give what are called constructive speeches that develop their side's case. Then they give rebuttal speeches that knock down the other side's arguments and rebuild their case. The speeches are timed. Debaters usually are given from 8 to 10 minutes for their constructive speeches and 4 to 5 minutes for their rebuttals.

There are many different formats for conducting debates. In the traditional debate format, the speakers will speak in this order:

Constructive Speeches	**Rebuttal Speeches**
1. First affirmative	5. First negative
2. First negative	6. First affirmative
3. Second affirmative	7. Second negative
4. Second negative	8. Second affirmative

Today, high schools participating in debating contests follow a format that allows each side to question the other after their constructive speeches. The cross-examination format is exciting because it lets the sides directly challenge each other's points in order to reveal weaknesses in their arguments. The usual format for a cross-examination debate is:

Constructive Speeches

1. First affirmative
2. Questions by second negative
3. First negative
4. Questions by first affirmative
5. Second affirmative
6. Questions by first negative
7. Second negative
8. Questions by second affirmative

Rebuttal Speeches

9. First negative
10. First affirmative
11. Second negative
12. Second affirmative

The only speakers who know exactly what they will say in a debate are the first affirmative speakers. After this, the other speakers have to respond to what the other side has said as well as to present their side's arguments.

How to Be a Good Debater

Good debaters have certain characteristics. They are both good speakers and good listeners. They are polite. Good debaters attack ideas, not people. Good debaters use evidence that can be proved. They are logical thinkers. They do not make faulty generalizations or confuse cause and effect. Study the following arguments. Can you find the errors in thinking?

1. "There are many injuries in contact sports. Larry Smith was injured in a sport. Therefore, Larry was playing a contact sport." (confusion of cause and effect)

2. "All the players on the high school basketball team are over six feet five inches tall. They ought to win the state championship this year." (faulty generalization)

Benefits of Learning to Debate

Learning how to debate may lead to an interest in a career like law or politics. It may inspire you to enter debate contests. It will teach you how to research and will encourage you to reason. But the everyday benefits of learning to debate may be even more important for you. You will find that you can present your case effectively in informal debates with family, friends, and teachers because you have learned how to organize your arguments and back them with evidence. If nothing else, learning how to debate will have taught you that there really are two sides to most arguments.

Oration

Patrick Henry, the distinguished American patriot, is most remembered for his words: "I know not what course others may take; but as for me, give me liberty, or give me death!" He used these words to urge the Virginia Provincial Convention to arm the colony against England. Patrick Henry was an orator. Orators are skillful speakers who try to influence listeners with eloquent speeches. The speeches that orators make are known as orations. An oration is a persuasive speech. It is just as much a work of art as the *Mona Lisa* or Beethoven's Fifth Symphony. Each word is as carefully selected by the orator as a color is selected by a painter or a note by a musician. Orators take the time to put their words into sentences and paragraphs that will grab their audience's attention and inspire them to action. Think about how these words from past orations have endured:

Ask not what your country can do for you—Ask what you can do for your country.

John F. Kennedy

Speak softly and carry a big stick.

Theodore Roosevelt

It is true that you may fool all the people some of the time; you can even fool some of the people all the time; but you can't fool all of the people all the time.

Abraham Lincoln

History of Oration

Today, people go to the movies or turn on the TV for most of their entertainment. They do not go to hear speeches. Long ago, people did go to hear public speeches. Orations were actually social events as well as political and educational events.

You can trace the start of oration back to the 460's B.C., when the Greeks set up rules for public speaking. Soon,

Demosthenes, one of the greatest orators of all time, speaking before the Greek assembly.

almost every male in Athens was attending the general assembly to hear public policies debated. After this, there was a long period of famous Greek and Roman orators. Demosthenes and Cicero are two of the best known. When Christianity came, the early preachers became the orators. In the 1700's and 1800's, political speakers became the important orators. You are probably familiar with such names as Daniel Webster, Henry Clay, Stephen A. Douglas, and William Jennings Bryan in this country. Today, oration is reserved for formal occasions such as graduations and speech contests. On other occasions, people seem to prefer shorter, less formal speeches.

Orations to Study

By listening to recordings of such famous speakers as Winston Churchill and Franklin D. Roosevelt, you can learn how to deliver an oration. By reading orations of great speechmasters, you can learn how these speeches are put together. Study the following speeches. Analyze the word choices that made them great.

In 1896 William Jennings Bryan was a delegate to the Democratic National Convention in Chicago. His speech defending the free-silver plank of the platform was so great that it resulted in his nomination for President, though he was only 36 years old. In the conclusion of this oration, Bryan said:

> **Having behind us the producing masses of this nation and the world, supported by the commercial interests, the laboring interests, and the toilers everywhere, we will answer their demand for a gold standard by saying to them: You shall not press down upon the brow of labor this crown of thorns, you shall not crucify mankind upon a cross of gold.**

In a speech delivered to Congress on January 6, 1941, President Franklin D. Roosevelt said that settlements following World War II should be based on "four freedoms." He asked Congress for laws that would allow him to lend or lease war materials to any countries whose defense was important to the United States. His speech was so effective that on March 11, 1941, Congress passed the Lend-Lease Act that he had requested. Roosevelt's words were:

In the future days, which we seek to make secure, we look forward to a world founded upon four essential human freedoms. The first is freedom of speech and expression—everywhere in the world. The second is freedom of every person to worship God in his own way—everywhere in the world. The third is freedom from want—which translated into world terms, means economic understandings which will secure to every nation a healthful peaceful life for its inhabitants—everywhere in the world. The fourth is freedom from fear—which, translated into world terms, means a worldwide reduction of armaments to such a point and in such a thorough fashion that no nation will be in a position to commit an act of physical aggression against any neighbor anywhere in the world.

Both William Jennings Bryan and Franklin D. Roosevelt were successful orators. Their speeches moved people to act. Their speeches are still remembered today.

Opportunities for Oration

You don't have to be a politician to make an oration. Nor do you need to be an ardent supporter of some movement like civil rights, temperance, or nuclear freeze. Opportunities to make orations exist right in your school and community. Don't let these opportunities slip by you. You can make orations to student and local government groups, to clubs, and to civic organizations. However, your best opportunity to make orations is to participate in local speech contests.

Speech Contests

Many large service organizations in your community sponsor annual speech contests. In order to be the local Demosthenes, you are going to have to make certain preparations. Begin by checking out the rules of the contest. There will either be a time or a word limit on your oration. There may be a limit on the number of quotes that you can use. Most contests require you to write out your oration and deliver it from memory.

You will be judged not only on the content of your speech but the delivery. A winning speech arouses emotion in you and your audience. It is well organized, persuasive, polished, clear, natural, and well articulated. Read the following speech. The speaker won first place in a local service club contest with it. Notice how the opening and closing paragraphs tie the speech together.

Freedom, Our Most Precious Heritage

They came from everywhere. They came from the north, the south, the east, and the west. They came on boats. They came on foot. Like a magnet, this vast and wonderful wilderness that is today the United States of America attracted many different kinds of people. They were different in many ways yet they had two things in common: They were all human beings and they all wanted a fresh start. They wanted freedom.

So often the United States is referred to as the "melting pot." Certainly our heritage is varied and diverse. In the beginning of our country, each person or each family was moving in a different direction. The "melting pot" was simply a black kettle without a flame beneath it. The unusual mix of people could have turned out to be a strange brew. Instead, their collective desire for freedom provided a uniform heat that created a heritage unique yet strong and patriotic. Each realized the other's differences but knew that within him was the same need to be free.

From time to time, the question "What is freedom?" surfaces. Is freedom being able to spend the night at Johnny's house when you're 5? Is it being able to take the car on Friday night? Is it being able to constructively criticize our government? Is it being able to march on Washington to further the position of American farmers? Well, the answer to all of these questions would have to be *yes*. But freedom as our precious heritage is much more than that. It is the one element that our forefathers rallied behind in their struggle against oppression. It is the one element that is responsible for the way we live today and the way we will live tomorrow.

Freedom is not like precious gold in that it doesn't glitter. People are willing to kill for both, but freedom is not a tangible, palpable item that symbolizes wealth. Thus, people sometimes take it for granted. I am guilty as well. We sometimes do not fully appreciate the national anthem, for example. But the moment someone or something threatens freedom's existence, we seem to come back to life. Once again, we rally behind it, precious freedom, just as Americans have done for hundreds of years.

Freedom is our most precious heritage, and if one other element deserves to be mentioned in the same sentence, that element is perseverance. In the face of adversity, our forefathers stood their ground. While fighting their battles, they could look into the future and see how

important the battle at hand actually was. They knew
freedom was precious. They knew it would be.

'America knows where it has been. America knows what
got her into the position she is in today—the desire for
freedom. It was the original spark, the original heat. It is
the eternal flame that continues to burn inside each of us.

Why do you think this was a winning speech? Was the
speaker's selection of words appropriate? Which words do
you remember? Read the speech aloud several times to
practice your delivery.

Graduation Speeches

In each graduating class, the valedictorian and salutatorian usually have the opportunity to make orations at the
commencement exercise. These orations are quite traditional. The speakers look back at the accomplishments of
their class and forward to the challenges of the future.
They thank the people who have helped the members of
the class and say farewell to the school.

In 1983 at Carmel High School in Indiana, five girls tied
for valedictorian and a girl was also the salutatorian. The
girls joined together to deliver this farewell speech:

Valedictory Speech

Fellow students, parents, faculty, and friends:

After twelve long years, we finally made it! In two hours,
our high school days will be over—after all the
celebrations, after all the ceremonies, we will be on the
outside looking in. Although commencement marks the
end of our high school years, the meaning of the word is
beginning. It is the beginning of our future, which will be
filled with challenges and major decisions, decisions
affecting the courses of our lives.

We cannot forget the friendships we've made and the
experiences we've had in high school as we sit here
together for the last time. We also must remember our
parents, who unselfishly gave their time, support, and
encouragement. These things we have taken for granted as
our parents' duties, but we all know they have stepped over
and above their obligations a countless number of times.

For many of us, this night is as sad as it is exciting.
Tonight is a night of mixed emotions; we are torn between
feelings of relief, joy, and apprehension.

It's a little sad, too. Sad because we are leaving friends
and familiar faces. Sad, almost frightening, because the
security of a set daily schedule is parting. The

Valedictory speeches are given at most high school and college graduation ceremonies. They are a form of oration.

overwhelming emotion, though, is excitement, excitement to continue our lives and reach for our goals.

As we go through life, we know we will not always succeed in what we set out to do; however, we should set our goals high and not be afraid to make mistakes along the way. For through our errors we gain insight and wisdom. Our learning does not stop with formal education. Each new experience brings a new challenge and a new opportunity to learn and grow. Don't cower from these challenges because you're afraid to fail. Succeeding is getting up one more time than you fall.

There are three kinds of people in life: those who make things happen, those who watch what happens, and those who wonder what happened. Don't be afraid to be a person who *makes* things happen. For it is people who make things happen who get the most out of life. As someone once said so well: A ship in a harbour is safe, but that is not what ships are built for.

Thank you and *good luck.*

Do you think the girls' speech upheld the traditions of past valedictory orations?

The Values of Oration

You may never have to make an oration in Congress or the valedictory address at your school. However, during your lifetime you will be called upon to make speeches. Don't avoid giving orations now. They are excellent practice for all kinds of public speaking. They let you take an idea that you really believe in and think about it, develop it, choose language to describe it, and share it with others. Giving a successful oration will give you the same sense of accomplishment that you get from succeeding in sports, school, or a job.

Other Speaking Occasions

All speeches at your school are not made in the classroom or at contests. There are many other occasions when you need to make a speech. In this part of the book, you will learn what you are expected to say when making announcements, introducing a speaker, or campaigning for an office. Most of these speeches will be brief. Frequently, you will have to memorize them.

Speeches of Courtesy

When you say things like "I would like to introduce," "Thank you," "You're welcome," and "I want to present you with this award," you are making a speech of courtesy. It should be brief and to the point. People often make the mistake of saying exactly the same thing that everyone else does in these speeches. Try to give your speeches of courtesy a personal touch that the audience will remember. Avoid trite words and overused phrases; be original.

Introductions

People will enjoy themselves better at a party if they are introduced to the other guests before the party begins. An audience will appreciate a speech more if they are introduced to the speaker before they hear the speech. If you are to introduce a speaker, you must tell the audience something about the speaker.

Include information about the speaker's profession and accomplishments in your introduction. Be sure to mention the speaker's name several times in the introduction, unless the speaker is well known to your audience. Finally, you should tell the subject of the speech. Remember that you are not the speaker. Don't bore the audience with too long an introduction or give part of the speech yourself.

Presenting Awards

If you have been selected to present an award to a fellow student, teacher, or member of the community, you must do it in a complimentary way. Take the time to find out interesting facts about the recipient's background. Always describe to the audience the award that you are presenting. Tell your listeners what the person did to receive this award. Be sure to mention the recipient's other accomplishments. If the award is being presented on a special day, you may want to begin by tying the day into the presentation.

Read the following speech that was used to present the student-leader-of-the-year award at a high school assembly:

It seems right that we present the student-leader-of-the-year award today on George Washington's birthday. George Washington was the first leader of our country. David Green is our new student leader of the year. We chose David because of his record as a leader. He has been a leader since his first day at our school. In his first year, after he was defeated for a class office, David became the chairman of the ninth-grade float committee. The float won first place. In his sophomore year, David was president of the French and science clubs. That year he helped the band raise money for new uniforms by selling the most candy bars. In his junior year, David was elected captain of the football team. Here is our leader of the year, David Green. Perhaps one day David will be leading the country like George Washington did.

Imagine you have been chosen to present the leader-of-the-year award to a student in your school. Select the student; then write your speech for presenting the award.

Accepting Awards

Often you know when you will be receiving an award, and you have time to prepare a short speech that expresses your feelings and your appreciation. What would you do, however, if your name was unexpectedly called at a school assembly to receive an award? It would be rude to just grab the award and run back to your seat. You need to say something. Take a minute now and think of all the acceptance speeches you have watched on television. Remember what the Emmy and Oscar winners said that you liked best. Use these words and ideas in your speech. Remember to just be yourself, as you express your appreciation and tell what the award means to you. No one is expecting to hear an oration. The audience knows you are surprised. Read what the surprised winner of a Spanish contest said:

> No one in this audience is more surprised than I to have won the Spanish speech contest. I want to thank my teachers and fellow classmates for spending all those hours listening to my many pronunciation errors. It is through their patience and understanding that I can stand here today and say, "Muchas gracias para este honor fantástico!"

Just for fun, turn on your tape recorder again. Now pretend you are David Green who has just been named student leader of the year. Give your own spontaneous acceptance speech for this award. Then listen to the recording. Check to make sure that your speech was brief and courteous, and that you showed your appreciation for the award. It's a plus if you were able to tie your speech in some way to the presentation speech.

Welcoming People

A welcome speech is used to make a visiting teacher, a new exchange student, or a special member of the community feel that the students in your school are glad that he or she is there. These speeches are usually given in front of the student body. If you are making a welcome speech, you will need to tell the name of the guest, something about the guest, and why the guest is at your school. You will also want to mention to the students why your school is happy to have the guest there.

Welcome speeches should be short and sincere. Read this speech welcoming a mayor to a school. Then think what you would say if you were to welcome a community leader to your school.

> Today's speaker is Joseph Jones, the newly elected mayor of our city. The mayor has lived here all his life and is even a graduate of our own Westwood Junior High School. He is visiting the school today for national government week. He is speaking in the government classes and will join everyone in the cafeteria for lunch. He has just returned from a mayor's conference in Washington and is going to share a few of the topics that the mayors discussed there with us. Now let us all give a big Westwood welcome to a fellow Westwood student: Mayor Jones.

Announcements

Announcements are made daily in your school. They are short, informative speeches that are usually broadcast over the school's public address system. These speeches are usually given by the principal or a faculty member, but frequently students are called on to make announcements about club meetings, pep rallies, plays, and other school activities. You may have to make an announcement sometime. Knowing the following information will prepare you to make that announcement.

Making announcements is simple if you just remember these rules: Speak clearly. Speak slowly. Be brief. Keep in mind that the reason for an announcement is to provide information. Answer the questions *who, what, when, where,* and *why* in your announcement. Take the time to create an announcement that will grab your listeners' attention as well as include the necessary information. What good is it to tell the student body about a pregame party if you forgot to tell them either the time or the place?

Read the following announcement for a pregame party. As you read it, notice if it provides sufficient information.

The Seniors say: All other students, don't board the bus tomorrow. Come party with us. Our class wants to say good-bye to you in the school cafeteria right after school. We're graduating on Friday. See you tomorrow.

Now write your own announcement for a party at your school. Make sure to include all the necessary information. Then tape your announcement and listen to it. Did it meet all the requirements of a good announcement?

Election Speeches

You stand up and say, "I nominate Jane Johnson," and an election is held to determine whether Jane or another candidate will be elected. Most school elections are rather informal processes. Class and student body elections are more formal. You may have to make a short speech nominating Jane, and Jane will probably have to give a campaign speech.

Nominating Speeches

In nominating a candidate, you are going to give a speech to inform the audience about your candidate. At the same time, you are going to persuade them to vote for your candidate. You will use glowing words of praise that would sound like conceit if the candidate were to use them. Keep your speech brief. Just tell the audience what the requirements of the office are and what your candidate's qualifications are. Two special reminders—sprinkle your candidate's name throughout the speech and don't criticize the opponents. The secret of a successful speech is your genuine enthusiasm for your candidate.

Candidates' Speeches

In many schools, there are no nominating speeches. In this case, the candidates must say what is normally said in the nominating speech as well as tell what they will do if elected. Study the following candidate's speech. Observe how the candidate sold herself to her class. She was elected president of the junior class.

Students running for class offices often must give campaign speeches to persuade students to vote for them.

What are *you* looking for when deciding the one person you want to represent you next year as class president? My name is Leslie Redman, and I know that I have the ability, the experience, and the desire to lead you as junior class president.

This year I served as an active member of Senate, doing many things, including running the publicity for the Halloween movie, having the number-one magazine sales team, and . . . (shouldn't putting up the flag and saying the pledge count for something?). A junior senator and I presented the bill to have girls' letter jackets, which was passed unanimously by the Senate. Recently, I have proposed three new bills. The first would have six-semester graduates' pictures included in the composite in the commons of the class with whom they graduate. Someone asked me about it; I didn't see why these early grads should be deprived of this recognition, so I did something about it! The second bill would have all class officer candidates, including Senate, give speeches at elections. It's only fair to you to hear what they have to say. Hopefully, that could be in effect by next year. The third bill will permit class presidents to act as nonvoting members of the Senate. That way, I can still be involved in the legislative aspect of student government. I can still take your ideas to Senate in the form of bills and be there to defend them. I can be aware of what is going on in the Senate and be involved in the planning and putting on of Senate-sponsored activities.

You've probably noticed on announcements more than once that I'm not afraid to call this class to action. I feel as if I learned a lot this year. I was chosen *the* sophomore to represent Carmel High School at Hugh O'Brian Leadership weekend, and I feel that I can use the knowledge I gained there to lead this class as president.

One thing I have learned this year is that to be a successful class, we all need to be involved! Everybody has something to contribute, and next year we need to unite as a class, to work together, and get things done.

What do *you* want next year? Do you want more concerts, such as the up-and-coming Roadmaster? If so, speak up! Your involvement is the single most important part of accomplishing something next year.

From a skating party, a skiing trip, to a pizza-talent night, or a weekend spent with other members of the Class of '88, we can do anything we set our minds to. The mentioned class activities are not impossible. It's just going to take some organization and planning. Some could be put on as Senate projects and others we could plan ourselves. All these things can happen. As many of them will as we want and are determined to make work.

I'm proud of this Class of '88. I'm enthused with this class! We've come a long way since those first days back in August. It says a lot for us that so many are running for office today. I hope you'll choose carefully those you want to represent you. You may think I'm talking of next year as a dreamer. But dreams become goals, and these are the people who can make those goals become reality! Let's not limit ourselves. I know together we can get things done next year, and I, Leslie Redman, would be proud to represent you, the Class of '88, as your junior class president. I can promise you I'll still be standing up for you, saying what I believe, and giving 110% of my effort. Thank you.

Trying Out for a Part

You can use what you have learned about your voice and how to speak when you try out for a part in a play. Before the day of the tryouts, read the entire play. Decide on the part that you would like to play. Practice reading it aloud. At the tryouts, read your part naturally.

Read this excerpt from *West Side Story.* Tony and Maria are dancing together. They appear to be in their own private world. Now, for practice, read one of the parts aloud. Try to imagine that you are that person.

Tony: You're not thinking I'm someone else?
Maria: I know you are not.
Tony: Or that we have met before?
Maria: I know we have not.
Tony: I felt, I knew something-never-before was going to happen, had to happen. But this—
Maria: (interrupting) My hands are cold. (He takes them in his.) Yours, too. (He moves her hands to his face.) So warm. (She moves his hands to her face.)
Tony: Yours, too.
Maria: But of course. They are the same.
Tony: It's so much to believe—you're not joking me?
Maria: I have not yet learned how to joke that way. I think now I never will.

Practicing and Learning

Speaking is like athletics. Skill comes with practice. Making announcements and giving speeches of courtesy are

Be sure to practice at home before trying out for a play at school.

good ways to practice speaking because they are brief speeches. Don't expect every speech you make to be a winner. Even with practice, an athlete doesn't always win. But if you keep practicing, you will have more winning speeches than losing ones.

Club and Committee Meetings

"The meeting is called to order."
"I move that the club hold a car wash."
"I second the motion."

You have probably heard words like these at club and committee meetings in your school. You can hear similar words in the United States Congress. These words are part of the parliamentary procedure that is followed at most meetings. Parliamentary procedure is a way to conduct a meeting in an orderly manner. The rules of parliamentary procedure bring order to meetings. They ensure that everyone will have a chance to speak. They limit the discussion to one matter at a time. They balance the rights of the majority, the minority, and the individuals at a meeting. By following these rules, a group is able to regard every member's opinion in arriving at a decision.

All groups do not use the same rules of order. Your state legislature and the Congress of the United States use complicated forms of parliamentary procedure. Your school clubs and committees will follow simpler rules of order. However, if all the members of a group do not understand and follow the rules, a meeting can soon become very confused. If you do not understand these rules, you will not be able to make good contributions to the meetings that you attend.

History of Parliamentary Rules

No one knows who first used parliamentary rules. It is known that the Greeks were using rules of order in their assembly of free citizens by 400 B.C. The Roman Senate had even more refined rules of order. Most of the parliamentary procedure of today was developed in the British Parliament. The colonists in America adapted these rules for their legislatures. It was Thomas Jefferson who drew up the rules that are still used in the Senate and the House of Representatives. Jefferson's rules did not work as well for clubs and committees. Yet it was not until 1876 that an effective handbook was developed for nonlegislative meetings. It was known as *Robert's Rules of Order.* It is still the official parliamentary guide for most organizations. In this part of the book, you will become acquainted with the most common rules of parliamentary procedure according to *Robert's Rules of Order.*

Terms to Know

The first step in learning about parliamentary procedure is to become familiar with the special terms that are used in meetings conducted according to these rules. Study these terms:

adjourn: to end a meeting.
agenda: the list of items to be considered at a meeting.
amendment: a change proposed in a motion.
chair: the name for the person running the meeting.

floor: the right to speak—no one else can speak when someone has the floor.

gavel: the small wooden hammer the chair uses to call the meeting to order and to quiet disturbances.

majority: one more than half of those voting.

minutes: an accurate report of what was done during a meeting.

motion: a proposal that is put before a group—it is made by saying, "I move . . . ."

order of business: the series of steps covered during a meeting.

out of order: speaking without the permission of the chair, or proposing an action that does not follow the rules of parliamentary procedure.

quorum: the number of members who must be present to transact business in a meeting.

recess: a temporary interruption of a meeting.

second a motion: to show support of a motion by saying, "I second the motion" or "Seconded."

table: to put a motion aside until another time.

Duties of the Chair

You have most likely attended lots of meetings. Most of them probably followed parliamentary procedures. But, if someone asks you to lead a meeting tomorrow, are you ready? Do you know what the chair's duties are?

First of all, it is important for you to know that it is the chair's responsibility to see that the people attending a meeting accomplish something. The chair prepares for a meeting by writing out an agenda. The chair budgets the meeting time in order to complete everything on the agenda. During the meeting, the chair must keep control at all times. When a disturbance occurs, the chair must see that order is restored. The chair must make sure that a group keeps on the topic that is being discussed and that a topic is completely discussed before a new one is introduced. The chair cannot voice an opinion. The chair cannot play favorites. The chair must recognize everyone's right to speak. If any of the members have difficulty in understanding what is happening in a meeting, the chair must clear up the problem before going on. As the chair, you play the role of judge, referee, umpire, and timekeeper at a meeting.

The person who runs a club or committee meeting is referred to as the *chair*.

Duties of the Secretary

It is not easy to be a good secretary. The job requires concentration and a lot of writing. Besides writing the minutes, the secretary's duties include keeping a membership list, checking roll at each meeting, and sending out notification of the time and place of meetings. The secretary also handles correspondence if the club does not have a corresponding secretary.

Writing the Minutes

The secretary's most important duty is writing the minutes. During the meeting, the secretary must quickly jot down notes on everything that is happening. These notes are rewritten into the minutes when the meeting is over. The minutes should be brief rather than lengthy. They should contain the important points of a meeting and be clear enough so that anyone hearing or reading them could tell exactly what happened at the meeting. Secretaries must make sure that the minutes do not contain their personal viewpoints.

Minutes should begin by telling the kind of meeting; the name of the organization; the date, time, and place of the meeting; who ran the meeting; and if the minutes from the last meeting were read. They must include all main motions and may tell who made these motions. The minutes should tell what happened to each motion. They always end by telling what time the meeting adjourned.

Reading the Minutes

Unfortunately, few members of a group are interested in hearing the minutes read. If you are called upon to read the minutes, there are several things that you can do to keep the attention of the group. First, read loudly enough so that everyone can hear the minutes. Next, show interest in what you are reading. Finally, if your notes are lengthy, ask permission of the chair to summarize the minutes.

Sample Minutes

Pretend that you are the secretary of a high school honor society. Tape yourself reading the following minutes of their last meeting. Then listen to the tape and ask yourself: "Did I race through the minutes? Would the members know exactly what happened at this meeting?"

The regular monthly meeting of the Southwest High School Honor Society was called to order by President Patty White at 3:05 on Friday, October 18, 19__ in room 101 in the high school. The minutes of the last meeting were read and approved.

Debbie Jones made a motion that the Honor Society take a leadership role in the cause of conserving energy. The motion was adopted. The members discussed several energy conservation projects. Chuck Smith moved to amend the motion by adding the words *by collecting*

aluminum cans. After discussion of where these cans would be turned in, the amendment was approved.
The meeting was adjourned at 3:30 p.m.

Making Motions

If you want a group to consider your idea about having a candy sale to raise money, you'll have to make a motion. If you want to postpone voting on a fund-raising activity, you'll have to make another motion. Committees and clubs usually carry on their business through a system of motions.

Main Motion.   Any motion that brings new business before a meeting is called a main motion. You can make a motion only when you have the floor. A main motion usually begins "I move that . . ." It should have only one idea. Make the motion brief and clear. Another member of the group must second it, and the chair must repeat it before the motion can be discussed. For a main motion to be passed, it must be approved by the majority. A vote can be taken by voice, by a show of hands, or by ballot.

Other Motions.   If members want to change anything about the main motion, they can make a motion to amend it. If they want to think about the motion for a while longer, they can make a motion to postpone discussing it until a later meeting. If the members want to have a committee study the main motion, they can make a motion to send it to a committee. The members can also make motions to lengthen or shorten the time to discuss a motion as well as to vote immediately. All of these motions center around the main motion.

Order of Business

Most meetings follow a fixed order. Your group has the right to choose what that order will be. This is the usual order that is followed:

1. **Call to order.** The chair says, "The meeting will come to order."
2. **Reading of the minutes.** The chair says, "The secretary will read the minutes." After the minutes have been read, the chair asks, "Are there any corrections

to the minutes?" Then the chair either says, "The minutes are approved" or "The minutes are approved as corrected."

3. **Reports of officers and committees.** The chair will usually ask for reports from all the officers and from the committees that have something to report.

4. **Unfinished business.** The chair brings up any matters that were not settled at the last meeting for discussion or a vote.

5. **New business.** After the unfinished business has been completed, the chair asks, "Is there any new business?" This is the time for members to bring up new business. It is helpful if the chair knows what the members are going to discuss so that the members can decide on the order in which they take up the new business.

6. **Announcements.** The chair makes or calls on members to give general announcements.

7. **Adjournment.** When there is no further business, or the majority of the members wish to adjourn, a member makes a motion to adjourn. After the motion is seconded, a vote on adjournment is held.

The pledge to the flag, the singing of the national anthem, and special opening ceremonies come right after a meeting is called to order. If a meeting is to have a speaker, film, or other activity, it usually takes place after announcements.

A Sample Meeting

Study this meeting of a Spanish club. Notice how the officers and president follow parliamentary procedure. Mark is the president, Ken is the secretary, and Jennie is the treasurer.

Mark: The meeting will come to order. Ken will read the minutes of our last meeting. (Ken reads the minutes.)

Mark: Thank you, Ken. Are there any corrections or additions to the minutes? (Pause) If not, the minutes are approved. Jennie will read the treasurer's report.

Jennie: The current cash balance is $49.78.

Mark: Thank you, Jennie. At the last meeting, we talked about doing something different to celebrate Pan American Day. Does anyone have any new ideas? Ken.

Ken: I move that we have a party.

Mark: Karl.

Karl: That's a great idea. I second the motion.

Mark: It has been moved and seconded that we have a party. All those in favor say "Yes." All opposed say "No." The motion is carried. Is there any discussion? Linda.

Linda: I like the idea of a party. But the motion isn't clear. What kind of a party should we have?

Mark: Matt.

Matt: No one ever comes to the club parties unless there is something to eat. I move to amend by changing the word *party* to *dinner.*

Mark: Ann.

Ann: I second the amendment.

Mark: It has been moved and seconded to amend the motion by changing the word *party* to *dinner.* Is there any discussion? Sue.

Sue: We could have a pitch-in dinner.

Mark: Jennie.

Jennie: That is a good suggestion, since the club does not have much money right now.

Mark: Is there any further discussion of the amendment? (Pause) Since there is no further discussion, all those in favor of amending the motion by changing the word *party* to *dinner* say "Yes." All opposed say "No." The amendment is approved. Karl.

Karl: I move that we adjourn.

Mark: Ann.

Ann: Seconded.

Mark: It is moved and seconded that we adjourn. All those in favor say "Yes." Opposed, say "No." The meeting is adjourned.

Think about what happened in the meeting. Do you know what the main motion was? Were there any other motions? Do you believe that you could conduct a meeting like this?

Parliamentary Procedure and You

You cannot play tennis, checkers, or video games without following certain rules. You cannot drive a car, cross a street, or mail a letter without obeying other rules. There are rules that must be followed for almost everything that you do. You cannot participate in a meeting without following the rules of parliamentary procedure.

Take the following true-false test to find out if you know the basic rules of parliamentary procedure. Check your answers by rereading the text.

1. A majority is two-thirds of those voting.
2. The chair calls a meeting to order.
3. A member does not have to be recognized by the chair to speak.
4. A main motion does not have to be seconded.
5. A main motion brings new business before a meeting.
6. A main motion cannot be changed by amendments.
7. The minutes are read in a meeting during the announcements.
8. The last order of business in a meeting is the adjournment.

Speaking with Others

Most of your speech at school is not planned. It is casual conversation with your friends, classmates, and teachers. There are times when you need to prepare to speak to someone at school in order to accomplish your goals.

Counselors.   Speaking with a counselor about career or college plans requires preparation on your part. Counselors are busy people. Before you meet with your counselor, make a list of the topics that you wish to discuss, and write down the questions that you want answered. Check the topics and questions off as you cover them in the meeting.

Teachers.   Speaking with a teacher about problems you are having in a class also requires preparation. Don't just say, "I can't get it" or "I don't understand." Instead, take the time to figure out and to write down exactly what the problem is. Your teachers will be able to help you when you ask questions like these:

"How do you bisect an obtuse angle?"
"What is the difference between the two past tenses in Spanish?"
"Can you help me identify the meter of these poems?"

Introductions.   Another time you need to be prepared to speak is when you are making introductions. The etiquette rules for introducing people need to be fixed firmly in your mind. Learn whose name to mention first in introductions. The rules for making introductions are based on three things: age, sex, and rank. Between sexes you should always mention the female first. If both people being introduced are the same sex, you will name the older person first. If you are introducing a visiting teacher to your school principal, don't worry about the age and sex rules, but name the person with the highest rank first.

Listening Carefully.   In speaking with your counselors and teachers, you will send accurate messages if you are prepared. Make sure that you receive their messages by listening carefully.

It is important to be prepared when you speak with a counselor at school.

Successful Speaking at School

You do not need to become a member of the debate team, win an election, or make the valedictory speech to be a successful speaker at school. Nor do you need to get a part in a school play, make announcements over the P.A. system, or welcome a visitor to the school. What you need to do is to use your speech skills to communicate effectively with all the people you deal with at school every day. You need to ask and answer questions thoughtfully in class, to participate actively in class and club discussions, and to read aloud in a way that interests other students in the material. If you do these things, you are a successful speaker at school.

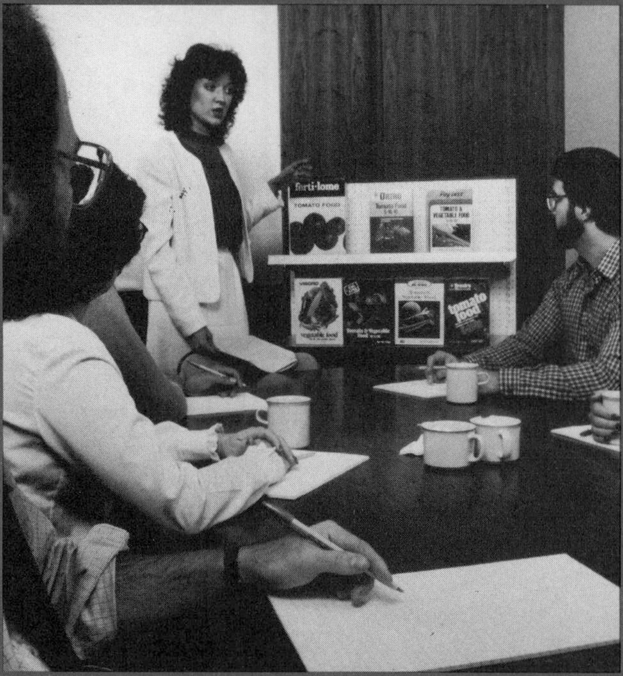
ferti-lome
TOMATO FOOD
tomato food

SPEAKING AT

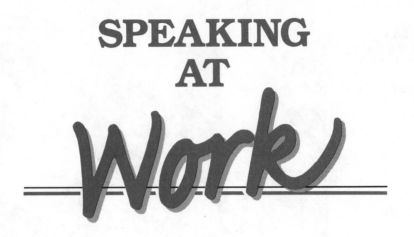

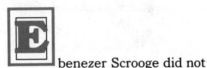

benezer Scrooge did not place much value on employer-employee communication in the business world. Poor Bob Cratchit couldn't tell him about new accounting practices, negotiate for a raise, or expect help in solving the health problems of Tiny Tim. The Ebenezer Scrooges of the past still run some businesses. They tell their employees what to do, and that is the sum total of communication between employer and employee. Today, however, most businesses place great emphasis on communication at every level and between levels of management and workers. In most companies, the cry is: "We must improve our communication."

The need for good systems of communication in the business world arises from the nature of today's businesses. Businesses are getting bigger. Most companies have more than one employee. In 1983, Eastman Kodak had 126,000 employees, and IBM had 354,936. As businesses get bigger, communications networks become more complicated. Information must flow between more people. It must get from top to bottom and should also get from bottom to top as well as across each level. Accurate information must be received at all levels for decisions to be made and for policies to be carried out. Some of this information is in the form of written messages. Much of it is oral communication—speaking and listening.

The fast pace of business today demands that you be able to speak well at work.

You must understand the communications network in your company. You are both a receiving and a sending station in this network. For example, if you are in the fleet department of a canning company, you act as a receiving station when you hear that a truck overturned this morning and a load of canned goods was destroyed. You act as a sending station when you pass this information along the chain of command. If you fail to communicate with the right person or persons, it can cost your company money. Good communication systems not only hold a company together, they also help a company make money.

All businesses, whether they are corporate giants or a husband-and-wife antique store, have communication problems. Sometimes they are even the same problems. Perhaps the wife tells the part-time employee in the antique store to dust the glassware, and the husband tells the employee to sweep the floor. The employee doesn't know which to do first any more than the worker in a large factory or office who has too many bosses.

At some point in your career, you are going to have to speak at work. You may, like Bob Cratchit, want to tell your boss about new practices, negotiate for a raise, or tell someone about health problems of a child. If your boss is a

Scrooge, you will probably want to interview for a new job, too. This section of the book gives you a close look at speaking at work to help you become a more effective communicator in your job. It covers all kinds of one-to-one communication between bosses, co-workers, and subordinates. It also deals with speaking to groups and at meetings, as well as how to make a sales presentation.

Communication in Business

During your working hours, you probably spend considerable time talking and listening to your boss, co-workers, and subordinates. Your success in business lies in your ability to communicate with them. Did you ever stop and look at the people who are successful in your company? They are the people who use their communication skills to sell their ideas, plans, and opinions to others.

Anyone who wants to make the most of their career opportunities must realize that poor communication skills are a barrier to their success. If you are unable to conduct a meeting, give a report, share your ideas, or understand what others are saying, you need to improve your speaking and listening skills. In this part of the book, you will see which of these skills you already possess and do exercises to help you acquire the skills that you need. You will also learn how to overcome barriers that may be interfering in your communication with others.

Speaking Skills

Social conversation or idle chatter is not business speech. Both require the same basic skills of appropriate rate, adequate volume, correct pitch, and pleasing voice quality, along with correct pronunciation and clarity of speech. However, business speech also requires certain special skills to get your message across. As you read this list of skills, select the exercises that you need in order to improve your skills.

Organizing Skills

Business speech is organized. Your ideas and plans should all be brought together and arranged in a logical fashion before you speak. Observe how an office manager organized the thoughts on tardiness that ran through his head before he brought the problem up at a meeting.

First, he listed all his ideas:

FREQUENCY   TARDINESS   HOW LATE

20 PEOPLE TODAY   WHO IS LATE

10 to 15 MINUTES   MORALE   HABIT

LAZY

PENALTIES   IRRESPONSIBLE

AWARDS   LOWER PRODUCTION

Then he organized the best ones into an outline to present at the meeting.

TARDINESS:

I. Description of tardiness problems
   A. Who is late?
   B. How tardy are they?
   C. How often are they tardy?
II. Why are workers tardy?
   A. Sick
   B. Habit
III. What is the effect of tardiness?
   A. Morale
   B. Lower production
IV. How to improve
   A. Awards
   B. Penalties
V. Discussion

You can practice organizing your thoughts in the same way. Jot down what you want to say before your next meeting with an individual or a committee. Then organize your thoughts into an outline to use at the meeting.

Motivating Skills

Machines work with the flip of a switch. It takes more effort to turn people on. You can always order or coerce people to do something, but they will do a better job if they are motivated. Of course, such things as salary increases, job security, and longer vacations are excellent motivators. Yet these aren't the only ways that people can be motivated. You can motivate those around you by what you say. With just a few words, like, "You did a great job on cutting costs," or "Let me carry your idea to the top brass," you can make people feel like they are a valued part of the company. By building up their self-esteem, you motivate them to do their best work.

Study the following statements. Choose the one in each pair that would be more successful in building up someone's self-esteem. Think about why it is better.

1. "The boss said you did a great job on pricing."
   "You figured the prices correctly."

2. "Your report gave a good picture of the problem."
   "Your report was satisfactory."

3. "I liked the job you did."
   "Joe, I liked the job you did."

4. "Did the company insurance take care of your daughter's broken leg?"
   "How's the family?"

5. "We met the deadline this month."
   "We all pulled together to meet the deadline."

Negotiating Skills

Negotiating is finding a way to reach an agreement with others. It involves bringing two sides together without either one losing face. Negotiating is not just labor-management talks. It is the informal give and take between two workers on the assembly line to decide which job each will do. It is a purchasing agent dealing with someone until the right quality corrugated boxes can be purchased for the best price. Negotiating is a speaking skill. Use it with your boss when you discuss the vacation schedule you want or when you try to reach agreement with a co-worker about who will stay late to write a report.

Successful negotiators may be able to win agreement by persuasion, reconciling differences, compromising, or finding a new joint solution. Which method or methods would you use to negotiate solutions to these problems?

Negotiating is a speaking skill that involves give and take between employees.

1. Les Goodrich headed the accounting department of a huge department store. He never received data he needed from the computer department employees to make his monthly reports on time. They complained that Les's department never gave them data in the form that they requested. How can the two departments negotiate a solution to their differences?

2. For five years the Fisher family had a produce stand on a lot the McQuarries owned in exchange for keeping the lot clear. Then the McQuarries decided that they wanted to be paid rent and have their new son-in-law keep the lot cleared. Both parties agreed. Soon the Fishers discovered that the son-in-law would not keep the lot cleared. They are losing business. How do they negotiate with the McQuarries?

3. Mrs. Herman bought carpet for two bedrooms and a hall at a department store warehouse sale. When the

installers arrived, they discovered that there was not enough carpet for one of the bedrooms. It was their measuring mistake, and additional carpet was not available. Mrs. Herman refused to let them lay any of the carpet. The company wants her business. How should they negotiate a settlement with her?

Handling-People Skills

People cannot all be handled in the same way. If you ask John, who is a whiz with computers, to devise a program to compare benefits offered by several health companies, he will not finish it unless you ask him how it is going every day. But if you mention a project to Patty more than once or twice, she will think that you are riding her. You have to adjust what you say and how you say it to the person you are talking to. In your dealings with people, respect the old adage that everyone is different.

Think now of the people you work with every day. Assign a descriptive word to each of them that says what characteristic of theirs you have to consider in your dealings with them. You will probably use words like procrastinator, perfectionist, go-getter, and sensitive.

Giving-Directions Skills

Directions must be exact. Tell your secretary to triple-space a special report, not just to type it. Directions should be given in the order that they are to be followed. Pause after each step to let your listeners take notes or follow your directions. Directions should only include the necessary information. Tell the new worker how to punch the time clock, not how much the time clock costs.

Study the directions below. Determine why people may not be able to follow them.

1. "Take highway 80 to the first gas station and turn."
2. "File the report. Type the new information up as a report. Look up information for the report."
3. "Go to the supply room. Say hello to Ted for me and ask him to give you one of those bolts for a model-260 fan that we should adjust."

Explaining Skills

Explaining is part of everyone's job. There are times when you have to explain to someone how to operate something, make something, or do something. In order to do this effectively, you should know how to do it yourself.

Explanations are no more than speeches to inform. You need to organize your information into steps, whether you are telling someone how to fill out an expense account, how to grease a coupling on a combine, or how to make an estimate. If possible, show your listeners what you are talking about. Explanations are simpler to make if you are holding a form in your hand or looking at a machine. Never rush through an explanation. Take the time to repeat the main steps. Encourage questions. Your explanation is successful if your listeners use the information they receive correctly. Take a minute and think about how you would explain your company's policy on vacations, office keys, or sick leave to a new employee.

Putting Your Skills Together

Just like stew is a combination of many different ingredients, you will need to combine your speech skills in order to successfully face all the different speaking situations that challenge you on the job. Effective speakers in the business world can organize, motivate, negotiate, handle people, give directions, and make explanations.

Special Qualities

More goes into business speech than skill. Your effectiveness as a speaker also depends on certain personal qualities. If your listeners regard you as a person who knows what you are talking about and they believe you, they will have confidence in what you say.

Knowledgeability

Business speakers need to be experts on what they are saying. They need specific as well as general knowledge. Employees and employers who do not know what they are talking about are not listened to for long. Study the following situations. What specific knowledge would you need to handle each one?

1. You are the owner of a restaurant. You are explaining how you arrive at prices to your accountant.

2. You are a computer salesperson. A customer wants to select a computer to handle his tax paperwork.

Credibility

Why do people believe certain newscasters and doubt others that tell them exactly the same news? Why can a certain salesperson convince you to buy a car when you wouldn't buy the same car from another? The answer is that some people project an air of credibility. People believe what they say. You will have this image if you keep your word and are honest in all your business dealings. You will have proven yourself credible.

Skillful Communicators

Every company has skillful communicators. Who are they in your company? Think about the special speaking skills that these people possess. Are their thoughts organized, do they explain clearly, handle people well? Do they know what they are talking about? Do people believe them? What about you? Are you a skillful communicator? Look back over this part of the book and decide whether or not you are.

Walter Cronkite projects an air of credibility. Most people believe what he says.

Listening Skills

Just because you can send a message does not mean that you will be able to receive a message. You are probably not receiving messages if you are always saying, "I didn't hear you say that," or "What did you mean?" To receive a message, you have to be a good listener. Check now to see if you are a good listener. A good listener will follow most of these rules:

1. I do not dominate conversations by doing most of the talking.
2. I am not easily distracted.
3. I do not interrupt frequently during conversations.
4. I react to the nonverbal message that is also being sent.
5. I take mental notes on what a person is saying.
6. I concentrate on what is being said.
7. I keep my opinions to myself.
8. I keep my eyes on the speaker.
9. I encourage others to talk by asking questions.
10. I do not interfere with a person's personal judgments.

Take the time some day at work to observe the people around you. How well do they listen? Notice how often someone breaks one of the good-listening rules above in a conversation.

André Gide, a well-known writer, once began a lecture by saying, "All this has been said before, but since nobody listened, it must be said again." You're lucky if you ever get a second opportunity to listen to something. Not listening the first time to an altitude change could cost an airplane pilot as well as the passengers their lives. Not giving your full attention to the instructions on how to run a new piece of machinery could cost your company money to repair the machine and a loss of production time. Listen carefully when the message is important.

It does not matter on what level your job is; you will need to concentrate when you listen. Many people don't realize that the average person only remembers 50 per cent of what he or she heard shortly after hearing a 10-minute presentation. Within a few days, retention has slipped to only 25 per cent.

Test to see how closely you really listen. You can do this activity alone or with someone. Close your eyes and listen to all the sounds you hear. Make a mental note of these sounds. Then open your eyes and write down the names of the sounds that you heard. If someone else is also taking the test, you can compare your lists. You can improve your listening skills by trying to:

1. pay attention to the speaker
2. eliminate or block out any distractions
3. keep eye contact with the speaker
4. have a good positive posture
5. concentrate on what you hear

Did you realize that phrases like "We don't have time" and "That's a terrible idea" turn people off from continuing a conversation with you? You should use positive phrases that encourage people to speak with you, such as, "I like that," or "That's great, how do we get started?" Read the following phrases and decide if they would encourage or discourage someone from talking to you.

1. "Sounds like fun, let's go."
2. "It won't work."
3. "Not now."
4. "That's fantastic."
5. "Good. What do we need?"
6. "The problem with your plan is . . ."

Good listening will provide you with an avenue of learning. It gives you insight into what makes people think and act.

It also helps to clear up misunderstandings that you may have thought you had. Over the next few days, concentrate on trying to improve your listening skills. When you feel you have improved these skills, take the final test. Attend a meeting without taking any notes. After the meeting, jot down all the main ideas and then compare your list to actual notes that someone took.

Barriers to Communication

Messages don't always get through. Sometimes there is a barrier that interferes with successful communication between the sender and the receiver. Of course, the sender can build this wall by sending a garbled message or speaking indistinctly, or the receiver can build the wall by not listening carefully. Let's look at some other barriers that interfere with communication.

Word, Words, Words

Most people have a working vocabulary of approximately 10,000 words and are acquainted with 30,000 to 40,000 words. If the sender and the receiver don't have the same vocabulary, a barrier will be built. Look at this list of words. Do you recognize all of them?

meliorate	lethargy	treatise
tranquil	remonstrate	chameleon
archaic	peripheral	esoteric

People with different business backgrounds can have problems communicating with each other because the same word can mean something different to the sender and the receiver. For example, to a computer operator a *header* is the first label on a tape file; but to a builder a *header* is a beam that fits between two long beams and supports the ends of short ones.

Look at this list of technical words. How many do you recognize?

tare	plurality	loader
mortar	quasar	salicylate
semiconductor	matriculate	starboard

Emotions

Have you ever been so excited that you could not think or so angry that you were trembling? Have you ever tried to talk to someone who was upset or unhappy? When emotions are running high in either the sender or the receiver, it is not the time to communicate. Emotions form a wall between sender and receiver that cannot be scaled until both calm down.

Sometimes people are so apprehensive about speaking that they scarcely talk at work. If you should fall into that category, look at the earlier suggestions for controlling stage fright. Try to accept the fact that your job is not on the line every time that you speak. Begin to communicate with people at work by greeting them. Instead of writing memos, start telling people what you would have written to them. Try this for a week; it should make you less apprehensive about speaking at work.

Outside Barriers

It is almost impossible to communicate over the noise of a siren or a jackhammer. It is difficult to compete with such distractions as a soccer match that your listeners can see. Before you begin any communication, make sure that you have selected the best place. The cafeteria is not the place to tell an employee about poor job performance. Your office or the employee's office is the place. Besides selecting the correct place to speak, you will need to select the correct time. During a problem-solving meeting is not the time to ask the boss for a raise. Make an appointment with your boss, co-workers, or subordinates to discuss matters like salary, advancement, or promotion. If you wish to communicate, eliminate the barriers that you can control.

Breaking Down the Barriers

So many things can interrupt the flow of ideas from sender to receiver. You can never be sure what response you will receive when you send a message. The secret to breaking down the barriers that interfere with communication is learning to recognize them so that you can either avoid them or deal with them when they appear.

Speaking Better at Work

In order to communicate well in business, you must have the desire to express yourself. Then you must know what you want to say, why you want to say it, where and when you are going to say it, and how you will say it. You must also know when to speak and when to listen. Don't let your co-workers' voices be the only ones heard when company plans and policies are being decided.

One-to-One Communication

"Have a good day."

"Did you hear about the merger?"

"What do you think of my department's budget?"

You might make any one of these comments to someone at work. Whatever your job—salesperson, secretary, supervisor, or vice president—most of your communication at work is on a one-to-one basis. Of course, you speak to groups, but the bulk of your speech is directed to individuals. It is this person-to-person speech that gets a company's work done. It is a back-and-forth kind of communication in which you take turns sending and receiving messages. Much of this communication is informal in nature. It is spontaneous, not planned. In this part of the book, you will find out about more structured one-to-one communications like interviews, performance appraisals, counseling sessions, terminations, and other business-oriented interviews in which some planning is essential to the success of the communication.

One-to-one communication is a very common—and important—form of speaking at work.

Employment
interviews are
important speaking
situations that call for
advance preparation.

Employment Interviews

Interviews are special conversations. They are planned
and have a purpose. There are many kinds of interviews.
However, when you say *interview* in the business world,
most people think of an employment interview that determines whether or not someone will get a job.

Interviewer and Interviewee

During your career, you will probably find yourself in the
role of both interviewer and interviewee in employment interviews. As an interviewee, you will be looking for a job.
As an interviewer, you may just be checking out how
someone would fit into your department rather than being
responsible for the complete selection process. For the interviewer, the purpose of the employment interview is to
meet the applicant, learn more about the applicant, and
ultimately determine if the applicant has what it takes for
a job. For the interviewee, the purpose is to learn more
about the job and the company and to get an actual offer
for the job.

Communication

The employment interview is an information-sharing
meeting. The interviewer and interviewee take turns sending and receiving information. The interview is also a
sales presentation. The interviewee has to sell himself or
herself to the interviewer. The interviewer is the buyer for
the company. Sometimes the interviewer has to sell the
company to a much-sought-after interviewee.

Interviews Are Important

Even though companies use other devices in selecting employees, the employment interview is the number-one determiner of which people are hired in most companies. Since it costs so much time and effort to train an employee, selecting the right employee for a job is doubly important to employers today. In the current tight job market, the interview has become more important than ever to the prospective employee. Unfortunately, the interviewer and interviewee are not always prepared for the interview nor do they always know exactly what is expected of them. So the employment interview sometimes becomes confusing or a waste of time.

The Interviewee's Preparation

There are few harder jobs in the world than finding a job. First, you have to go out and find a company that is looking for someone like you. You study newspaper ads, ask friends for leads, contact companies, and visit employment agencies to find a prospective employer. Once you have a job lead, you fill out application forms and send in a résumé to tell a company about yourself. If the company is interested in learning more about you, someone will call you in for an interview to see if you really are the right person for the job. Prepare yourself thoroughly for an interview. You can't wing your way through one and expect to get a job.

Begin with the Résumé

A résumé is a short history of a job applicant's qualifications and experiences. There is no set pattern for writing a résumé. What you include in the résumé does depend on the job that you are seeking. Usually a résumé has the job applicant's name, address, and telephone number at the top of the first page. Then there normally are sections describing your education, job experiences, and accomplishments in the business world. In these sections, list your most recent experiences first. Everyone should have an active résumé in their files, whether or not they expect to look for a new job soon. Otherwise, they may find it difficult to remember years, jobs, responsibilities, and accomplishments if they ever have to seek a new job. Why don't you write your résumé now? It will give you a good picture of what you have accomplished in the business world.

Résumés should always be typed or typeset. Arrange your information in them attractively. Make sure the résumé looks professional. Proofread your résumé and then have others proofread it. Spelling and punctuation errors must be avoided. They are job losers.

Research the Company

A question that is frequently asked during an interview is, "Why do you want to work for this company?" You won't be able to answer it satisfactorily unless you have researched the company and know what it is like. You should know these basic facts about a company:

Background. Who owns the company? Where is it located? How large is the company?

Product. What does the company sell? How is it sold? Who are the customers?

Financial facts. Is the company making money?

It is often very difficult to find out much about small companies. Try local newspapers and the chamber of commerce for information. You can find information about large companies in their annual reports, company brochures, newspapers, magazines, and trade journals at the library. You can also find out a lot about a company by talking to someone who works for the company. The more knowledge you acquire about a company, the more comfortable you will feel during an employment interview.

Research the Job

First, make sure that you know the requirements for a job. Find out what education levels and kinds of experience are expected from the applicants for this job. Do not interview for a job if you obviously do not meet the requirements. Try to find out what the duties are for this job. Investigate what the salary is for similar jobs.

Anticipate Questions

Before press conferences, politicians often have their staffs ask them questions that they think the press will ask. Prepare yourself in the same way for an interview. Study this list of some of the most common questions that employers ask during interviews with college seniors. The questions on this list are from a survey of well-known business and industrial firms that was published in the "Endicott Report 1975" by the Placement Center at Northwestern University. Write out your answers to these questions before a job interview. Writing your answers forces you to organize your thoughts and gives you valuable experience in answering questions that the interviewer will probably ask. Be sure to relate your answers to the job you are seeking. To make sure that you can answer the questions comfortably, ask someone to read the questions to you before an actual job interview. Then practice answering the questions without looking at your written answers. You may even wish to tape them in order to see how they can be improved. Rehearse your responses because they may get you the job that you are seeking.

1. What are your long-range and short-range goals and objectives, when and why did you establish these goals, and how are you preparing yourself to achieve them?
2. What specific goals, other than those related to your occupation, have you established for yourself for the next 10 years?
3. What do you see yourself doing five years from now?
4. What do you really want to do in life?
5. What are your long-range career objectives?
6. How do you plan to achieve your career goals?
7. What are the most important rewards you expect in your business career?
8. What do you expect to be earning in five years?
9. Why did you choose the career for which you are preparing?
10. Which is more important to you, the money or the type of job?
11. What do you consider to be your greatest strengths and weaknesses?
12. How would you describe yourself?
13. What motivates you to put forth your greatest effort?
14. Why should I hire you?
15. What qualifications do you have that make you think that you will be successful in business?
16. What do you think it takes to be successful in a company like ours?
17. In what ways do you think you can make a contribution to our company?
18. What two or three accomplishments have given you the most satisfaction? Why?

19. Why did you decide to seek a position with this company?
20. What do you know about our company?
21. What two or three things are most important to you in your job?
22. Will you relocate? Does relocation bother you?
23. Are you willing to travel?
24. Why do you think that you might like to live in the community in which our company is located?
25. What have you learned from your mistakes?

Prepare Your Own Questions

It is almost inevitable that at some point in the interview, the interviewer is going to ask, "Do you have any questions?" Think long and hard about what else you would like to know about the company and job. Interviewers consider your questions important. They are also another opportunity to sell yourself. Below is a list of questions that company recruiters expected and recommended interviewees to ask. These questions are from the "Northwestern Endicott Report 1983."

1. What are the opportunities for advancement?
2. Is the company stable and financially sound?
   followed by
3. What then are the company's plans for future growth?
4. Describe the typical first-year assignment.

More than half of the recruiters chose the first question as the most important question because it showed that the candidate was looking for a long-term commitment, not just a job. Think now of the questions that you asked when you interviewed for your present job. What questions should you have asked?

The Interview Day

Dress for your interview as you would dress for the actual job. If anything, be conservative in your dress. Not only should you be pleasing to the eye, you should be agreeable to the nose by avoiding overpowering scents. Arrive early for the interview, so that you can sit down for a while and absorb the atmosphere of the company. Arriving late to an interview puts you into an impossible position from which you may never recover.

The Interviewer's Preparation

Good interviewing is an art. It includes knowing what information you want to find out about the job candidate and knowing how to obtain that information. Interviewers, just like interviewees, should prepare for the interview. They should begin by reading the candidate's application and résumé. Then they should think about the direction that they want the interview to take. They should ask themselves if they want to find out more about the candidate's skills, background, or how the candidate works with other people. When they know, they are ready to develop a few key questions to ask during the interview. Imagine now that you were to interview a person for a position in your department. Which questions from the list of commonly asked questions would you want to ask the candidate?

One caution in preparing questions for an interview: there are questions that should not be asked because laws forbid discrimination on the basis of certain information that the interviewer might obtain. Make sure that you know and are following the Equal Employment Opportunity Commission's guidelines on this information. Avoid questions that would give you information on national origin, religion, type of discharge from the military service, and personal questions not related to job requirements.

The interviewer may also want to prepare a checklist to use during the interview. It could include such items as promptness, dress, speech, interest, and enthusiasm to be rated during the interview. What other items do you think should be on a checklist?

The Actual Interview

If an interviewee has prepared well for an employment interview, he or she should feel confident in approaching the actual interview. If the interviewer knows what he or she wants to find out, the interview should give a good picture of what the interviewee is like. Let's look now at how an interview is structured. It has a definite beginning, middle, and end.

The Beginning.   This is the warm-up period. General greetings and conversational clichés about the weather can be exchanged. At this time, the interviewer should try to make the interviewee feel comfortable. The interviewee should try to make a good first impression. The purpose of this part of the interview is to establish rapport.

The Middle.   This is the heart of the interview. Most of the time of the actual interview should be spent on this part. Here the interviewer will be evaluating if the interviewee is a good candidate for the job. Interviewers should control this part of the interview. Interviewees should sell themselves.

The End.   At this time, interviewers tell the interviewees how and when they will be notified about the outcome of the interview. Both should try to close the interview on a positive note.

The interview is a speech situation. Both participants in an interview share the responsibility for making it a successful communication. They should not only share the speaking responsibilities, but they should also extend their antennae and listen to what the other is saying and how it is being said. Emotional speech should be avoided, as should negative comments and exaggerations. Politeness is essential. The tone of speech in an interview should be more formal than casual.

Why People Don't Get Jobs

Sometimes people don't get a job because there are better qualified applicants. Sometimes it is because they are guilty of one of these speech faults:

1. They did not give specific answers to questions.
2. They did not express their views clearly.
3. They rambled on without purpose.
4. They used poor language in their speech.
5. They did not pay attention to what the interviewer was saying.

Performance Appraisals

When you take a ring to the jeweler's to get an appraisal, you want to know its value. The jeweler makes a close examination of the ring before determining its value. Employee performance appraisals are much the same. They let employers know the value of employees to the company. Employees are closely looked at, and their performance is evaluated before they receive their personal appraisal.

Just as employers want to know the value of employees, the employees need to know how they are doing, where they are going, and if they have a future in the company. There must be communication between the employer and

Don't ramble on without a purpose during an employment interview.

the employee to answer these questions. The performance appraisal interview is this form of communication. It is done after formal or informal appraisals have been made. There are many different types of appraisals and ways to make them.

Informal Appraisals

Just because your company does not have an appraisal form does not mean your performance on the job is not being appraised. It is being evaluated informally every day. Your boss and co-workers can't help observing the job that you are doing. They notice when you arrive late, take long coffee breaks, cut through red tape, negotiate successfully, or complain to co-workers. Notes are sometimes made of these observations. This informal appraisal will often be discussed in a performance appraisal interview.

Formal Appraisals

Formal appraisals are not a surprise. Employees know that sometime during the year their work is going to be evaluated. Formal appraisals have the same purpose as in-

Appraisal interviews allow employers and employees to exchange ideas and feelings about job performance.

formal appraisals. The only difference is that these appraisals are made on a standard form that is filled out before an interview is scheduled. Companies use different methods to conduct formal appraisals. The most widely used method is to have the employee's supervisor do the appraisal. Appraisals can also be made by the employee's co-workers or even by the employees themselves.

The Appraisal Form

Most standard appraisal forms have a scale that the appraiser uses to rate different categories of performance such as attitude, cooperation, attendance, quality of work, quantity of work, and so on. On many forms, your ability to communicate is evaluated. Appraisers rate under communication both your verbal and nonverbal communication. They also rate the accuracy of your communication.

Take the time to rate your current job performance on the following standard appraisal form. Are you pleased with your performance? Now, use the form to rate a subordinate's performance. Are you pleased with his or her performance?

The Appraisal Interview

It does not matter whether information has been gathered informally or formally for a performance appraisal interview as long as it was gathered carefully. What does matter is how this information is discussed with the employee in the interview. If you are conducting a performance appraisal interview, you must be completely prepared before

Performance Appraisal

Employee	Appraiser	Reviewer	
Department	Job Title		Date

Category	Check the appropriate rating						Comments
	Exceptional		Satisfactory		Unsatisfactory		
	1	2	1	2	1	2	
Productivity							
Dependability							
Cooperation							
Attendance							
Communication Skills							
Job Understanding							
Job Performance							
Comprehensive Rating							

Appraiser's Comments:

Contact

Daily ☐

Freq. ☐

Infreq. ☐

Signature	Department	Job Title	Date

Reviewer's Comments:

Contact

Daily ☐

Freq. ☐

Infreq. ☐

Signature	Department	Job Title	Date

Date Reviewed with Employee:	Employer's Comments:
Employee's Signature	

A sample appraisal form.

the actual interview. Study the employee's current appraisal. Then review old performance appraisals and make careful notes of any major changes in the employee's work performance.

When you conduct an employee performance appraisal interview, you have the responsibility to set the tone of the discussion. Stress that this is a conversation between just the two of you. You should begin the interview by pointing out areas in which the employee is doing exceptionally well. Give praise where praise is due. Also remember to thank the employee for the job he or she is doing. Always let employees know that the company appreciates the efforts that they are putting into their jobs. Then you will be able to bring up any problem areas without causing employees to feel threatened. Also keep in mind that if an employee is upset, not much will be accomplished during the interview.

One of the purposes of appraisal interviews is to identify areas of weakness so that they can be improved. Discuss specific job problems, not the employee's problems with the job. Don't say: "David, you are not getting the invoices out on time," but "David, why do you feel that there is difficulty in your department in getting the invoices out?" This lets David propose a solution rather than be defensive. In the most effective interview, you will get the employee to do most of the talking. Your role should be that of an active listener. Do you wonder how this can be done? It is really quite easy; ask the employee open-ended questions, for example:

1. "We have discussed ways to increase production in your area before. How do you feel production is doing now?"

2. "A lot of time and money used to be wasted taking the mail to the post office daily. Now that we have the postal pickup service, what benefits are you getting?"

If you enlist the employee's cooperation, job problems will be solved much faster. By encouraging employees to discuss problems, you are also opening the communication door and letting them know you want their help in solving problems. During the interview, you must make notes of how the employee reacts to the problems that were discussed. Don't try to solve the employee's problems, or worse yet, lead the employee to expect things from the company that may not happen.

After all the points on the performance appraisal have been discussed, you should give a summary of the discussion to the employee. Don't forget to express your thanks for his or her time and effort. Point out that you will be doing follow-up checks to make sure the employee solves any problems that were discussed. A good way to end the interview is by finding out what the employee's career goals and plans are.

Knowing Where You Stand

Performance appraisals have their good and bad points. It is up to you as the appraiser to make these evaluations of an employee's work truly a valuable experience for both the employee and your company. If you use an open, non-threatening form of communication, both parties will benefit. If your job performance is being appraised, be sure to find out what the company considers your strengths and weaknesses to be. Then make a list of any areas that are weak so you can try to improve them.

Correcting Employees

Unfortunately, employees do not always perform as they should. They violate safety rules, quarrel with other employees, are repeatedly tardy or absent, and do not follow company policies in many different ways. To keep the business running smoothly, you are going to have to correct an employee. In a correction interview, you are in charge of the flow of messages. You must listen to the employee's side after stating the problem because it may bring new light to the situation. Make sure that the problem area is clearly defined. How would you clear up these rather fuzzy statements of common problems?

1. "Smoking isn't good for your health, you know. You must be a two-pack-a-day person. I realize it's hard to wait for a cigarette, but sneaking off to smoke by the gas pumps sounds kind of dangerous to me."

2. "I like to park in the shade, myself. I suppose you do, too. Did you know that two visitors to the company today couldn't find a place in the visitors' lot?"

The final step in this kind of communication is to spell out to the employees exactly what will happen because of their actions. Although you are judge and jury in this type of problem, try to work for an attitude of fairness that will help the employees understand the company's position.

Handling Grievances

A grievance interview is the other side of a correction interview. Employees sometimes complain about things they
don't like. They may be unhappy about such things as
overtime, starting and quitting times, other workers, their
supervisors, or working conditions. If there is a union,
there is usually an established procedure for handling
grievances.

If you are an employee with a complaint, calm down before you do anything. Then arrange to talk to the correct
person in the chain of command. You will need to gather
your facts and present them in a clear, organized, unemotional manner at the interview for your grievances to be
handled with respect.

If you are handling a grievance, you must always try to
take the emotion out of the situation. Let employees give
their complaints before you begin looking for solutions together. Sometimes all they want to do is air their views.
Listen carefully to the employees; make sure that what
they are complaining about is their real complaint. Once
you and an employee have decided how to resolve a grievance, do so promptly.

Think now of a problem or a series of problems at work
that are bothering you. Write down the facts as you see
them. Just getting them off your chest may be enough to
reduce your complaints.

Counseling Employees

"My wife is divorcing me."
"The supervisor is picking on me."
"I can't meet the house payment this month."

You may find yourself listening to similar conversational
openers when a job or family problem interferes with an
employee's work. In this type of one-to-one communication, you play the role of listener. When you speak, you offer understanding. You do not propose solutions but help
the employee determine what he or she can do to find solutions. You do tell the employee about help that is available
within the company, like credit unions or alcohol counseling. If the problem is severe, you help the individual find
professional help. You do not assume the role of a professional psychologist. To be effective as a counselor, you
must keep what is said in counseling sessions confiden-
tial. Try to end a session on an upbeat note.

Look at the following conversation. Imagine the types of things the person counseling could say to get these responses.

Employee: I'm really in hot water with the auditor.
Counselor: (Seek more information in a sympathetic way.)
Employee: I didn't get the report auditing needed for taxes done on time, and the auditor just didn't understand.
Counselor: (Be receptive to the problem.)
Employee: I was so tired that I kept falling asleep at my desk, and I'm just as tired today. I can't get any sleep at home, with the new baby crying all night and my wife with the flu. Now I'm further behind than ever with the reports. And the auditor says he's ready to get me fired.
Counselor: (Help employee identify solutions.)
Employee: Well, those reports have to get done. I'll need to get some help at night. Maybe my sister could help watch the baby.
Counselor: (End on a positive tone.)

Firing Employees

Sometimes things have to be done that no one enjoys doing. Firing an employee is one of those things. Often the employee knows what is coming, but you still need to make an official termination speech.

Arriving at the Decision

People are fired for different reasons. Constantly breaking the rules, fighting, or inability to get work done are some of the reasons why people get fired. Whatever the reason, most companies follow certain steps to prevent the final dismissals.

When a problem is first noticed, the employee is told or helped to correct it. If, after a reasonable period of time, the problem has not been corrected, the employee is notified in writing that the problem is serious and needs to be corrected. A time limit is then normally given for correcting the problem. All transactions, both oral and written, with the employee about the problem are placed in the employee's file. If a problem continues, the employee may suffer a salary cut or be passed over for a promotion. If an employee still fails to correct a problem, the employee is usually given a final notice which says that if the problem is not corrected by a certain date, the company has no other alternative but to dismiss that employee.

If you are involved in firing people, you need to read the Civil Rights Act of 1964 before you terminate any employee. There are laws that protect the employee. If employees feel their rights have been violated, they can contest their firing in court. That is why it is essential for you to keep records that show how problems were handled. These records protect the company against lawsuits and can also be used in discussing the dismissal with labor unions.

What to Say

When an employee has had every opportunity but has failed to correct a serious problem, a company has no choice but to fire the employee. Someday you may be the person who has to give a termination speech. What should you say? How should you say it?

Meet with the employee in private for the termination speech. Look the employee in the eyes; then tell the employee that he or she is fired and why. Don't defend your actions. The employee has usually been given ample opportunity to correct the problem. Try to state your message in such a way that the employee knows that the company is justified in the firing. For example, if an employee makes every weekend a three-day weekend, you could easily justify the firing by saying something like, "Your frequent absences have placed too great a burden on the other employees in your department for you to continue working for this company."

Do not leave any hope that the employee can still keep his or her job. To do so is avoiding your job and giving the employee false hope. The employee must realize that the decision is final. This way, the employee will be better able to deal with the future. Read the following comments and decide which ones you feel would be appropriate to use in a termination speech:

1. "You're fired."
2. "Due to the circumstances, I am sure you must agree that . . ."
3. "Pick up your walking papers."
4. "You have tried hard, but our company does not seem to be the best place for you."
5. "Your career opportunities will increase with a different company."
6. "I called you in to ask for your resignation."

7. "It is not working out."

8. "You are a conscientious worker, but we cannot depend upon you to be here."

9. "Management has made decisions that go beyond personalities."

10. "The bottom line is that we can't have people who don't communicate effectively."

Once an employee realizes that the firing is a fact, it is time to discuss the financial aspects of the situation. Then explain the other details that are involved to the employee. You are in charge of this interview. Don't let the employee make you feel guilty.

Layoffs

Sometimes employees must leave a company through no fault of their own. The company simply must cut back and lay off people permanently. The people who are laid off usually do not have sufficient seniority to keep their jobs. This is a hard speech to make. Stress how the employee has been a valued worker. Point out how the company will help the employee find another job and what financial benefits he or she will receive. Let the employee take an active role in this communication.

After the Employee Is Fired

Sometimes you feel relieved when you have finished a speech, especially a difficult speech like a termination speech, even though it was justified. Be convinced that you have handled this situation well if you did not speak with great anger, emotion, or apology, and you put a touch of kindness in your speech.

Exit Interview

Just because you work for Ross Plumbing today does not mean you will work for that company tomorrow. You may be a plumber now, but you may decide to become a salesperson for a hardware store. Or you may decide to move back home and manage your parents' flower shop. Things come up; people's plans change. They also become dissatisfied with their jobs and leave for a variety of reasons.

Every year, thousands of people change their jobs. It costs companies millions of dollars when this happens. It means new people will have to be interviewed, hired, and trained. That is why companies conduct exit interviews. Companies want to know why an employee is leaving. They want to eliminate problems that cause good employees to leave.

Exit interviews are usually difficult interviews to conduct because employees are reluctant to give their real reasons for leaving. They want to make sure that they get good recommendations from the company, and they want to leave on good terms in the event that they want to return some day.

If you are conducting an exit interview, you will want to review the employee's record before the interview to see if this is the first job the employee has left or if there is a regular pattern of job hopping. Also notice the employee's age, since younger employees change jobs more frequently. Look for previously expressed grievances or problems on the record.

As the interview begins, it is up to you to set the tone of the interview as a fact-finding interview for the company. This task will be accomplished by asking probing questions tactfully. During the interview, watch to see if there is a hidden reason for the employee's departure. It is not advisable to hold the exit interview on the last day, since the employee's mind probably will be preoccupied with thoughts about the future.

Using the Phone

Employees misuse the phone constantly. It should be a business communication tool. Conversations should be short and to the point. Courtesy and good speech are essential.

Read the following list of reasons explaining why people used the phone at work. Which ones do you feel benefit the company? The phones were used to:

1. set a date for a new job interview
2. chat with a spouse
3. make a luncheon appointment with a supplier
4. order new invoices from the printer
5. read a long report to a co-worker
6. find out when the painter will be at a home
7. call personnel to find out more about an insurance policy

8. buy airplane tickets for a vacation
9. ask a secretary to take dictation
10. get a price quote for a customer

Effective One-to-One Communication

All structured communications have a definite beginning, middle, and end. In these communications, you are both a sender and a receiver. The communication should usually be balanced between these roles.

For any communication to be effective, both participants must be prepared with facts. Not much is accomplished when people just chat their way through performance appraisals, terminations, and employment interviews. These communications must be approached seriously. Their outcomes are important. Records should always be kept of these communications.

Speaking well on the telephone is an important part of business communication.

Communication in the Company

One-to-one communication is sufficiently complicated. However, compared to group communication, it is very simple. In a job interview, the interviewer talks to the interviewee, or the interviewee talks to the interviewer. Add another person to this group and all kinds of communication patterns emerge; now the interviewer can talk to the new person or to both people, and so on. A group of five people can communicate with each other in 75 different ways. Much of the communication in the business world is within groups. Because your share of communication time is much smaller in groups, you must make sure that everything you say counts.

Speaking at Meetings

Over a million business meetings are held every day. Yet few people are ever enthusiastic about attending a meeting. Are you? Most people leave a meeting saying, "What a waste of time and energy." So why do people keep organizing and attending meetings? It's because at good meetings, ideas, information, and opinions can be shared, problems can be handled, and policies and strategies can be developed. If meetings can be worthwhile, then why do so many fail? They fail because many people haven't learned how to communicate within groups. They don't know how to lead or how to participate in a meeting. If you want to do your part to make a meeting a success, you will need to acquire these skills.

Leading a Meeting

A group tends to act like its leader. If you are rude and shout, so will they. If you act friendly, calm, or thoughtful, so will they. Think of the last three meetings you attended; did the group behave in the same way as the leader? How will a group behave if their leader sounds like one of these leaders?

Leader #1: I think we'll start with Mark's report. No, it's probably better to hear from Russ first. Or maybe we should get Frank in here to clue us in on what he thinks about hiring the consultant.

Leader #2: We'll start with Mark's report. Then we'll hear from Russ before we vote on hiring the consultant.

Note how the first leader sets the tone for a disorganized meeting. Soon the participants will be running out to bring additional people into the meeting. The participants will tend to stay on track in the second meeting, since the leader is organized.

The Leader's Job. Almost every study of leadership assigns the same functions to a leader. What a leader does before a meeting is to choose the time, place, agenda, participants, and goals. To start a meeting, the leader tells a group the purpose of the meeting. During a meeting, the leader guides the discussion and summarizes it frequently. At the end of the meeting, the leader reviews what has happened in the meeting and thanks the participants.

In running a meeting, a leader might begin by saying, "Let's see today if we can decide on how to package our frozen corn." After stating the goal, the leader could clarify the problem further by saying, "We have the choice of staying with the traditional boxes or starting to use polyethylene bags." To open the discussion, the leader could begin by asking, "How does the cost of the boxes compare to the cost of the bags?" The leader might then summarize the answers to this question by saying, "It appears that it

To run a business meeting, you must be prepared and you must keep the discussion on the right track.

would be more expensive to use the bags." To add interest to the discussion, the leader might throw out an opinion like, "I think the bags have less consumer appeal." Finally, the leader will summarize the meeting by saying, "The consensus is to go with the bags to meet the competition."

To keep a meeting going, a leader needs to ask questions. They can be addressed to individuals or to the group at large. When the leader is asked a question, he or she can answer it or direct it back to the group. Not all questions are effective. Good questions usually cannot be answered with a simple *yes* or *no*. Good questions keep to the subject of the meeting, they are brief and clear, and they do not cover several topics. Which of the questions below are good questions that could be included in the discussion on packaging frozen corn?

1. "Have you studied the durability of bags?"
2. "What size bag is most popular with the consumers?"
3. "Where shall we test-market the bags?"
4. "When shall we begin to manufacture the bags, and where shall we start selling the product?"
5. "What do you think we should do about the work schedule for the Thanksgiving holiday?"

Only questions **2.** and **3.** are good questions.

Disrupters.   The hardest part of being a leader is to handle the participants who intentionally or unintentionally disrupt the flow of a meeting. See if you can identify who the jokester, the interrupter, the delayer, the left fielder, and the ego deflater were at a meeting from the following bits of conversation:

George: Do we really have enough information to make a decision to enter the artificial flower business at this time? Why don't we wait until the first of the year and see what the economy is like then?

Maria: George, are you saying that we should—

Tom: You know what George is saying. Let's review who our distributors would be.

Gene: Artificial people, for sure.

Maria: Whatever happened to our idea to repave the visitor's parking lot?

Bill: Trust Maria to know what the topic of discussion is.

Gene is the jokester. Tom is the interrupter. George is the delayer. Maria is way out in left field, and Bill is the ego deflater. Did you identify the disrupters correctly?

To make sure that a meeting goes smoothly, leaders have to handle these difficult personalities as well as the talkers, repeaters, axe-grinders, whisperers, fighters, and socializers. To do this and keep to the agenda, a leader has to be strong and assertive. The leader needs to remember to always attack the problem and not the person causing the problem, or the meeting will disintegrate into a mudslinging contest with the participants taking sides.

Here are some time-tested tips for dealing with difficult people at meetings. Give the talkers a role in the meeting. You can even let them talk first. When they pause for a breath, give another speaker a chance by saying something like, "Let's find out what Charlotte thinks." Another way to handle talkers is to simply avoid calling on them. You can frequently silence the whisperers and socializers by merely looking at them pointedly. Seat two antagonists side-by-side so they can't glare across the table or room at each other. Keep participants on the subject by saying firmly, "Today we are discussing so and so, not such and such. We will take that subject up at a later date."

Never let a group stray far from the subject before calling them back to the business at hand. Discourage the constant jokesters by refraining from laughing at their humor. In handling some of these people, you may find phrases such as these effective:

1. "I don't see how that relates to what we are currently discussing."
2. "I believe that point was already settled earlier in the meeting."
3. "I can't hear what Mary is saying."
4. "What does everyone think of Chet's ideas?"

Characteristics of a Good Leader.   Good leaders are prepared. They take charge of the meeting but do not hog the show. They keep a meeting moving and decide how much time to spend on each item of the agenda. Good leaders balance participation between the talkers and quiet members of the group. They try to keep a friendly, informal atmosphere during the meeting. After the meeting is over, they check on the progress of any plans or decisions that were made during the meeting.

Participating in a Meeting

A good leader is not enough to make a meeting a success. The members of the group also share this responsibility. In fact, if a leader is weak, other members of the group must help with this function. Being an effective participant does not mean sitting like a bump on a log at a meeting. It means actively participating in a meeting. When should you speak? Whenever you have something to contribute. Don't wait until the end of the meeting to suddenly give your views; that is not participating effectively in a meeting.

It is the participant's responsibility to prepare for a meeting by gathering information about what is going to be discussed. Notes should be written to take to the meeting. You should also decide what you want to say. At the meeting, you should follow the agenda, stick to the point, make purposeful contributions to the discussion, and above all else, listen to what is being said.

Roles in Groups.   During a meeting, people usually take on one of two roles. They either work toward accomplishing the task or toward helping the group work together. Study these statements made by participants at the previously discussed meeting and determine whether they are people- or task-oriented.

Be sure to speak up if you have something to contribute at a meeting.

Dick: Well, what Janet is saying is really not too far from the basic thrust of Larry's report.

Luis: What Larry said is that larger households prefer the polyethylene bags to the boxes.

Anne: Both Janet and Larry agree that we will have to start selling the bags, even though they do not agree on a time schedule for getting them into stores.

Kent: Let's set a date for getting the bags into stores.

Dick and Anne are group-oriented, while Luis and Kent are task-oriented. Which role do you usually play? At the next meeting that you attend, study which roles the people are playing. Both roles are valuable.

How to Start Participating.   There are advantages to participating in meetings. Not only do your bosses become aware of you as a valued employee, but you also begin to feel that you are playing a part in the operation of your company. If you have always been tongue-tied at meetings, give yourself confidence by really researching a subject before a meeting begins. You don't have to initiate an area of discussion, but you should be able to add additional information. If even this frightens you, begin to participate by showing your support for others. Use such phrases as, "I agree with Larry's ideas about the bags," and "You really showed the advantages of using bags over boxes."

Communication at Meetings

More and more of the business at companies is being conducted in small group meetings. This means that more and more people are participating in decisions and that more views are being considered in making decisions. It also may mean that originality is being stifled for consensus and a lot of time is being wasted on talking. The value of meetings lies in what information the leader and participants bring to them and how everyone interacts to make decisions. There is no value to having a meeting if one person dominates it.

Making Reports

When the company chemist tells the new-products committee about the gasoline substitute that is being developed, the chemist is making a report. When the sales manager describes the new sales territories to the board, the manager is making a report. Reports are nothing more than speeches to inform in a business setting.

Content of a Report

Reports must be accurate because the information that is given in them is frequently used in making decisions. They are concrete. They deal with facts and figures—not guesstimates. Reports focus on one subject. Everything that you say in a report should tie back to that subject. Tailor the information in a report to fit the audience. If you are an engineer talking to a group of engineers, go with all the technical details of your subject. But don't include these details for the finance committee, unless you clarify what they mean. If you are a specialist, watch using the jargon of your particular field, or you may have the same results as the scientists did in the following story:

A plumber wrote to a government agency, saying he found that hydrochloric acid quickly opened drainpipes. Was this a good thing to use? A scientist at the agency replied, "The efficacy of hydrochloric acid is indisputable, but the corrosive residue is incompatible with metallic permanence."

The plumber wrote back, thanking him for the assurances that hydrochloric acid was all right. Disturbed by this turn of affairs, the scientist showed the letter to his boss, another scientist, who then wrote to the plumber, "We cannot assume responsibility for the production of toxic and noxious residue with hydrochloric acid, and suggest you use an alternative procedure."

The plumber wrote back that he agreed—hydrochloric acid worked fine. Greatly disturbed by this misunderstanding, the scientists took their problem to the top boss. He broke with jargon and wrote the plumber, saying, "Don't use hydrochloric acid. It eats hell out of the pipes."

Arrange the information in your report in such an organized way that one step follows another. In the introduction, you should tell the background for your report, the subject of the report, and the main points that you will be talking about in the report. Try to capture your listeners' attention so that they listen carefully to the body of the report, which is the information they need to know. Conclude by summarizing the report and leading into the question-and-answer period that usually follows a report.

Presenting a Report

A report is not an oration. Don't present one in the dramatic manner of a Laurence Olivier. Nor should you use the humor of a Johnny Carson. A report is designed to inform. Deliver it with sincerity so that your listeners will know that you believe what you are saying. Avoid being wordy. Be concise. What could you eliminate from the following sentences without losing the sense of the report?

1. "You are probably aware of the fact that sales were down last year."

2. "It really pleases me to stand up here today and tell you that for the first time ever, our company reached a million dollars in sales this quarter."

3. "To end this report, I would like to leave you with this conclusion as my final words of wisdom: the higher rates on bulk mail are reducing the number of mail order businesses."

Personalize Your Report

An oral report is less formal than a written report. Your audience is sitting right in front of you instead of reading a report in an office. Personalize your report by saying, "John's" or "Martha's" department instead of the personnel department. Use the more friendly "We found" instead

When presenting a report at work, you are giving a speech to inform.

of "The report is based on these facts." Give a report from an outline or note cards instead of reading it; you will be talking more directly to your audience.

Effective Group Communication

In communicating to groups, you should focus on clarity in how you speak and on accuracy in what you say. The end product of leading or participating in a meeting or giving a report should be communication between you and the group. Communication provides a mutual understanding that lets you work together effectively and efficiently.

Outside Communication

Communication in the business world is not limited to the exchange of messages within a company. Companies send messages to, and receive messages from, the outside world of other companies, the government, and the public. Persons in business also talk to each other at lunches, banquets, and conventions. Let's explore what is involved in some of these communications.

Companies and the Government

Companies need to plan their communication with other companies and the government. They must decide who sends and receives different kinds of messages. A regular network must be established. For example, the marketing department may handle communication with customers, the finance department with banks, and personnel with the Civil Rights Commission. Without a network, chaos will result because messages are sent and received by the wrong departments or persons.

Speaking to Customers

In communicating with your customers, these old clichés hold true:

> Keep the customer happy.
> The customer is always right.

People are not always pleased with the products or services that they have bought from a company. Things break, wear out, or don't satisfy the customer in some way. The customer wants the problem corrected. Frequently, the customer is upset and angry when he or she is speaking about the problem to someone at a company. If you are that person, handle the problem unemotionally. Remember that the customer really may have reason to be upset. Hear what the customer has to say. When you speak, be sympathetic, courteous, and respectful at all times. Try to find out the reason for the problem. Admit that there is a problem and express your company's interest in resolving it to the customer's satisfaction. Emphasize that your company is sorry for any inconvenience that the customer may have experienced. Then negotiate a settlement with the customer.

Formal Communication

You may have to make a speech at a dinner, convention, conference, or workshop. These speeches must be well prepared because you are representing your company. Use notes. Choose speaking tools that will add interest to your speech. Whether you give a speech to inform, persuade, or entertain, make whatever you say enhance the public image of your company.

Informal Communication

No matter where you are speaking in the business world, you speak for your company. What you say and how you behave reflects on your company. Learn to handle casual conversations well; they count in the business world.

Business Lunches.   Divide your conversation at a business lunch or other meal into the three traditional parts of a speech—introduction, body, and conclusion. Handle the business part of your lunch after exchanging greetings and small talk. Be sure to conclude your meeting in some way by summing up what plans or decisions have been made. Always watch your manners. Don't turn off your companion or companions by talking with your mouth full or by eating peas with your knife. People usually notice bad manners.

Banquets.   Business banquets give you an opportunity to socialize with people you deal with in the business world. However, they are not completely social functions. There are things that you must do. You must greet and thank

What you say and how you act at business lunches, banquets, and conventions reflects on your company.

the people hosting the function. You must introduce yourself to and converse with everyone at your table. If you are shy and cannot initiate conversation, you must add comments to what others are saying and smile a lot. Be careful about what you say. Don't bore people, argue, monopolize the conversation, or interrupt others. Read the following conversational bits from a banquet. Decide which ones should never have been said.

1. "The president of our company is getting a divorce."
2. "Your company's new sales approach seems to be successful."
3. "Why didn't your children go to college?"
4. "What an old-fashioned idea! *Buyer beware* is out in today's world."
5. "It's great to have a banquet in a museum."

Avoid comments like **1.**, **3.**, and **4.** Gossip, invading people's privacy, and insults are not acceptable.

Convention Small Talk. At conventions, if you don't know people but want to speak to them, introduce yourself. Do include the name of your company and your position in the company in your introduction. When you introduce others, always label them by their jobs. Conventions aren't the time for long conversations. If you have a purpose to a conversation, make your point quickly.

Making Your Speech Count

Whenever you speak in a business setting, make your speech count. There is no such thing as idle chatter in the business world. Everything you say at lunches, banquets, and conventions builds up or tears down your image and your company's.

Effective Selling

There are many different types of people in the business world, but nearly everyone fits into one of two groups: *paper-people* or *people-people*. One group works mostly with paper and the other mostly with people. Salespersons are people-people. They make their living by selling a service or a product to people. Not everyone who reads this book will make a living by selling. Many of you are probably paper-people. However, it is highly likely that at some point in your career, you will be asked to sell something. Then you will have to know the three *P*'s of effective selling that successful salespersons know. They are:

1. Principles of selling.
2. Preparation for selling.
3. Presentation of the product or service.

Read on and see if you already have mastered these three *P*'s of selling or if you need to do a few of the practice exercises in order to brush up or improve in some of these important areas.

Principles of Selling

Buying is an important part of everyone's life. Almost everything that you own or use is bought. You buy food, clothing, appliances, cars, houses, and insurance. And someone is selling everything that you buy. It is not easy to sell things today. The competition is tough. You expect many things from salespersons, whether their product is candy bars or hot tubs. Plenty of persons sell things, but

Successful salespersons strive to establish a good rapport with customers.

the persons who get your sales are the ones who know the principles of selling. As you read the following list of these principles, ask yourself if you really follow them when you are selling something:

1. Know your product or service thoroughly.
2. Believe in your product or service.
3. Know your competition.
4. Know where your sales are.
5. Establish yourself as an honest, reliable salesperson.
6. Establish your company as a dependable and trust-worthy one.
7. Show enthusiasm for your product or service.
8. Arouse a need for the product or service within the customer.
9. Identify the reasons why people should buy from you.
10. Respect your customer.
11. Develop a pleasing voice and effective body language.
12. Adjust your approach to fit the customer.

Preparation for Selling

To be successful at anything, from gourmet chef to salesperson of the year for an insurance company, requires preparation. Any salesperson can ring doorbells, make phone calls, or see prospective customers; but it is the salesperson who is prepared who gets the sales. Don't schedule any sales appointments until you are adequately prepared.

The Product or Service

Preparation means knowing what your product or service can do or won't do and how to use it. Some companies have to train their employees for months to teach them about products or services. Think about what you would need to know in order to sell a simple product like a smoke detector. Did your list include the ionization principle, the monitoring circuit, the low battery signal, the housing, the installation, and the price?

Preparation also means knowing what makes your product or service so much better than the competition. That includes knowing things that go beyond the sales, like service, reliability, and warranties. It means knowing how to justify the price of your product or service, especially if the price is higher than the competition's. Remember, a sale won't be made just because you tell what your service or product can do for the customer. You must be able to prove what it can do for them. Be prepared to back up your product or service with testimonials from satisified customers.

The Company

Know your company. You represent the company, so you should know its philosophy, how long it has been in business, and whether it is a member of the local chamber of commerce, the Better Business Bureau, or state or national organizations. Do you know this information about your company? You should.

The Customer

Preparation also includes knowing your customer. Know who has the authority to buy in a company. Keep a record of your dealings with this person. Since you build up your business through repeat customers, you want your customers to remember you. So don't forget to have business cards prepared and ready to pass out whenever you talk to a customer.

The Speech

Sales presentations are speeches to persuade with a little bit of informing and entertaining in them. You have to persuade customers that they need the product or service you are selling.

Adjust your speech for each customer. Use terms that the customer is familiar with. If you're selling a personal computer to a systems analyst, high-tech vocabulary is appropriate. If you're selling the same machine to the manager of a hardware store, it isn't. Explain everything the machine will do to the systems analyst. Tell the manager how the machine can be used effectively in the hardware store.

People buy products or services for the benefits that they receive from them. So point out benefits in your speech. Don't sell a pool as a hole in the ground full of water; sell it as a place for fun, relaxation, and exercise.

Show your customer what you are selling. If you don't have the actual product, show pictures. How many door-to-door salespersons sell vacuum cleaners or encyclopedias without letting their customers see them? Not many. Samples and brochures are your speaking tools; use them in your speech.

Before you ever talk to your first customer, practice your sales speech on anyone who will listen. Be sure to record it and check whether you have any speech faults that need correcting. If so, go back to the appropriate parts of "Improving Your Speaking Voice" and do the exercises.

Presentation

You're ready to go. You're all prepared and have an appointment with the appropriate person. Now is the time to give your presentation. A presentation is a lot like a business letter. Both begin with a warm and friendly greeting that introduces the salesperson and product or service to the customer. Next comes the body of the speech or letter, which creates a need or desire in the customer for the product or service that you are selling. Give your persuasive speech here to sell the customer on why the product or service should be bought from you. Use your speaking tools in this part of the speech. In the conclusion of the speech or business letter, you ask for the order.

Helpful Hints

You want your presentation to be stimulating, informative, and brief. Remember that it does not matter how well you speak; if you don't also listen to the customer, you can lose a sale. Be flexible enough to adjust your sales approach to meet the needs of the customer. Respect the customer. Never talk down to one no matter how bored you may be or how ridiculous the questions are that the customer may ask.

Honesty is important at all times. For example, if this is your first sales call ever, tell the customer. Explain that this is your first call, and you know the customer will find out through your presentation that you are very inexperienced. Honesty extends to believing in your product. You will find it very hard to sell a product that you don't fully believe in.

If a customer brings up any small objections to a sale at the last minute, quickly eliminate the objections. The customer is really asking you to convince him or her of the value of the sale. For example, a couple has finally found their dream home and are ready to close the deal with the real estate agent when the husband says, "I bet the utility bills are high on this house." Which of the following answers should the agent use to banish this objection?

1. "Two thousand dollars a year."
2. "Really, for this area, the bills are not bad."
3. "On the utility company's budget plan, you would pay less than $200 a month."

The last answer will convince the husband that the bills are reasonable and help the agent close the deal.

Sample Presentation

A good salesperson, as you may have heard, can sell a refrigerator to an Eskimo. Another story tells of a real estate agent in Florida who wanted to know if he should refund a couple's money for land that they had purchased a few months before. The land was now under water. The salesperson's boss was furious and wanted to know what kind of salesperson the employee was. The boss pointed out that the couple now had a great need, and it was the salesperson's job to fulfill that need by selling them a boat.

As you read this sample presentation, study what the salesperson said in each part. Be sure to notice how the salesperson identified the customer's need and filled it.

A well-organized presentation is an important part of effective selling.

Introduction. "Good morning, Mr. Brown. Fantastic weather today. Spring is finally here. I don't think that we have met before. I am Doug Young, representing the Brian Chemical Company. We manufacture cleaning compounds and solvents for industrial use. I've just been assigned to this district, and I noticed that you were not on our customer list. Perhaps that is because no one has called on your company recently. You may not be familiar with our company's name. However, we just bought out Industrial Cleaners, which has been selling cleaning products for over thirty years in this state."

Body. "I notice that your floors are tile and probably quite difficult to keep clean, with people tracking in mud from the construction next door. Is slipping a problem after mopping? Would you like to have a high gloss that stands up to heavy traffic? The detergent floor polish we manufacture has such a high level of solids, only one coat is necessary for a bright shine. Then damp mopping with just water will keep floors like yours clean for weeks before another application is required. Our product has polyethylene, which no other product has. This stops slipping accidents. Here, let me demonstrate on one tile for you." (Actual demonstration.) "The floor looks great. Notice you can't slip or leave a black heel mark on it.

"We also have a cleaner that you can use to remove oil and grease from your concrete sidewalks. Just brush it on where it is needed and allow it to stand for 10 minutes. Then sweep the area clean. No scrubbing or bending is needed. Many local machine shops, like Herman's and Ford's, use it."

Conclusion. "I'd like to enter your order for a trial case of the floor polish and five gallons of the cleaner. What, you're worried about storing the products? They're perfectly safe. Neither are flammable. Both meet OSHA standards." (Customer orders the product.) "Thank you for your order. I know you will be pleased with how easy it is to keep your floors looking good. Your order will be delivered on Friday. I'll stop by in a few weeks to make sure that you are satisfied with the products."

Practice

You get the best practice in selling by actually going out and selling. No selling situation is ever exactly like another. Give yourself a little advance sales practice now by reading the following descriptions and selecting the better salesperson in each one by deciding which one best followed the principles of selling:

1. Two interior decorators were helping a woman decorate her home. She had wanted her couch and chairs re-covered. After the re-covered furniture was delivered, here is what each decorator said:

   a. "Let me show you how well these carpet samples would go with your furniture."

   b. "I can measure your room for carpet."

   Decorator **a.** is the better salesperson because **a.** tried to arouse a need for a product within the customer.

2. A prospective customer, looking at a lawn mower, said that he thought he could do better at a nationally known chain store because their prices were better. The better salesperson answered:

   a. "I've never heard that before."

   b. "It's true that their prices are lower. But their warranty is only good for 30 days, and ours covers the first 2 years on both parts and labor."

   Your answer should be **b.** because **b.** knows the competition.

3. A man is asking about the possibility of returning a chain saw if it is too heavy for his son to use. Two salespersons responded quite differently:

   a. "Let him come down to the store and lift it."

   b. "Our company has been in business for over 30 years. We have never failed to return a customer's money if they were not completely satisfied."

   Salesperson **b.** is the better salesperson because **b.** established the company as dependable and trustworthy.

4. The customer wanted to know how the company could ensure that her heating system would be regularly maintained. The salespersons explained what their companies had to offer by saying:

   a. "What you need is our company's service contract. You receive a complete checkup for your system in August. Then, if you have a problem during the heating season, you pay only for the parts."

   b. "We do have a service contract."

   Choose **a.** as the better salesperson, since **a.** showed a thorough knowledge of the company's service.

5. Two salespersons were selling an herbicide to a farmer. After explaining how to use it, they added:

   a. "This weed killer is unbelievable. The Ontario Nursery was reluctant to use it at first by their young trees. Now they have tried it and are completely sold, since not one of their trees was damaged and every single weed was killed. They have even started using it around their shrubs. This is a great product!"

   b. "This weed killer works."

   Since salespersons should show enthusiasm for what they are selling, **a.** is the better salesperson.

Positive Thinking

There is more to selling than knowing the three *P*'s of selling. Besides knowing the principles of selling, being prepared to sell, and making a sales presentation, you have to practice positive thinking. You can't be discouraged because you don't turn every prospective customer into a buyer. After all, a baseball player has a great season when he hits .300. In selling some products, you have a great season if you get 15 sales out of 100, which would only mean a .150 batting average. For some products, one sale a year is a great season. There is no room for negative thoughts in the minds of successful salespersons. Get rid of customers' negative comments by treating those comments as questions and answering them in a positive way. Think of yourself as unlike any other salesperson in the world. Then use this uniqueness to your advantage in going after sales.

Successful Speaking at Work

Can you think of a job in which speaking is not useful? It may be impossible to do so. Speaking may not be as important in some jobs as others, but what job doesn't require that you speak to a co-worker, a boss, or a subordinate? Even Bob Cratchit and Scrooge spoke to each other, although there wasn't a lot of communication between them. Speaking is your strongest vehicle for communicating in the business world. The better you speak at work, the further you are likely to advance in your career.

SPEAKING IN THE

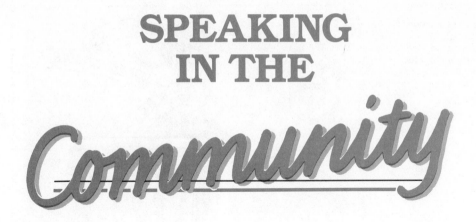

Community

I f you are going to play an active role in your community, then you are going to have to speak up. You will have to speak to the planning commission to protest the building of a service station in your neighborhood. You will have to speak to your neighbors to solicit for charity or get petitions signed. You will have to speak up in organizations to make motions. Unless you speak up, no one will know what your ideas are.

Whether you choose to play an active role or not in your community is your choice. However, every time you step out of your home, you probably will speak to someone in the community. It's almost impossible to avoid speaking to tradespersons, professional persons, salespersons, and neighbors and get anything done in a community. This section explores ways to become an effective speaker in the community by learning how to speak to both groups and individuals.

Clubs and Organizations

In the United States, there is no shortage of clubs and organizations for people to join. There are groups for almost any purpose. Think of any interest or hobby that you have; there is probably a group of people somewhere in

There are thousands of clubs and organizations, representing a wide variety of interests, thoughout the country.

this country that has joined together to share that very same interest. There are groups for people who are dieters, gourmets, history buffs, skiers, poker players, river rafters, teachers, realtors, neighbors, veterans, and on and on. All these groups vary enormously, not only in their purposes but in the size of their membership and their structure. Still, to participate effectively in any of these groups, it helps to know something about leading a meeting, fund-raising, publicity, the rules of parliamentary procedure, speaking to groups, and getting speakers for groups.

Leading a Meeting

Obviously, there are differences between leading the Rotary or Lions clubs in a large city and leading a small investment group in the suburbs. Still, the person who gets the praise or blame for the success of any group's activities is the leader. The secret of being a successful leader is not just planning a meeting, but knowing what to say and when and how to say it.

Planning a Meeting

Whether you are leading a large, formal meeting or a small group sitting around the coffee table in your living room, you must have a plan for the meeting. The plan is the agenda. It may be a formal outline that is sent to the members of a group before a meeting, or it may be items written on the back of a piece of paper for your own use. When you write an agenda, set time limits for each item on the agenda. This will keep the meeting from lasting too long or having the group spend too much time on any one item. The agenda for the business meeting of an organization follows a standard order:

1. Call to order
2. Reading of the minutes
3. Reports of officers and committees
4. Unfinished business
5. New business
6. Announcements
7. Adjournment

Notice how this standard form is used in making the agenda for the meeting of a parent-teacher association:

1. Call to order (2 minutes)
2. Pledge of Allegiance—Jane Adams (1 minute)
3. Inspirational message—John Quinn (1 minute)
4. Reading of the minutes—Paul Rich (2 minutes)
5. Treasurer's report—Carol Green (1 minute)
6. Report of the traffic safety committee—Claude Jones (5 minutes)
7. Announcements—The annual flower sale is Saturday, May 10th. The sixth grade won the magazine subscription sales contest. (1 minute)
8. Spring song program—Miss Louis (45 minutes)
9. Adjournment

The casual agenda below for a homeowner's association is just as necessary to keep a meeting running smoothly as the formal agenda above is for the parent-teacher meeting.

1. Garbage service (10 minutes)
2. Bus route change (5 minutes)

To lead a meeting effectively, you must keep order in the room and stick to the agenda.

3. Mail box vandalism (5 minutes)

4. Installation of sidewalks (10 minutes)

5. Local florist (30 minutes)

When you plan an agenda for a meeting, try always to include something that will make the meeting special. It could be a program following the formal part of a meeting. It could be showing the posters for a publicity campaign. It simply could be an interesting report from one of the standing committees. Something should happen at each meeting to set it apart from other meetings. At the parent-teacher meeting, the presentation of the spring song program will make the meeting special. At the homeowner's association meeting, the special event will be a demonstration on how to make unusual centerpieces from home-grown flowers.

Running a Meeting

Leaders must always run meetings, whether the meetings are large or small, formal or informal. They need to take charge of a meeting from the start. They do this by beginning a meeting on time. When it is time for a meeting to begin, a leader should walk briskly to the front of the room or to the speaker's stand, face the group, and wait calmly for the members to come to order. If this approach does not quiet the membership, the leader should use a gavel to gain the attention of the group. A leader should not have to speak to bring a meeting to order. Once a leader has brought a meeting to order, the tone of the meeting should be set by his or her opening remarks. Which of the following remarks do you think would be effective to open a meeting of a ski club?

1. "Fellow skiers, the slopes are ready. There are 12 inches of snow on Mt. Pleasant. There are 2 feet of powder on Mt. Mohawk. Tonight, we're going to decide on the place for this month's ski trip. Let's begin by discussing the advantages that Mr. Pleasant offers."

2. "Um, do you want to get started? Does everybody know everyone here? What do you want to talk about first?"

Obviously, the first set of remarks would show that the leader knew what he or she was doing. An informal atmosphere was established for the meeting. The members were greeted with friendliness and told the reason for the meeting. Then the leader opened the discussion. In any meeting, the leader's opening remarks must tell why the meeting is being held and how it will be conducted.

Once a leader has opened a meeting, he or she cannot let up. The meeting must move from item to item of the agenda. Which of the following comments will keep a meeting flowing?

1. "What shall we discuss next?"
2. "Let's move on to the next item on the agenda."
3. "We're discussing item 3 now. Does your remark tie into that point?"
4. "So far, we have discussed the advantages of going to Mt. Pleasant. What are some of the disadvantages of going there?"

   5. "Have you heard the joke about the skier who lost his bindings?"

Comments **2.**, **3.**, and **4.** will keep a meeting moving. Frequent summaries of what has been said also keep meetings running forward. For example, after the first discussion, the leader of the ski club meeting could have said, "The advantages of going to Mt. Pleasant seem to be a short trip, inexpensive ski rentals, and good cross-country skiing."

To keep a meeting moving toward its goal, it is essential for the leader to override disruptions. A leader cannot allow people to talk out of turn, move away from the topic, verbally attack others, or monopolize the discussion. When people get out of line, the leader must bring them back on the right track. To do so, the leader must try to change behavior instead of arguing with those who create disturbances. Read the following pairs of remarks that were used to handle disruptions. You will find it easy to see which ones attack problems instead of people.

   1. a. "We'll get done faster by sticking to the agenda."

   b. "Harry, if you'd follow the agenda we might get done before midnight."

   2. a. "Stop reading the paper, Mark, and start participating in the discussion."

   b. "Participation by everyone would make this a more interesting discussion."

   3. a. "Ann, don't mumble. It sounds like your mouth is full of food."

   b. "The members will find the meeting more interesting if they can hear what everyone is saying."

The old adage, "You get more flies with honey than vinegar," holds true in a meeting. A leader needs to sprinkle genuine praise and heartfelt thanks throughout the meeting for the work the members are doing. The ski club leader should praise the member who created the Hansel and Gretel ski race contest and thank the member who brought a former Olympic skier to speak to the club.

The leader cannot let up before formally closing the meeting. Just before closing, the leader should summarize what has been accomplished in a meeting. This is also the time to tell the group the plans for the next meeting.

A meeting is not really over until the leader closes it in some way. People like things tied up neatly. The leader of the ski club could wrap the meeting up effectively by saying: "We have decided to go to Mt. Pleasant for our ski trip because it is closer. We hope to be able to use some of the tips that our speaker gave us about using the right wax for the conditions. At our next meeting, we will have a guest expert on conditioning for skiing. See you on the slopes next Saturday."

Parliamentary Procedure for Leaders

Business meetings of clubs and organizations must be run in an orderly fashion if anything is to be accomplished. The system of rules for making decisions in a group is known as parliamentary procedure. Leaders of clubs and organizations must know and follow the basics of parliamentary procedure in order to run a meeting as democratically and efficiently as possible. To run any group, a leader should know how to handle motions, since it is through motions that the business of most clubs is transacted.

A motion is a brief, precise statement of a proposed action by a member of a group. A member can only make a motion if the leader has called upon the member to speak. Before any motion can be discussed by a group, it must be seconded. The leader usually restates the motion for the group. In groups that strictly follow parliamentary procedure, discussion can occur only after a motion has been made. However, in more casual groups, discussion usually precedes the making of a motion. During a discussion, the members may decide they want to change a motion. To do this, they must propose and approve a new motion that amends (changes) the original motion. When everyone has had a say about a motion or an amended motion, the leader restates the motion or has the secretary read it. Then the leader calls for a voice vote. He or she begins by saying, "All those in favor of the motion say 'aye.' " Next, the leader says, "All those opposed say 'nay.' " If the leader cannot tell which side has the majority, the leader should ask for a show of hands.

Each motion must be disposed of in some way before the group can take up another item of business. The members can dispose of a motion by voting to take it up at another time. The leader can dispose of a motion by sending it to a committee to study it and report back at a later date. Of course, most motions are disposed of by having the members vote on the motion. Eventually, all motions must be either approved or disapproved by a majority of the members of a group.

All motions can be classified into one of four types:

Main Motion. Most of the action in your club or organization will center around main motions. A main motion brings new business before a meeting. It takes up a matter that has been previously tabled. It lets the members strike out a motion that was previously passed. It also lets the members consider a matter out of its scheduled order.

Subsidiary Motion. This is the other motion that will be most frequently used by the members besides the main motion. A subsidiary motion is any other action that may be taken on a main motion. This type of motion can only be made when a main motion is being discussed. Motions to change a main motion, send it to a committee, discuss it later, or limit the discussion time of a main motion are subsidiary motions.

Incidental Motion. This type of motion grows out of other business that a group is considering. It is used to handle procedural problems, like correcting an error in parliamentary procedure, objecting to the ruling by a chairperson, withdrawing a motion, and requesting information.

Privileged Motion. This motion is used to deal with the welfare of the group. Besides being used to adjourn or recess a meeting, members use it to complain about noise, room temperature, and similar emergencies. A privileged motion is not connected in any way with a main motion.

Leaders must be able to answer the following questions about each of the four motions:

1. May a member interrupt a speaker to make the motion?
2. Is a second needed?
3. Is the motion debatable, or must it be voted upon right after it is proposed?
4. Can the motion be amended?
5. What vote is needed for the motion?

The following chart provides you with the answers to the above questions.

Chart of Selected Motions Used in Parliamentary Procedure

The following frequently made motions are listed in order of their rank. When a group is considering any one of them, a member may not introduce another that is listed below it. But a member may introduce another that is listed above it.

Type of Motion	Interruption of Speaker?	Second Needed?	Motion Debatable?	Motion Amendable?	Vote Needed
Privileged Motion					
Adjourn the meeting	no	yes	no	no	majority
Recess the meeting	no	yes	no	yes	majority
Complain about noise, room temperature, etc.	yes	no	no	no	none, chairman rules
Subsidiary Motion					
End debate	no	yes	no	no	2/3 majority
Limit length of debate	no	yes	no	yes	2/3 majority
Postpone consideration of a matter to a specific time	no	yes	yes	yes	majority
Have a matter studied further	no	yes	yes	yes	majority
Amend a motion	no	yes	yes	yes	majority
Incidental Motion					
Correct an error in parliamentary procedure	yes	no	no	no	none, chairman rules
Object to a ruling by the chairman	yes	yes	yes	no	majority
Obtain advice on proper procedure	yes	no	no	no	none, chairman rules
Request information	yes	no	no	no	none
Withdraw a motion	no	no	no	no	majority
Main Motion					
Introduce business	no	yes	yes	yes	majority
Take up a matter previously tabled	no	yes	no	no	majority
Strike out a motion previously passed	no	yes	yes	yes	majority
Consider a matter out of its scheduled order	no	yes	no	no	2/3 majority

A leader who answers all of the following true-false statements correctly would be able to lead a group that uses considerable parliamentary procedure. Rate your knowledge of parliamentary procedure by taking the following short quiz:

1. A member may introduce a motion to adjourn when a group is ready to take a vote.

2. A member makes a motion complaining about noise. The leader should let the group discuss the motion.

3. The motion to recess is in order any time.

4. A majority vote is required to end a debate.

5. A motion to amend requires a second.

6. A vote does not need to be taken in order to withdraw a motion.

7. Incidental motions can be amended.

8. A main motion that introduces business can be debated.

9. A main motion that introduces business can be amended.

10. A main motion that introduces business requires a majority vote.

Statements **2.**, **4.**, **6.**, and **7.** are false. The others are true. Throughout any meeting, the leader's job is to run the meeting rather than to participate in the discussion. In formal meetings that strictly follow parliamentary procedure, a leader wishing to participate must select someone to sit in the chair. In informal or casual meetings, leaders frequently participate in the discussion.

Other Officers Speak

The essential officers for a group are the president and secretary. The secretary will speak at each meeting to read the minutes. If a group pays dues or raises money, a treasurer is also necessary, and the treasurer will at times speak at a meeting to give a financial report. Large organizations with many activities have additional officers. A vice president speaks for the president when the president cannot carry out one of his or her duties. Whenever any officer speaks to friends or people in the community, the officer should make it a rule to speak well of the other officers as well as the club or organization.

Participating in a Meeting

When should you speak at a meeting? You should speak at
a meeting any time that you have something to contribute. At a small meeting of 10 people, a good rule of thumb
is that you should do one-tenth of the talking. If you are
talking much more or less, you are either monopolizing
the meeting or not doing your share.

At large, formal meetings, you will probably find it easier
to speak toward the beginning of a meeting. Otherwise,
you may sit and worry until you have built up so much
speech anxiety that you will never attempt to speak. Always keep in mind that it is necessary to keep to the topic
and to be concise in what you say; avoid personal confron-
tations.

Parliamentary Procedure for Participants

It's not just the leader of a meeting who needs to know
something about parliamentary procedure. Participants
must also know basics of parliamentary procedure to keep
a meeting moving toward its goal. First, participants
should know not to speak at formal meetings and most informal ones until they are called upon to speak by the
chair. All participants in a meeting should at least know

Don't be afraid to
speak up at a
meeting. It's the best
way to let others
know what your
views are.

how to make basic motions; which of these motions require a second; and how motions are amended, discussed, and passed or voted down. There are standard phrases that are used to make or begin certain common motions. Can you find the correct things to say for the following situations in a meeting?

Situations	Phrases
1. to complain about noise	a. I move that we adjourn.
2. to change a motion	b. Point of privilege
3. to limit discussion of a motion	c. I move debate on this matter be limited to ___(time)___.
4. to object to a ruling by the chair	d. Point of information.
5. to end a meeting	e. I appeal the chair's decision.
	f. I move we recess until ___(time)___.
	g. I move this motion be amended by _____.

The correct answers are: 1.-b., 2.-g., 3.-c., 4.-e., and 5.-a.

Main Motions

Since most of the business of clubs and organizations centers around the main motion, it is very important for the participants in a meeting to know how to make good main motions. A main motion is brief and clear and contains only one idea. This motion is expressed positively. You do not make a motion to not do something. A main motion should begin, "I move that . . ." Study the following main motions. Which ones do you think are good main motions?

1. "I move that the club hold a car wash, a hayride, and a pitch-in dinner as fund-raising activities."
2. "I move that the club not hold a picnic on Labor Day."
3. "I move that the club contribute $25 to the new book fund at the high school library."
4. "I move that the club hold the annual barbeque on the first Sunday in June."
5. "I move that the club pay for the officers' trips and expenses to the national convention and the officers' expenses only to the state convention."

Only the third and fourth main motions are good
motions. The first main motion has more than one idea.
The second is expressed negatively, not positively. The last
main motion has more than one idea and is confusing.
See if you can improve the poor motions.

Announcements and Reports

Besides making motions and contributing to discussions
at a meeting, club and organization members are frequently called upon to make announcements and reports.
These speech assignments fall under the heading of
speeches to inform. If you receive such an assignment, try
to avoid the triple pitfalls of being long-winded, imprecise,
and boring. As always, preparation is the key to effective
speech. The secret of giving a successful announcement or
report lies in making and following an outline.

Introduction.   In the introduction of an announcement or
report, you must grab the group's attention and tell them
what you are going to be talking about in just a few lines.
You might use an approach like one of these to introduce
a report to an investment group:

> "You've all heard 'Don't count your chickens before
> they hatch.' Well, our chickens are hatched. Here's the
> report on the money we made from our speculation in
> silver futures." (story)

> "The good news is we doubled our investment in our
> speculation in silver futures. The bad news is we sold
> too soon." (humor)

> "My report today will satisfy your curiosity about how
> the club's speculation in silver futures turned out."
> (traditional)

Body.   Whether you are giving an announcement or a report, the body is where you give the facts. An easy way to
make sure that you include all the facts in an announcement is to answer the questions *who?, what?, when?,*
and *where?* The order in which these questions are answered is usually not important. However, the questions
must be answered in considerable detail. What details are
missing from the body of this announcement?

> The next meeting of the investment club is at the Jolly
> Crow restaurant a week from today at 5 o'clock.

The speaker making this announcement did not mention
that it was a dinner meeting that would cost each member

$7.50 for a buffet supper. The location of the restaurant and needed directions were forgotten. The speaker also neglected to give the exact date of the meeting.

Most club and organization reports tell members what committees have been doing. The members use the information that they get from these reports to make decisions. If you are making a report, limit the number of points in the body to no more than five.

Conclusion.   Whenever you give an announcement or a report at a meeting, you should end by summarizing what you have said. It is ideal if you can conclude with a line that will be remembered. Since many reports are studies of a particular problem, they often end with a recommendation for a specific action as well as a summary.

After a group has heard a report, the members have to decide how to handle it. They may decide to accept it, reject it, discuss it again later, refer it to a committee for further study, or simply to file it. They finalize their decision through a motion.

Speaking Up in Committees

The serious business of most large clubs and organizations is accomplished in committee meetings. There are two kinds of committees—standing and special. Standing committees meet regularly to handle a continuing task such as membership, finance, or publicity. Most groups have only a few standing committees. They can also have several special committees. These committees are created to do a specific job and are then dismantled. The head of a committee, or chairperson, is normally appointed by the president of the group. The members of a committee may be chosen by the club president, or the chairperson of the committee, or both.

Role of Chairperson

The chairperson of a committee plays almost the same role as the chairperson of a meeting. Both have to keep the members of a group moving toward a goal. Both must follow agendas and handle disruptions. It may be difficult to keep the attention of the smaller group focused on the task of each meeting. There will always be members who try to turn committee meetings into social events.

The chairpersons of committees do not have to follow the rules of parliamentary procedure as closely as the

The chairperson of a committee runs the committee meetings and also participates in the discussions.

chairpersons of meetings. However, it is usual to have the members of the committee make motions to formalize major decisions of the committee. The main difference between the roles of the two chairpersons is that the chairperson of a committee participates in the committee's discussions and decisions.

Role of Members

Members of committees need to remember that their role is a working role rather than a social role in an organization or club. The size of most committees is approximately five members and a chairperson, which means that each member should do about one-sixth of the talking. Committee members need to avoid the speech fault of talking too much or too little. As a member of a committee, do your speaking at a meeting in short bursts rather than a couple of long speeches. Make an effort to stay on the topic that is being discussed. Be sure to prepare for meetings, if necessary.

Being a Guest Speaker

Some day you may be called upon to make a speech at a club or organization. You may have been invited because you have acquired a reputation as a speaker, or because you have an interesting hobby or unusual job, or because you have just returned from an exotic locale. The club or organization may give you a topic or ask you to choose one of your own. Four kinds of speeches that are frequently given at meetings are book reviews, travelogs, how-to talks, and talks about humorous experiences. Whatever the topic of your speech, you will need to research the audience and setting and prepare an outline. Use the outline when giving the speech. The average length of a speech for a meeting is 15 to 20 minutes, except for travelogs, which last longer.

Book Reviews

A book review is a speech to inform. It should also entertain. The purpose of a book review is to stimulate group discussion of a book or to stimulate their interest in reading the book. In giving a book review, you will normally take about 10 minutes to pursue major ideas in the book or events in the life of one of its characters. You might trace the conflict of a mother and a daughter or tell about different tests of courage a character meets in his or her lifetime.

You should begin your review by giving the title, author, publisher, and year of the book's publication. You will find it effective to read passages from the book that describe characters or tell what they say. You never retell a story. You don't dwell on the life of the author or the setting. You don't have time to do these things.

You may choose to review a novel, a biography, an autobiography, or a work covering some current issue. Most reviewers choose contemporary books, but at times it is effective to review a popular classic.

Travelogs

If you ever visit Nepal, Somalia, Tahiti, or any other interesting or unusual place, you may be asked by some group to give a travelog telling about your trip. Like a book review, a travelog is a speech to inform that should also entertain. Travelogs are complicated speeches to give because you usually must coordinate what you say with slides or movies.

Good travelogs are tailored to their audiences. You would include lots of slides on flowers for a travelog on the Netherlands that you give to a garden group. But for a travelog on the Netherlands that is given to a parent-teacher group, you should show a number of slides of

To give a good travelog, you must give your audience a feel for the place you visited.

schools and points of interest. Think of the slides or pictures you took on a recent trip. Which ones would you select to show these special audiences?

homeowner's association   service organization
church study group   hiker's club
Future Farmers of America   a sixth grade class

An effective way to begin a travelog about an area that is not well known to your audience is by comparing it in several ways to places the audience knows, for example:

"Think of an area the size of Arkansas, covered by mountains like the Rockies, and having the same number of people as Texas, and you are thinking of the place that I visited—Nepal."

In giving a travelog, make sure that the audience knows where the place is. Either point out where it is on a map or show a slide of the area where it is located. Few people really know where places like Nepal are.

The major mistake made in most travelogs is making them too long. Thirty minutes is ample time for a travelog. Forty-five minutes is the absolute maximum.

How-to Talks

Because you are an expert at wallpapering, making quilts, or decorating cakes, or because you possess some other skill that people would like to acquire, you may find yourself asked to give a speech about your skill. It will be a speech to inform. Nothing makes one of these speeches easier to give than to actually demonstrate your skill. It is possible to show people how to hang wallpaper, blow glass, make candles, do karate, or perform cardio-pulmonary resuscitation. If you can't show all the steps in a process, show several of the steps as well as the finished product. If you can't show any of the steps, use charts or a chalkboard to give the audience a clearer view of your skill.

There are a couple of things that you need to remember when giving a how-to talk. Be sure to practice your speech with your tools. Make sure that you speak to the audience and not your tools.

How-to talks are made easier and more informative by an actual demonstration of your skill.

If you think that you don't have a skill that you could share with others, look at this list of how-to speeches. People have made speeches on how to:

make a mask	grease cars
put a ship in a bottle	iron clothes
play chess	dehydrate fruit
dwarf trees	write books
paint china	make movies

Which skills of yours could you add to this list?

Humorous Experiences

You don't have to be a comedian to make a speech that entertains. Just keep a record of the things that have made you laugh in your own life recently. You should be able to weave these stories together to make a speech that entertains. Think about how this series of disasters could be put together to describe an average day in the life of a family with four children under 5 years of age:

a red sock in the washer
gum in the hair
the sitter has chicken pox
a car with a flat tire in the garage

Successful Guest Speakers

A speech to a group or organization tends to be short. The audience is usually made up of people you know. They do not expect you to deliver a show-stopping speech. These factors join together to make speaking to local groups or organizations a pleasant experience.

Finding a Speaker

There is no shortage of people in a community who are willing to speak to clubs and organizations. The secret is to use your ingenuity to find them. The following people are frequently called upon to make speeches:

local politicians	police and fire personnel
school personnel	members of Toastmaster Clubs
librarians	religious leaders
health workers	government employees
sports figures	local TV personalities
members of the chamber	newspaper employees
of commerce	historical society employees

Speakers from Businesses

Your club does not need to be limited to the above group in choosing its speakers. Any business, large or small, that sells a product or service probably will have employees who can make interesting speeches. Large organizations, like utilities, automobile companies, and department stores, frequently have lists of speakers who give informational talks. It is the small business firms that provide an unlimited source of possible speakers for your club or organization. You will have to suggest a speech topic when you call these smaller companies. You can't just call a Japanese restaurant or a bakery and ask for a speaker. You will find a speaker if you ask the firm for someone to talk to your group and show the members how to stir fry or make a torte. The following firms could probably provide speakers for your group. As you read the list, think of a topic you might request the firm's speaker to talk about.

flower shop	clothing store
travel agency	craft store
beauty or barber shop	sporting goods store
jewelry store	insurance agency
real estate company	antique store

Speakers from Diverse Sources

You are not limited to finding speakers in traditional places. Call a theater group and ask for several actors to do a scene from a current play. Call the Red Cross and ask for a speaker to talk about their organization's disaster preparations for earthquakes, blizzards, or tornadoes. Call a golf course and ask the golf pro to give a demonstration. Call a sky-diving club and ask several members to tell about their experiences and show how their parachutes work. Just about anyone who has an interesting job, hobby, or skill can be considered a potential speaker. If your group is able to pay for a speaker, you will be able to find an unlimited number of speakers by calling a lecture bureau. These bureaus can be found by looking in the yellow pages of the telephone directory of a large city.

Handling a Speaker

Once your club or organization has found a speaker, the speaker needs to be told several things before the actual date of the speech. To be properly prepared, the speaker should know:

People with interesting or unusual hobbies or professions often make good guest speakers.

1. the time and place of the speech
2. the amount of time allotted for the speech
3. the format the speech is expected to take—will there be a question-and-answer period, a panel discussion, a debate, etc.
4. the program of the meeting—especially when the speaker will speak
5. the size and interests of the audience

Someone in a group should be assigned the responsibility of greeting the speaker when he or she arrives at the meeting place. This person should help the speaker check out the room, set up any necessary equipment, and introduce the speaker to people in the group.

When a speaker is from out-of-town, arrangements must also be made for transportation and accommodations. The speaker needs to be met when arriving in town and taken to where he or she is staying. Before arriving in town, the speaker should be told of any luncheons, dinners, or receptions that he or she is invited to attend.

Being a Director of Ceremonies

If you are the president or the program chairman of a club or organization, at some time you will be called upon to introduce guests and speakers, acknowledge helpers, give inspirational messages, or make toasts. Each of these tasks requires a speech. These speeches may be part of a business meeting, a luncheon, or a banquet. They should be brief, yet they need to be prepared. They should be light in nature. You do not need to tell jokes or funny stories unless you are skilled at doing this.

Introducing Guests

At luncheons or banquets, the people sitting at the head table need to be introduced. Be enthusiastic in introducing each person. Be sure you pronounce names correctly. Identify the people with labels that explain why they are at the meeting. For example, a dentist at a school function would be identified as a school board member, but the same person at a sports banquet would be identified as a coach of a local Little League team. Think of the different ways in which you could be identified at a club meeting, a school function, or a political fund-raiser.

In introducing a series of people, keep things flowing by asking the audience to hold applause until everyone is introduced. It is also smart to remind the people being introduced to stand up when their names are called.

Introducing Speakers

The introduction of a speaker should create an interest in the audience to hear the speaker. If you limit your introductions to three minutes or less, the audience will probably be told enough about the speaker and his or her topic to whet their appetites. Never tell so much about the speech that the speaker doesn't need to make the speech. Tell about the speaker's accomplishments, not virtues. Don't be so complimentary in your introduction that the speaker could not possibly live up to your description.

Read the following introduction of a local high school coach to a scout banquet. Then reread the introduction, eliminating the phrases in italics. Which version do you think is better? Why?

> "It is my honor *and great pleasure* to introduce tonight's speaker—Ray Simmons. Ray coaches the high school wrestling team. Last year, the team won the

state championship. *Ray is the best high school coach to ever coach in this state. He puts more effort into his job than any man has ever done.* Ray is going to tell you how the boys trained to win that championship. *He will tell you how George Smith learned to press 220 pounds. He will tell you that the Tyson twins skip rope for 15 minutes each day.* Ladies and gentlemen, here is *the greatest coach to ever walk the streets of our town*—Ray Simmons."

You should have picked the version without the italicized phrases because those phrases build up the speaker too much and give away some of the contents of the speech.

Acknowledging Helpers

Some time during a meeting, luncheon, or banquet, the members who have worked to make the gathering a success need to be acknowledged. Rarely is a blanket acknowledgment, like "I want to thank everyone who helped make this meeting a success," an adequate acknowledgment of the members' help. You will need to name names. Group the names together in some way, such as, "Bev Allen, the chair of the hospitality committee, along with members George and Louise Trout, arranged for this evening's table decorations and door prizes." Recite your list of acknowledgments quickly. Only include those who really should be acknowledged. Tell what they did. Ask the audience to hold their applause until everyone has been named.

Giving Inspirational Messages

Many clubs and organizations no longer have anyone give a prayer at the beginning of a meeting or banquet. Instead, you may be called upon to give an inspirational message that is nondenominational in nature. Such messages usually request a divine being to help guide the members of the organization in some way. Here are a couple of suggested messages.

Before Meals. "We are thankful for the bounty of our table. We are thankful for the fellowship that we will share with each other during this meal."

Before Meetings. "We ask that we work together in harmony in making today's decisions. Let these decisions be the product of our collective wisdom. Let them reflect the highest standards of our organization."

Toasting is a
standard method of
speechmaking at
banquets, weddings,
and celebrations.

Making Toasts

At the conclusion of a meal, the director of ceremonies as
well as several members of a club or organization may
make toasts to honored guests. It is customary for the
toastmaster to stand up and raise a glass while giving the
toast. It is not essential for a toast to be either lengthy or
witty. A sincere expression of good will usually makes an
excellent toast:

> "Here's to Mayor Niles, who has guided our city to a
> role of prominence in the sports world."

> "I propose a toast to Geraldine Harvey, who has served
> so effectively as president of our club this year."

Fund-Raising

Money makes the activities of clubs and civic groups possible. Because members' dues and pledges often will not
provide sufficient funds for activities, like buying play-
ground equipment for a local park or new beds for a hospital's burn center, there is scarcely an organization that
does not have some kind of fund-raising project. Girl
Scouts are famous for their yearly cookie sales. Nearly
every civic and parent-teacher organization has some kind
of fund-raising activity, from candy sales to raffles.

The success of any fund-raising project, from selling Girl Scout cookies to light bulbs for your club, rests on the energy, commitment, and speaking skills of each member of an organization. The parents of a Girl Scout who is afraid to go out to sell will have a freezer full of cookies, while the parents of a Girl Scout who enjoys selling will be helping the child deliver cookies all over town.

Selecting the Cause

The first step in fund-raising is for a club or organization to select a cause. Large organizations, like the March of Dimes and the American Heart Association, have one cause that they support. Many local organizations also have specific causes that they regularly support. There are groups that support zoos, museums, orchestras, hospitals, animal shelters, and thousands of other worthy causes. Some groups, however, wish to make a contribution in some way to their community but do not have a special cause. If you are a member of a group like this, you will have to make a persuasive speech if you wish to convince your fellow members to select a cause you favor. Can you think of three causes that you believe in sufficiently to ask the members of an organization to hold a fund-raising project to support?

Selecting the Fund-Raiser

Once a cause has been decided upon, a club or organization must select the appropriate kind of fund-raiser. The group must take into account the amount of money they want to raise, the number of members they have, and the amount of time that the group has to raise the money in. Study the following list of fund-raising activities. Which ones have been used in your community? Which ones would you like to participate in?

raffles	door-to-door solicitations
auctions	sporting events
social activities	providing services (car
movies, dances	washes, lawn cutting)
fairs	putting on a show
garage sales	feeding people (pancake
concerts	breakfasts, fish fries)

After a fund-raising activity has been selected, a club or organization must find an appropriate time in which to hold the fund-raiser. To do this, a group must check what is happening in the community on the day or days that have been selected for the fund-raiser. To hold a garage sale on the same Saturday as a big home football game could be a disaster, just as it would be ineffective to hold a car wash on the same day that five other groups also hold car washes.

Solicitations

The task of soliciting funds or items to be sold for raising funds depends largely upon the ability of the members of a group to speak to people. When you are making a solicitation, make sure that you wear a badge or carry a letter to show people that you are an authentic representative of a club or organization. Also be sure to dress appropriately for the situation. Casual dress is fine for door-to-door fund solicitation in your neighborhood. Dress more formally to speak to local merchants or businesspersons. No matter where group members are speaking, they should all have similar speeches. You should develop your own speech from the general outline that a group has given to you.

Door-to-Door Solicitation.   If you are going door-to-door to solicit funds for a well-known group, you will probably be given a sample speech like this one that the March of Dimes gave its solicitors in 1984. The organization asked their marchers to say the following speech with a smile:

> "Hi, I'm your Mother's March Volunteer. I would like to share this educational message with you and ask for your contribution to the fight against birth defects."

The March asked their volunteers to give an educational flyer to every home and reminded them to say a big "thank you" to everyone.

   You will probably need to make a speech much like the one above for any door-to-door solicitation. You should be prepared to answer the question, "How much should I give?" Do not answer, "Any amount would be all right," or "It's up to you." The best answer is, "Most of the people in this neighborhood are giving (name an amount) or more." To answer any other questions, you need to be familiar with the facts and figures and other information that a group has given to you.

Merchant Solicitation.   As a volunteer, you may be assigned to visit local merchants to ask them to give items or money for some cause. Before you visit a merchant, find out if the merchant has contributed to your group before and how much money or what item was donated. When you go into a store, begin by saying something like, "I am David Stein from the Youth Soccer League. Our playing field is two blocks away on 103rd Street. Is it possible to speak to the manager?" If you are speaking to the manager, go on to the purpose of your visit. Otherwise, repeat your introduction to the manager, then state your purpose. "I am working on the Youth Soccer League's fund drive for uniforms. We are seeking the contributions of merchants in our community to support this worthwhile activity." Next, you will remind the merchant of past contributions. "Last year, your company donated 25 dollars, which let us buy uniforms for three children." Then you will request a contribution. "May I put you down for a similar contribution this year?" If a merchant seems reluctant to contribute, it is frequently helpful to describe the contribution that other merchants are making. "Several of the merchants in this shopping mall are giving 25 dollars again this year."

If you are timid about approaching merchants, work as a team with another member of your club or organization. In this case, you will need to rehearse your speech roles with a third person playing the part of the merchant. Think now about what you would say as solicitor #2 in this role-playing situation:

Solicitor #1: Good morning. We're from the Youth Soccer League, and our playing field is two blocks away on 103rd Street. Is it possible to speak to the manager?

Manager: I'm the manager.

Solicitor #2: (State the purpose of your visit.)

Manager: I don't think that our store contributes to this group.

Solicitor #2: (Remind the manager of last year's contribution.)

Merchant: Business isn't as good this year.

Solicitor #1: Several of the merchants on this mall are helping again because the names of the participating stores will be listed in the programs for every game.

Merchant: How much should I give this year?

Solicitor #2: (Suggest a contribution.)

Merchant: We'll give the same amount as the other stores.

Solicitor #2: (Give a big "thank you.")

Your spoken thanks should always be followed with a written thank-you note.

Larger Solicitations.   Whether you are asking an individual, a business, or an organization for a large contribution, you must make an appointment. Since many groups wish these people to contribute, you may find it easier to get an appointment if you say, "I have already talked to Mr. A., company B., or organization C." Or "I worked with you in ____(name of group)____." In talking to these people, you must not only know the facts, you must have your sales pitch prepared. At the start of your speech, establish rapport with the prospective contributor. Then go on to argue the case for the person to contribute to your cause. Be sure to let the person ask questions. Finally, you must ask for a contribution.

The Successful Fund-Raiser

You are not alone when you are out fund-raising. There are thousands of people competing with you. The successful fund-raiser really believes in the cause, works harder, and speaks more effectively than the unsuccessful fund-raiser. How would you respond to these negative comments from potential contributors:

1. Door-to-door: "I'm too busy to listen right now."
   a. "I'll be back in this neighborhood tomorrow. May I talk to you then?"
   b. "I'll just leave this envelope and you can mail in your contribution."
2. Merchant: "Our store contributes to too many groups already."
   a. "Maybe you can contribute to us next year."
   b. "Would you consider giving a gift certificate, since it would bring customers into your store?"

The successful fund-raiser would answer **1.-a.** and **2.-b.** These answers demonstrate the fund-raiser's willingness to work hard and ability to come up with innovative ideas that benefit both the donator and the cause.

Publicity

Clubs and organizations need to publicize what they are doing, especially their fund-raising activities. Trying to hold any event without publicity is like trying to swim without water. Publicity committees tell people about their group through radio, television, and newspapers. To select the correct medium, it is necessary for groups to think of the audience they are trying to reach. To find out more about local radio and television stations, obtain a media handbook for public service organizations from a station. Most large cities have these handbooks that tell you exactly how to present your group to the public.

Radio

Imagine that your club is holding a pancake breakfast to establish a burn center at the local hospital. Where would you begin if you were asked to arrange for a radio spot to publicize the event?

The first step is to select a radio station that is reaching the listeners you wish to contact. Don't choose the local rock station if you want to reach people over 40 years old. Once you have selected a station, call the station's public service director and find out how to submit a public service announcement. Ask whether the station wants a written or a prerecorded message. Find out how long your announcement should be. Be sure to learn how far in advance the station will need to receive the announcement from your group.

When you know what the radio station's requirements are, you are ready to write the announcement to publicize the pancake breakfast. *Be brief.* Public service announcements vary in length from 10 seconds to 60 seconds. *Be informative.* Announcements must answer the questions *who?, what?, when?, where?,* and *why?*

Making Announcements.   The announcement that you send to the station will probably look something like this:

FROM: Northwest Community Club—
Contact Dwayne Jones, 891-6203

_____ seconds   Starting date: _____

_____ words   Stopping date: _____

The Northwest Community Club is holding a pancake breakfast at Davis Hospital on Saturday, June 4th from 8 to 12 to raise money to establish a burn center.

If you had written the pancake breakfast announcement for a 10-second spot, your next step would be to count the number of words. A 10-second spot will usually have about 30 words. Now read the announcement at a normal speaking speed, and use a stop watch to time your reading. You may need to adjust the number of words in the announcement, or your speaking speed, to meet the specified time requirement.

Once your announcement meets the station's time requirement, you are ready to record it. Remember that you are not speaking to a large audience but to individuals. Be yourself. Adjust your voice to fit the message. Record your announcement for the pancake breakfast. Then check the time. Make adjustments until you have a 10-second recording that you would be able to send to a radio station.

Now expand the announcement about the pancake breakfast to make a 30-second recording. Use the techniques of persuasion you have learned in this book to really *sell* the breakfast. A 30-second announcement usually has about 60 to 80 words.

If you were sending one of the pancake breakfast announcements to a radio station, you would include the name of your club and your name and phone number as the contact person in case the station wanted additional information. You would also include the starting and stopping dates, so the station would know when to use your announcement. Finally, be sure to address the letter to the public service director of the station.

News and Special Programs.   Although spot announcements are the most popular way to obtain radio publicity, there are other ways to obtain publicity for a group. Listen to local radio stations, and learn the format of each station. You may be able to get coverage on news programs, or call-in programs, or have someone from your club appear on a talk show. To get coverage on a news program, you will need to call the news director of a radio station and find out how to submit copy. To appear on a talk show, you will need to talk to the producer of that show. Before you go on a program, you will normally talk with the program producer and discuss what you are going to say. You will also be shown how to speak into a microphone right before the actual program.

Television

If what your group wants to say on television takes more than 30 seconds, you will want to get the message on a program rather than on a spot announcement. If this is the case, learn what features are presented on the news programs and what types of guests appear on the local shows. Then contact the appropriate producer to find out how to get your group's story on television. If you are asked to appear on television, the program producer will give you help with what to say before the actual program. You will not usually meet the host or hostess of a program until you are on the air. You will need to establish instant rapport with this person. You should be pleasant, chatty, and informed. It is a good idea to watch a program several times before you appear on it.

Spot Announcements.   Each television station has its own requirements for the submission of public service spot announcements. The station's public service director will tell you exactly what the station's requirements are. Generally, 10- and 20-second spots are preferred. Sometimes 30- or 60-second spots may be available. You should prepare your copy in exactly the same way as for a radio spot, except that with a television spot you may also be expected to provide video material. This can take the form of slides, photographs, 16-mm film, or video tape.

Most stations use a standardized format for all slides that requires them to prepare the slides for your group. They also will make films to accompany your announcements. You will need to contact television stations well before an announcement is to go on the air. One month is the recommended time period.

Sample Announcement.   If you were sending a public service spot announcement to a television station for the pancake breakfast, it should look like the following one. Note that it is almost identical to the radio spot announcement.

FROM: Northwest
    Community Club
    863 Olive Street
    Indianapolis 46209
    10 seconds
    30 words
    Slide # _____
    Northwest
    Community Club

Contact: Dwayne Jones
    891-6203
Starts: 5-28-87
Stops: 6-4-87
Start your day at the
Northwest Community Club
pancake breakfast at Davis
Hospital on June 4th from
8 to 12. Help the club raise
money to establish a burn
center.

Newspapers

The newspaper is the most popular way to get your message to the public. If you phone in your information, be sure that you have the answers to those well-known questions: *who?, what?, when?, where?, why?,* and *how?* Also be sure that you have the correct spelling of the names of the people you mention. It is a good idea to follow your call with a written news release.

Speak Up and Contribute

Clubs and organizations in the United States have always played an important part in communities. There may be as many as 100,000 meetings of clubs and organizations every day. To participate, you need to speak up. Participating lets you share your interests with others. It is one way that you can make a valuable contribution to your community.

Day-to-Day Communication

In today's busy world, you have to communicate effectively with many people in your community in order to get things done. You have to tell the doctor about your pulled muscle to get medicine that will ease the pain. You have to tell the plumber where the leak is in order to get it fixed. You have to tell the person selling shoes what your size is to find a good fit.

Just think about how many people you communicate with every day. Have you ever taken the time to analyze how effectively you communicate with them? Does your child's teacher really understand what you told her about your child? Does the mechanic fix what you say is wrong with your car? If the things you want done are not being done, the problem may be poor communication. This part of the book deals with effective day-to-day communication with people in your community.

Speaking to Receptionists

When you enter an office, don't just go in and sit down in a waiting room. No one will know why you are there. Greet the receptionist, and tell who you are and what you want. Don't be secretive, but don't give your life's history either. Without basic information, a receptionist cannot help you.

Read what the following people said to a doctor's receptionist. Who told the receptionist what he or she needed to
know?

1. "I'm Monica Rogers and I have a 10 o'clock appointment with Dr. Jones."

2. "Hello, I am Mark Miller."

3. "You'd never believe what a hard time I had getting
   here. I can scarcely walk on my foot. Thank heavens I
   had an appointment with the doctor today."

When speaking to a
receptionist, be sure
to state your name
and why you are
there.

Only Monica Rogers gave the receptionist the appropriate
amount of information. The receptionist would have to
find out more in order to help the other two. Mark Miller
could have been a patient or a salesperson. The third person did not identify himself even though he apparently
had an appointment. If a receptionist needs more than
basic information, supply it willingly. Receptionists aren't
just curious, they have been told how to screen people
wishing to see their employers.

Speaking to Tradespersons

Plumbers, jewelers, mechanics, and other tradespersons are specialists in their fields. Remember this when you are talking to them. If you are experiencing a problem with something, describe the problem as accurately as you can. They are the experts in repairing things; let them diagnose what's wrong. Don't tell a mechanic that your car's timing is off or the carburetor needs adjustment. You are making the diagnosis for the mechanic. Instead, give symptoms, like the car is stalling or the car does not have as much pickup as after it was tuned last year. The mechanic can use these symptoms to diagnose the problem.

If tradespersons are installing or repairing something in your home or office, do not give advice unless it is requested. Just tell them where you will be if they have any questions. Keep in mind that many tradespersons work by the hour. Unless you like to waste money, don't tell the tradespersons things that are not important. For example, if someone comes to your home to fix the air conditioner, you don't need to tell the person about how much your family likes air conditioning or what your neighbor's air conditioner is like. Show the person where the air conditioner is and then get out and let the work get done.

Whatever you take in for a repair, set a limit on what you will pay. Be sure this amount is written on the service form. Leave a phone number where you can be reached if the repair cost will be higher than the estimate. Study the following comments that were made to a jeweler. Which do you think were most effective?

1. "I have had this watch for years. My grandmother bought it for me on a trip she took to Switzerland. Don't you think the face is really beautiful on this watch? The band is quite unusual too."

2. "My watch is losing about two minutes every hour. It is still under warranty. I have all the papers right here."

3. "The stem has broken off my watch. Could you please give me an estimate of how much it will cost to fix the watch?"

4. "Would you clean this watch for me so it will keep accurate time again?"

Comments **2.** and **3.** effectively describe what was wrong with the watch. The first comment was merely a descrip-

Give symptoms, not your diagnosis, when you are speaking with tradespersons about repairs.

tion of the watch. The last comment was a diagnosis that might or might not have been correct.

The keys to speaking to tradespersons are: be brief, be accurate in your descriptions, be courteous, and let them diagnose the problem when there is one.

Speaking to Civic Workers

You may see some civic workers, like mail carriers and bus drivers, almost every day. Remember that when you see these people, they are working. Greet them each day, and let them continue their work.

When you talk to civic workers in their offices, don't chit-chat; they are there to talk business. Introduce yourself, and tell the nature of your business. If you have a complaint, don't blame the civic worker. You won't get a stamp faster or cheaper from a postal worker by complaining about the mail delivery to your home or office.

Speaking to Public Figures

Many people in public life are regularly addressed by a title other than *Mr., Miss, Mrs.,* and *Ms.* Even long after they have held an important title, many still like to be addressed by these titles. For example, generals may want to be addressed as generals for as long as they live. This is also true of judges, senators, members of congress, and cabinet members. Often in government, a person may have held two or more titles. Always address the person by the most lofty title, unless he or she states a preference. Can you match the titles to these well-known people?

1.	Pope John Paul II	a.	Mr. Secretary
2.	Ronald Reagan	b.	Senator
3.	Henry Kissinger	c.	Mr. President
4.	Edward (Ted) Kennedy	d.	Your Highness
5.	Queen Elizabeth II	e.	Your Holiness

The titles that you will probably need to use on the local level are *judge* and *mayor*. In some areas, the police and fire chiefs like to be addressed as *chief*. When you are speaking to educators who have their doctorates, many want you to use the title *doctor* in addressing them. Don't make the mistake of addressing someone by the wrong title. If you don't know how to address someone, call his or her secretary.

Speaking to Religious Leaders

Books of etiquette once laid out quite clearly how religious leaders of different faiths should be addressed, and people addressed their leaders according to these rules. Today, the relationships between religious leaders and members of their congregations have become more informal. Instead of addressing ministers by titles and last names, many ministers are now addressed by titles and first names. You will hear ministers addressed as Father Mike, and Pastor Bob; but until you know religious leaders, address them formally.

Speaking to Professionals

You don't always know how to solve problems that you have. Frequently, you have to call upon the specialized knowledge of others. That is why the world is full of professionals like lawyers, doctors, accountants, and dentists. Many people are nervous about talking to professionals because they feel overwhelmed by the knowledge these people have and are puzzled by the specialized vocabulary professionals often use. Do you know what the following terms mean?

legal	*medical*	*accounting*
lien	abdomen	assets
injunction	colic	liabilities
probate	spasm	overhead
perjury	degenerative	audit
tort	pulmonary	debits

If you heard a professional use one of these terms and didn't know what it meant, what would you do? What you should do is to ask the professional to explain the term. No one is expected to know all the jargon of each profession. Professionals often forget and use the same terms when they are talking to both clients and colleagues. So don't be afraid to ask for explanations of terms you do not understand.

Speaking to Doctors

Most doctors like to be addressed as *doctor*. Like tradespersons, they prefer to make their own diagnosis. They do not like to hear "I have an ulcer," or "The boss says that I have a strep throat." Instead, tell doctors what your complaints are. They are trained to translate symptoms into diagnoses. Limit your complaints to the most important ones. A list of 22 complaints can be confusing. When you visit a doctor, a good way to describe your symptoms is by answering the question: "What is the one thing I want the doctor to get rid of today?" When medical professionals ask you questions, don't say things just to please them. Answer their questions honestly.

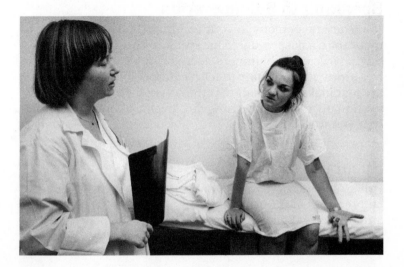

Doctors are trained to make their own diagnosis. Explain your symptoms and answer their questions honestly.

Speaking to Accountants

Accounting professionals usually charge by the hour. Be sure to bring the documents you need for a meeting with an accountant. Don't use accounting terms unless you know what they mean. When you visit an accountant for help with your income tax, it will be helpful if you know what the following terms mean:

exemption	receipts	dividends
interest	depreciation	dependents
W-2	FDIC	IRA

If you don't know what some of these terms mean, look them up in a dictionary.

Speaking to Lawyers

Lawyers work on an hourly or a flat-fee basis. They help their clients with wills, divorces, contracts, and business matters. They give advice to keep their clients out of trouble. When you talk to a lawyer, the main rule is be frank. Before you visit a lawyer, try to summarize the purpose of your visit in one statement like:

"I want to write my will."
"I want to stop my neighbor from using my driveway."

Be sure to answer all your lawyer's questions honestly. They need all the information they can get in order to help you effectively.

Speaking to Salespersons

There are no persons in your community that you speak to more than salespersons. You speak to them when you are buying sweaters, hammers, food, or medicine. If you are in a store, it is only fair to tell a salesperson whether you are just looking or wish to purchase something. If you wish to purchase something, be specific about what it is that you want.

Speaking to the Police

Police officers serve your community in many ways. They enforce laws and work to prevent crime and to protect lives and property. You will probably speak to the police only when you are asking for help with various problems or when you are stopped for a traffic violation.

If you have a problem and require the assistance of the police, state your problem. Address the police officer as *officer* or *sir*. Try to remain calm when you describe an emergency situation.

If you are driving and are stopped by an officer, what the officer says to you is almost standard throughout most communities:

> "Good morning. May I please see your driver's license and car registration? Do you know why I am stopping you? Have you received any tickets recently for traffic violations?"

Police officers expect you to reply in a courteous manner. They do not want you to get out of the car or to make any sudden movements toward a purse or glove compartment.

Police officers want you to be honest in your responses. They classify people by their responses. Can you identify how the police would classify the following drivers?

1. "Did you know the mayor is my brother-in-law?"

   a. hostile   **b.** namedropper   **c.** belligerent

2. "Yes, sir. I was going a little fast, sir. But it is the first time, sir."

   a. overly polite   **b.** illness faker
   c. suffering mechanical problems

3. "My grandmother just suffered a heart attack and I am dashing to the hospital to see her."

   a. namedropper   **b.** overly friendly   **c.** illness faker

4. "The throttle is stuck, and I cannot control my speed."

   a. suffering mechanical problems   **b.** overly polite
   c. belligerent

5. "Why are you stopping me? Why aren't you out catching real crooks?"

   a. hostile   **b.** why me   **c.** illness faker

Police officers would probably classify the drivers making these five statements as **b.**, **a.**, **c.**, **a.**, and **b.**, respectively. The only acceptable responses to police officers are illness and mechanical problems, if they are true. Always avoid being overly polite, hostile, or belligerent if you are stopped for a traffic violation.

Follow These Rules

No matter who you are speaking to in the community, you need to follow these speech rules:

1. Look at the person to whom you are speaking.
2. Use good manners.
3. Don't argue.
4. Be sensitive to people's moods.
5. Don't be shy.
6. State what you want clearly.
7. Listen to what people say to you.

Speaking to School Personnel

Are you apprehensive about speaking to your children's teachers, counselors, and principals, as well as other people at school? Do you still feel intimidated by these people from your own school days? Are you afraid to talk to your child's math teacher because you did poorly in math, and your child appears to be following in your footsteps? Does talking to the principal make you feel as uncomfortable today as it did 10 or 20 years ago? Do you still think of high school deans as stern people who dispense discipline? If your answer to any of these questions is *yes,* you will probably be surprised to learn that many of these school personnel also feel apprehensive about talking to you.

Speaking to Teachers

Whether you want to know how your children are doing in second grade or in high school English, the people you want to speak to at school are their teachers. In fact, the National Committee for Citizens in Education (NCCE) recommends that you schedule annual education checkups with your children's teachers to find out how your children are doing at school. An education checkup is rather like a medical checkup, except you are checking for possible educational problems instead of health problems.

The heart of an education checkup is the parent-teacher conference. Many schools recognize the value of these con-

Prepare in advance a list of questions that you want to ask at a parent/teacher conference.

ferences and automatically schedule these meetings between parents and teachers. If your children's school doesn't, you should schedule conferences for your children in the fall after they have been back in school for six weeks or more. You can't just walk into a school and expect your children's teachers to be prepared for a conference. You need to make an appointment ahead of time. When you set up the appointment with a teacher, be sure to explain the purpose of the meeting, and mention specific areas that you want to discuss. To prepare yourself for the conference, review your children's past and present report cards, look over their current schoolwork, and talk to your children about the school year. Only then are you ready to prepare a list of questions that you want answered at the conference.

Checkup Questions

The NCCE has prepared a list of questions that should be addressed at a parent-teacher conference. Be sure that they are included on your list. As you read the list of questions below, check the ones that you asked the last time you took part in a parent-teacher conference.

1. Is my child performing at grade level in basic skills? Above/below?

2. What achievement, intelligence, or vocational aptitude tests have been given my child in the past year? What do the scores mean?

3. What are my child's strengths and weaknesses in major subject areas?

4. Can we go over some examples of my child's classwork together?

5. Does my child need special help in any academic subject? In social adjustment?

6. Would you recommend referral to other school specialists?

7. Has my child regularly completed homework you assigned?

8. How well does my child get along with classmates?

9. Have you observed any changes in learning progress during the year? Has learning improved or declined dramatically?

10. Have you noticed any changes in behavior, such as squinting, extreme fatigue, or irritability, which may be signals of medical problems?

11. Would you advise any of the following summer activities: Summer school for remedial help? Enrichment courses? Career-related summer job? Home learning activities? A complete rest from school pressures?

12. Will you advise any special programs or placement for next year?

After you attend a parent-teacher conference, you will want to schedule follow-up conferences with the teacher and other school personnel if they are necessary.

What You Should Say

Whether you are speaking with a teacher at a regularly scheduled or specially arranged conference, try to develop a team spirit to help your child succeed at school. What you say and how you say it make a great difference in establishing a parent-teacher relationship that will truly benefit your child. Study the following remarks that parents made to teachers. Select the ones that should never have been made.

1. "Teachers have a difficult job today."

2. "Teachers just don't put in the time they used to."

3. "I know what I'm talking about; after all I taught school for four years."

4. "I'm so mad about Tricia's report card that I could scream."

5. "My child really enjoyed the assignment on TV com-
    mercials."

6. "You pick on my child all the time."

7. "You have helped my child learn to control his
    temper."

8. "It's your fault my kid hasn't learned fractions."

9. "Did you hear that the music teacher has declared
    bankruptcy?"

10. "If you don't change my child's grade, I'm talking to
    the principal about this matter."

Remarks **2.**, **3.**, **4.**, **6.**, **8.**, **9.**, and **10.** should never have
been made. They leave teachers defensive and perhaps
hostile and may make an effective dialogue between you
and the teacher impossible. Gossip, threats, undocu-
mented accusations, and disparaging remarks about a
teacher's ability or effeciveness do not belong in a conference. Nor do strong emotions like crying, yelling, and
shouting. Instead, express your areas of concern and give
the teacher insight into what your child is like and what
he or she is concerned about at school. Discuss how your
child is doing and how you can help your child. Keep to
this topic, and really listen to what the teacher says; you
should have a successful conference.

Speaking to Counselors

Counselors are usually found on the junior high school
and senior high school levels rather than on the elemen-
tary level. Their primary job is working with students.
They help students with their schedules, learning problems, career choices, college admissions, problems with
teachers and classmates, and adjustment difficulties. If
your child has a general problem that he or she cannot
seem to resolve, or you would like test results interpreted
or special tests given to your child, you will want to talk to
a counselor. If your child is having a problem in a particular subject area, however, talk to the teacher, not to a
counselor.

Be sure that the counselor knows what you want to discuss before the meeting or at the start of a telephone conversation. Spell out the problem by saying things like:

> "I'm calling because I am concerned about my child's
> progress toward graduation."

Conversations with your child and a student counselor are helpful in solving problems at school.

"I think that my child may be having a problem finding friends."

"I would like to know what a score in the 40th percentile on the recent achievement tests means."

Most of your conversations with counselors will be problem-solving sessions. Join with them in looking for solutions to your child's problems. Both you and the counselor should focus on the specifics of a problem and explore ways in which it can be solved. Always end conversations with counselors by thanking them for their help and making plans to check back with each other to find out if a problem is truly resolved.

Speaking to Principals

Don't automatically call the principal every time your child has a problem at school. Most problems can probably be handled by a teacher or counselor. Do call the principal when you want questions about overall school policy answered, when you want to know if disturbing rumors are true, when your child is having problems on the bus or with bullies on the way to school, or when a child and teacher simply cannot work together effectively. Principals would rather hear about problems than to have them fester in the community.

If you are speaking to a principal about problems that your child is having with a teacher, don't begin by criticizing the teacher. This puts the principal on the defensive and forces the principal to defend the teacher. Instead, begin by describing the situation and ask the principal if he or she can help you.

Unfortunately, one reason that you may be talking to a principal or dean is that they have called you about your child's behavior. If this happens, stifle your first reaction to defend your child. Instead, listen to all the facts. Before you react, ask your child to explain how he or she sees the situation. Three-party conferences between student, parent, and school administrators are often very effective ways to improve a child's behavior. They let the child have input into how his or her behavior can be improved.

If your child has broken some rule at school and a penalty has been invoked, like detention, suspension, or expulsion, don't ask for exemptions to established school rules for your child unless there are unusual circumstances that make such a request reasonable. Be aware of the fact that if your child is suspended or expelled from a public school for any reason, he or she is entitled by federal law to a hearing and due process.

Positive School Talks

Remember that it is natural to feel upset when you are talking to a teacher, counselor, or principal about your child's problems at school. It may be quite difficult for you to be calm. Try to calm yourself before a difficult talk by vigorous exercise—it helps. If you find it impossible to calm down, just say something like, "Let me get this off my chest before we really begin to discuss this matter," or "Bear with me for a minute." Try to have an open mind once you begin to talk to school personnel. Don't let your child's complaints about school shut the door to what a teacher, counselor, or principal has to say about the child. Remember, don't just talk to school personnel; also listen to what they have to say. Keep in mind that many teachers, counselors, and principals are reluctant, even fearful, about talking to you.

Speaking and Politics

Some day, you may find yourself wanting to take a more active part in the political world than just voting. Like most people, you may enter the political arena at the local level by working for a candidate or supporting an issue. If "Potomac fever" grabs you, you may soon find yourself running for local office, from school board member to mayor. Once you have been part of a winning campaign or have won an election, the lure of politics may capture you forever. Your success in the political world will depend greatly on your ability to speak to people.

The Campaign Worker

Your first job as a campaign worker may be going door-to-door to find out what issues voters are interested in and to find out whether your candidate's name is recognized. This is an easy assignment because your candidate will probably provide you with what you should say. It could be something like this:

> "Good morning, my name is Matt Douglas and I am helping take a survey about the coming city council election. Would you answer two brief questions?"

People will usually agree to this request—partly out of curiosity about what the questions are. Your voice should show an eagerness to hear the person's answers. Continue by asking the survey questions. Be sure to ask the questions slowly and to emphasize the important words.

> "What do you think should be the *number one issue* in the city council race this year?"

Write down the answer, then emphasize your candidate's name in the final question to increase voter recognition of the name.

> "Did you know that *Larry Scott* is a candidate for city council?"

Note the answer. Then thank the person graciously for co-operating.

Besides conducting surveys, a frequent assignment for campaign workers is campaigning for a candidate door-to-door or at a shopping center. Often, you must wear a badge to identify yourself. You will begin by introducing

yourself and telling which candidate you are supporting
for an office. Then you will want to find out whether a person knows your candidate. You continue by asking whom
the person would vote for if the election were held today.
The answer to this question determines what you say
next. If the person is for your candidate, you find out if the
person is registered, and you offer party services to help
them vote on election day. If the person is undecided or for
another candidate, you will need to make a direct sell of
your candidate.

The most important thing to remember is to always ask
the person to vote for your candidate. It seems to place an
obligation on people to vote for the candidate that they
have agreed to support. Before you hit the campaign trail,
be sure to practice what you will say on other campaign
workers. You may find it helpful to begin campaigning in
your neighborhood with people you know.

Whether you are conducting a survey or campaigning
for a candidate, there are several things that you must
never do:

1. Never walk across lawns.
2. Never chew gum.
3. Never argue.
4. Never look sloppy.

The Campaigner

Whether you are running for dogcatcher or mayor, you
must go where the people are. Then you must greet them
and speak about your candidacy. You don't have to be a
backslapper to succeed in politics. You do have to develop
a comfortable speaking style. You will have to learn to say,
"Hello, I'm Rita Smith and I'm running for city council. I
would be happy to answer any questions that you may
have." The most important thing that you must say to
everyone is, "I would like your vote on election day."

When you are speaking to small groups at a coffee,
breakfast, or meeting, try to get to know your audience before you speak to them. Try to find out what issues interest them so you can bring up these issues in your speech.
Keep your speeches brief. Ten to twenty minutes should
be ample time to tell a small group the following things:

1. Who you are
2. Something about the office you are running for

As a campaign worker, you must be friendly and interested in the opinions of community members.

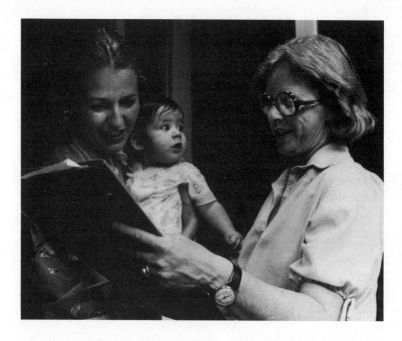

3. Why you feel you are qualified for the office
4. What you would like to accomplish in office (Tie this to what you have learned about the issues that concern your audience.)
5. That you would like their vote

Political Speaking

Political speeches are, of course, speeches to persuade. Persuasion is the business of politicians. To succeed in persuading people to vote for you, you should use these three tactics:

Establish Character.   Your first tactic is to establish your character. This means you are going to have to convince the voters that you are the kind of person who knows what he or she is talking about and can be trusted. To do so, you can talk about your past, modestly describe your credentials, and tell of your association with people who have positive qualities. If this is your task, consider whose names you could give voters as your associates.

Arouse Emotions.   As you establish your credibility, you can also begin the second tactic of persuasion: arousing the emotions of the voters toward supporting you. Most politicians do this by making emotional appeals for peace, prosperity, liberty, justice, and other ideals that everyone wants. How did the persons you voted for in the last election succeed in gaining your emotional support? Was it because the candidates promised to ban the bomb, bring prosperity, or save the environment?

Be Logical. The final tactic in all speeches of persuasion is to lay out the logical reasons why an action should be taken. Here, politicians give the logical arguments for their election. The arguments cannot be too lengthy or complicated. Generalizations can be used effectively.

Winning Speech

Although political speeches are persuasive, parts of them can be informative or entertaining. Back up your statements with facts. Use humor only if you are comfortable with it. Instead of telling a joke, you may find it easier to tie humor into funny things that have happened during the campaign. Develop a general outline for your speeches. Adjust it for each audience. You will feel more comfortable as the campaign continues because you are using a familiar speech. Be concerned with your delivery. Eye contact is especially important. Also, always watch your appearance; you must look professional.

Speaking in Court

You may find it necessary some time in your life to speak in a court. Perhaps you will be a plaintiff, defendant, or witness in a lawsuit. You may be selected to serve on a jury or need to appear in a traffic or small claims court. Whatever the reason, you will find that what happens in a courtroom is not too different from some of the courtroom activity that you see on television. You may not find your appearance in court as dramatic as the ones shown on television, but the basic procedure will be similar.

Serving as a Juror

There are two kinds of juries—grand juries and petit juries. A grand jury is a body of up to 23 members that serves for a period of time. The grand jury hears evidence presented by a prosecutor or others and determines if there is sufficient and probable cause that a crime has been committed. A petit jury is the trial jury. Since most people serve as petit jurors, the following discussion is about serving on a petit jury.

The Petit Juror

Prospective jurors are chosen by lot. If your name is picked for a particular court, you will receive a letter telling when and where you are to appear to serve as a juror. Frequently, a questionnaire will be included, which is to be mailed back to the court. Questionnaires typically ask your age, address, and occupation, as well as the occupations of immediate family members. The questionnaire will be used by the judge and attorneys in selecting you as a juror for a particular case.

If you are a prospective juror in a court that serves a small population, the bailiff may informally explain how the jury selection process works. The approach will be more formal in large cities, where jurors are usually being selected for several trials. In either case, you will normally be sent to a courtroom and sworn in. The judge will then come in and talk to the prospective jury. The judge will tell the jury what the case is about and go into the mechanics of a trial.

When serving on a jury, you must listen closely to everything that is said in the courtroom.

The Judge Questions

In some states, the judge begins the selection of the jury by asking the entire panel of prospective jurors a series of questions. The first questions will concern excuses from jury duty for cause. You will hear quesions like:

1. "Is anyone over 65 years of age?"
2. "Does anyone have a medical reason for not serving as a juror?"
3. "Does anyone have a religious reason for not serving as a juror?"
4. "Is anyone not a citizen of the United States?"
5. "Is anyone a law enforcement officer or a spouse of a law enforcement officer?"

You will only need to speak if you answer *yes* to one of the questions. Then the judge will ask you more specific questions to determine if you should be excused for cause. As most people are quite nervous, it is a good idea to think of your answers ahead of time if you feel you should be excused from jury duty.

The Judge and Attorneys Question

The next series of questions that the judge or attorneys may ask the entire panel deal with the case. You will hear general questions like these:

1. "Are you acquainted with any of the parties in the case?"
2. "Do you know anything about the case?"
3. "Have you ever been involved in a similar case?"

Again, if you answer *yes* to any of the questions, the judge or attorneys will ask specific questions of you.

Finally, you may be asked individual questions by the judge or either attorney. The questions are not asked to find out details about your personal life, but rather to determine if you have a particular bias. This question period will probably be longer for a criminal than a civil case. Expect to be asked lots of questions if you are a prospective juror for a case that has been highly publicized or one that deals with rape, murder, or child abuse. Jurors are just questioned, not grilled as shown on television. Once you have been selected for a jury, you will probably end up loving every minute of it. Most people do. Besides, you will have an excellent topic for future conversations.

Serving as a Witness

If you are to be witness in a court case, you may be given a subpoena, which is a court order mandating you to appear. Before you actually appear in court, you may be subject to a deposition, which is a sworn examination of a witness by both attorneys. Depositions can be taken anywhere, even in your home. You are subject to cross-examination at a deposition. It is similar to the procedure at a trial. The purpose of depositions is to let each side know what the other's witnesses will say. If you give a deposition, you may not have to appear in court as a witness.

Before giving a deposition or appearing in court as a witness, you will talk to the attorney who has asked you to be a witness. This attorney will probably ask you some of the same questions that he or she will ask you during a deposition or in court. The attorney may also give you an idea of what the opposing attorney will ask you. In most cases, your answers should be brief—perhaps no more than *yes* or *no*. Avoid rambling answers; they can confuse a case. It is acceptable to carry notes if you need them, but you may be required to show them. Dress and act appropriately if you are to serve as a witness.

Serving as Your Own Lawyer

Technically, you can be your own lawyer in any court, including the Supreme Court; but you will probably choose to be your own lawyer only in a traffic court or a small claims court. How you express yourself in any court is important.

In most traffic courts, a bailiff calls your name. Your traffic violation is read, and you are asked how you plead. If you plead guilty, your speaking is done. If you plead not guilty, a time will be set for a trial. Whether you act as your own lawyer in a traffic court trial or a small claims court, the key word is organization. You will have to gather evidence and prepare your case. Then you need to make a persuasive speech.

Jury Service and You

For most people, speaking in a courtroom is a rare experience. No matter why you are in a courtroom, it is an opportunity to see how the judicial system works. Consider jury service as a special opportunity to participate in the judicial system.

Don't give long-winded answers to questions when you are serving as a witness.

Community Communication Counts

Whenever you talk to a mail carrier or a clerk in a local store, you are communicating in your community. You are communicating when you make a motion at a club meeting, solicit for funds in your neighborhood, or have a conference with your child's teacher. How well you communicate depends upon how well you speak. People cannot read your mind. Take the time to send careful messages in order to play a vital role in your community.

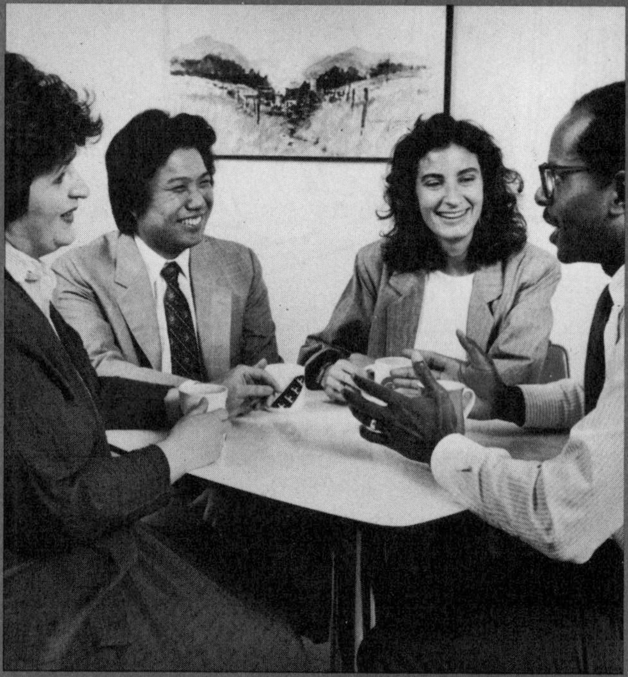

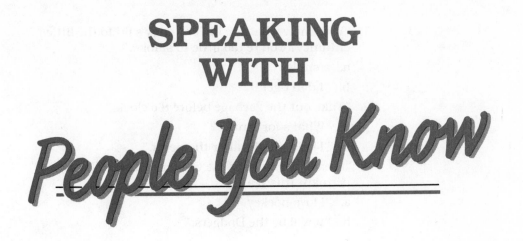

SPEAKING WITH
People You Know

ou speak at work, and you speak in the community. What you say in these places certainly affects your career and daily life. But nothing affects the quality of your life more than the communication you have with family, friends, and acquaintances. You spend some part of every day in communication with these people. You speak to them of your doubts, fears, complaints, successes, worries, likes, dislikes, and innermost feelings. And they respond to you in the same way. This section of the book discusses ways to have successful personal communication with people you know.

Sending and Receiving

Personal communication is far more than sending and receiving a message. Without some kind of response or feedback from the receiver, the sender doesn't know whether or not the message was received. The receiver's response could be a smile, a nod, a frown, a yawn, a puzzled look, or an encouraging or discouraging remark. Study the following messages. Which responses show that the actual messages were received?

1. "You know what the big chimney said to the little chimney? You're too little to smoke."

   a. a smile

   b. "I don't get it."

2. "Take out the garbage before 8 o'clock."

   a. "What's for dinner?"

   b. "I'll do it right after the news."

3. "I really believe that the Chicago Cubs will win the pennant this year."

   a. "I love hockey."

   b. "It will be the Dodgers."

Responses 1.–a., 2.–b., and 3.–b. show that the message was received.

Effective personal communication takes place only when the sender knows that his or her message has been received. It can be diagrammed like this:

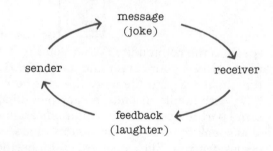

Interference

Sometimes, barriers come up that stop the receiver from getting the message. At other times, barriers come up that stop the sender from getting feedback. These barriers that interfere with communication can be in the form of interference from the sender, receiver, or surroundings. If a barrier is not removed, personal communication will be ineffective. You need to find out what is interfering with your communication in order to improve it.

Interference from the Sender

Your message is not going to get through to the receiver if you have bad speech habits. This includes speaking too fast or slow, too high or low, or monotonously, which

OH, WOW, IT WAS TOTALLY FAR OUT AND GROOVY TO THE MAX. CAN YOU DIG IT ?

Don't use slang when speaking to someone from a different background or generation.

turns the receiver off. Nor is your message going to get through if you use language that the receiver does not understand. Which of the following words and terms do you understand? Which ones would your parents or grandparents understand?

haberdasher	VCR	laser
Prussia	microchip	czar
Zaire	jitterbug	spats

You should especially watch the use of slang. Not everyone will know the meaning of words like *punk, laid back, uptight,* or *nerd.* Be aware that certain words can be offensive to your receivers and for this reason will block communication.

Interference from the Receiver

Sometimes, you may not receive a message because of your attitude toward a speaker. If a speaker is dressed in an unusual outfit or has a very different hairstyle, you may not listen as seriously to that person's talk about world trade. Your emotions and past experiences can also play a role in interfering with communication. Think about how emotions and experiences might affect the communication of the following messages:

sender	message	receiver
18-year-old son	decision to join the army	mother
teacher	holding a child back a grade	parent
parent	family is moving	teen-ager

Interference from Surroundings

It's hard to communicate effectively with someone if a phone rings, a child cries, someone comes in a room, or a timer buzzes. Noise is one of the major barriers to effective personal communication. Look at the following list of barriers to personal communication. Can you add barriers that you frequently encounter to this list? What barriers commonly stop communication within your home?

barking dogs	sirens
low-flying planes	radio, TV, and stereo
running water	slamming doors

Removing Interference

The first step to removing interference is to find out what the interference is. Then you must determine how you are going to eliminate or lessen the interference. You can im-

Some of your most meaningful and important conversations are with your family and your friends.

prove bad speech habits, and you can choose words that your listeners understand to lessen interference. You can dress and speak in ways that are acceptable to your listeners to lessen interference. You can stop trying to talk over a noise and wait for things to quiet down. It is usually possible to reduce interference. It is not always possible to eliminate it entirely.

Feedback

There is good feedback, and there is poor feedback. Just because the receiver indicates in some way that a message was heard does not mean that the message was understood. The best feedback restates what the message was. Study these examples of feedback in a conversation about vacations. Which ones really show understanding of what was said?

1. "Nice plans."
2. "You mean you are going to camp out every night?"
3. "I get the picture."
4. "You'll be pulling a trailer over 1,000 miles, is that right?"
5. "I know."

Feedback comments **2.** and **4.** tell the sender exactly what the receivers think the message was. Perhaps the receivers who made comments **1.**, **3.**, and **5.** also really understood what was said. The senders cannot be as sure from these comments and may wish to send the message again. The receiver should always acknowledge that the feedback was correct in order to complete a communication.

Feedback is not always essential. The message may not be that important in a casual conversation. Or there may not be any time or need for feedback after a message like "Fire!," "Help!," or "Watch out!" However, you probably should give more feedback than you do to increase your understanding of what is being said to you. You should make it a point to give feedback when you are talking about something that is very important, like wedding arrangements or watching a pet. At times like these, it helps to say things like, "You mean you want me to cut the cake," and "I should feed the cat at 5 o'clock every day, right?" Also, it is always wise to use feedback when you feel upset about what is being said. For example, "You told your boss that I would cook dinner for the entire office?"

Body Language

Many people don't realize that they communicate with more than words. Their gestures, posture, and facial expressions all send messages without any assistance from their vocal cords. What messages do these gestures or expressions send to you?

shrugging shoulders   frowning
nodding head   winking
yawning   clenching fists

The quality of your gestures is extremely important. It has been estimated that only a small percentage of social meaning in communication comes from words, while most of the meaning comes from different forms of non-verbal communication.

Successful Sending and Receiving

Successful communication with people you know means expressing yourself clearly. You will be more effective if you avoid clichés. Successful communication means listening to more than what is said. As people listen, they must learn to look at the meaning behind what is being said. To

Body language, such as yawning or clenching a fist, is an important part of nonverbal communication.

do this, they need to observe the tone of the speaker's voice, the expression of the speaker's face, and the gestures the speaker makes. Communication is truly effective when what the listener thinks the speaker said, is what the speaker actually said.

Speaking with Family

Have you ever given serious thought to how you talk to members of your family? Take a minute now, and consider whether they would have the following complaints about your conversations with them:

1. You speak too loud or too soft.
2. You speak too fast or too slow.
3. You mumble.
4. You speak too much or too little.
5. You always interrupt.
6. You never complete your sentences.
7. You finish other people's sentences.
8. You nag.
9. You criticize endlessly.
10. You never praise.
11. You are always correcting.
12. You are overbearing with your advice.
13. You complain frequently.
14. You whine.
15. You shut people out.

There is no place like home. This is where you can let your hair down and relax. This should also be the place where you speak with the greatest skill, since you are speaking to your family, which is a constant source of love and personal satisfaction to you.

Family Speech Manners

Manners are a code of behavior that help people get along with one another. Family members should not leave their manners at the front door when they enter their homes. They must treat each other with consideration, tact, and courtesy in both their actions and speech. Each family should have an informal speech code that every member knows and follows. The basis of this code is politeness. Family members should be able to expect politeness from each other. They may not always find it in the outside world. Here are some basic rules of family speech. Do you and the members of your family usually follow most of these rules?

1. Family members should address each other by appropriate names or titles.
2. Family members should greet each other at the start of the day and when returning home.
3. Family members should say good night to each other.
4. Offensive language is not acceptable family speech.
5. Family members must not be rude to each other.
6. Family discussion is preferable to argument.
7. Family members should always ask before using each other's possessions.
8. Family members should knock and ask for permission to enter one another's bedrooms.
9. Family meals are the time for pleasant conversation. Mealtime is not the time to complain, to nag, or to criticize each other.
10. Family secrets may not be revealed outside the family.

You may wish at this point to take the time to discuss with your family what the unwritten speech rules in your home are or should be. It is just as important to have everyday family manners as to have company manners used in the presence of nonfamily members.

Family Communication

The best family communication is like a good game of tennis. The conversation goes back and forth several times between the members of the family like a tennis ball does in a good rally. Family members must take turns sending and receiving messages to keep communication going.

Much family communication is like a game of singles. It is a one-to-one exchange between parents, between parent and child, or between two children. Sometimes, the communication is like a game of doubles, with several members of the family taking turns hitting the conversation ball. Just as good tennis players study the techniques of

There are many
different lines of
communication
within a family.

the game to improve their skills, you can study the following techniques of praising, criticizing, advising, and making decisions to improve your family communication skills.

Praise

Parents are continually advised by psychologists to praise their children and each other. Since almost everyone is convinced of the value of praise, it is curious that family members often find it difficult to praise each other. They seem to find it hard to discover something to praise and to select the appropriate words.

What to Praise. No one believes exaggerated compliments. If you are going to praise someone in your family, you must find something believable to praise. It is helpful to look for something specific rather than something general. General praise is not as personal. Look at the following general and specific comments. Decide which ones you would prefer to receive.

1. a. "You look nice today." (general)
    b. "Your new hairstyle is quite becoming." (specific)
2. a. "Your landscaping is attractive." (general)
    b. "The new flower bed adds so much color to the yard." (specific)

3. **a.** "You are a great student." (general)
   b. "We're so proud you received straight *A*'s this grading period." (specific)

Praise need not be limited to the way people or things look. Praise ideas and actions, and don't forget to praise what family members say. You may not like everything that someone is saying; however, try to find some part that you can praise. When you are praising someone, look for one thing at a time to praise. It is not necessary to string together a series of compliments. Stop now and think of one specific thing that each member of your family has done today that you could have praised.

What to Say.   It is a good idea to personalize your praise. To do this, you can begin with such phrases as "I think that . . .," "I believe that . . .," "I like . . .," or "It seems to me . . ." Reread the previously listed general and specific comments. Note how they would sound if you began them with a personal phrase. For example, "I think that you look nice today," is more personal than "You look nice today."

Criticism

People ask you for criticism, but they only want praise.
Somerset Maugham

No one will deny that negative criticism can make family members feel hurt and unloved. After all, you are asking people to change in some way when you criticize them. Still, something worthwhile can come out of constructive criticism. Members of the family can find out where they made mistakes. They can also find out what others in the family thought of their ideas. Since criticism has some benefits, some criticism of family members should take place. What the members need to do is to learn how to give criticism in such a way that it can be tolerated. However, don't expect family members to say "thank you" when you criticize them.

Criticism is Opinion.   Don't give criticism as if it were fact. It really is only your opinion. You could be wrong. Try to let family members see this by beginning with a phrase like, "It appears to me . . .," "I believe that . . .," "In my opinion . . .," or "I thought you should know that . . . ."

Don't be overly
negative when
criticizing someone.

Avoid Personalities.   Family members do not like to be
criticized. However, they can handle criticism better if it is
aimed at their actions, ideas, or beliefs, not at their personalities. Imagine that the following criticisms were directed at you. Would you find it easier to accept the ones
that do not criticize you personally?

1. "I think that you're a very sloppy person."
2. "I feel quite unhappy about the way you disagreed
   with me in front of the children."
3. "It really hurt me that you ignored me at the party."
4. "As far as I am concerned, you're a bigot."
5. "In my mind, what you said to the neighbors will not
   stop them from parking in front of our house."

Comments **2.**, **3.**, and **5.** were not directed at people but
at what they said or did.

Avoid Generalities.   Like praise, criticism should be specific. Point out exactly what you are criticizing. Don't say,

"It seems to me that you never get anything done around the house." Instead, say, "It seems to me that you haven't cleaned the garage as you promised." To avoid generalities, you should not use words like *never, always, every time,* and *constantly,* which imply no exceptions are allowed. Instead, use words like *sometimes, frequently, often,* and *occasionally.*

Include Praise.   Rarely is something all bad. Learn to soften your criticism by including praise. Most people find accepting criticism easier when they know what they have done or said is partially acceptable. Note the difference between these two methods of criticism:

1. "I don't like the way you left the mess for me to clean up after you painted the kitchen." (without praise)
2. "I like the way you painted the kitchen; on the other hand, I don't like the way you left the mess for me to clean up." (with praise)

Final Cautions.   When you criticize someone, limit your criticism to one area at a time. Don't overwhelm someone by naming all the person's faults at once. Select the appropriate time and place for giving criticism. Avoid criticizing family members in front of others.

Advice

You can help members of your family by giving them advice. Just be sure that you don't give them so much advice that they feel they cannot make their own decisions. This is especially important with teen-agers. The first premise of advice giving is to give advice only when it is requested. The second is to give the exact kind of advice sought.

When you give advice, make sure that the recipient understands that you are only expressing your opinion. Do say something like "If I were you, I would . . .," "In my opinion the thing to do is . . .," or "From my point of view it would be a good idea to . . . ." When you give advice, don't expect others always to take it. The Earl of Chesterfield, an eighteenth-century wit, gave everyone good advice when he said: "Advice is seldom welcome, and those who want it the most always like it the least."

Making Decisions

Decision making in families is a constant process. Many decisions must be made each day. Some are recurring decisions, while others are one-time decisions. Some deci-

Mealtime is a good time for families to have pleasant conversation. It is not a good time to make major family decisions.

sions are of minor importance, while others are of major importance. Some decisions must be made by the parents, while others should be made by the entire family. Classify the following decisions as minor or major decisions. Think of who would make each of these decisions in your home.

1. Should grandmother go into a nursing home?
2. Should the family buy a new car this year?
3. Who will walk the dog tonight?
4. What time should we leave for the movies?
5. Where should we go on our yearly vacation?

Improving Decision Making.   Most families would benefit from improving their decision making. Following certain rules can enhance the decision-making process in a family. You may want to try using these rules in your family:

1. Decisions should be made when the family members are rested and free of emotional disturbances.
2. Set aside special times to make decisions. Use only these times to make major decisions.
3. Decision-making times should be used for that purpose alone. Do not include other activities like eating or watching TV.

Solving Problems.   One of the purposes of decision making is to resolve problem situations. To solve problems, families will find it helpful to follow John Dewey's six steps, which were introduced in the chapter on speaking at school. All of these should be used to make decisions.

1. Family members should identify the problem precisely.
2. They should analyze the problem.
3. They should bring up possible solutions. (Brainstorming is a good way to do this.)
4. They should evaluate different solutions for the problem.
5. They should decide on the best solution.
6. They should verify the solution by observation or practice.

Family Council.   Many families set up a family council for making decisions. A council is a group of people called together to give advice and to discuss or settle questions. Since a family is an organization, a council gives a family a formal body for making decisions. Families should schedule regular council meetings and set up rules for operating their council. Even the smallest children can participate effectively in a family council if the topics of discussion are carefully chosen.

Levels of Communication

Within a family, the members communicate on several levels, from the shallow level of casual small talk to the deep level of discussing true inner feelings. To communicate on deeper levels, family members have to learn to reveal their feelings to each other. Just saying, "I feel . . .," does not necessarily mean you are revealing your feelings. Study these comments, and decide which ones really communicate feelings:

1. "I feel we should buy a new car."
2. "I feel absolutely crushed from losing by one point."
3. "I feel comfortable about leaving early."
4. "I feel as happy as if I had won myself."
5. "I feel so mad that I could chew nails."

Comments **2.**, **4.**, and **5.** communicate feelings. They accurately describe a person's emotional responses. Use such comments when you wish to communicate with the members of your family.

Toward Better Communication

So often, important communication within a family takes place at odd times and in haphazard ways. During a TV show, family members may decide where a child should go to college. As her husband is driving in freeway traffic, a wife may elect to discuss her frustration with being home-bound. Family members need to make the effort to find special times to make important decisions and to involve themselves in discussions with each other.

Family members also need to encourage each other to really communicate. One way to do this is by asking questions or making comments that encourage members to expand on what they are saying. Get family members talking by saying things like:

> "What is your opinion?"
> "Would you go into more detail about that?"
> "What do you have in mind?"
> "I'd like to hear more about that."

Besides finding time to communicate and encouraging others to communicate, family members will begin to communicate better with each other when they learn to listen to each other. When family members talk, they really want others to listen and understand what they are saying.

Speaking with Friends

People are gregarious. They need companionship. Their families cannot completely fill this need. People also enjoy being with friends. They like to talk and listen to their friends. They use their conversations with friends to share ideas and feelings, good and bad times, joy and grief, triumphs and failures, pleasure and pain, as well as to simply pass time in an agreeable way. It is conversation that cements the bonds of friendship.

Conversation Secrets

One of the greatest pleasures of life is conversation.
Reverend Sydney Smith

Since conversation with friends provides so much pleasure, it seems sensible to look at ways to improve these conversations. Are you guilty of any of the following conversation faults when you speak to your friends?

1. Do you monopolize conversations?
2. Do you overuse the word *I*?
3. Do you gossip?
4. Do you get to the point quickly?
5. Do you encourage others to talk?
6. Do you interrupt?
7. Do you listen?

Study the following ways in which you can eliminate any conversation faults that may damage your relationships with your friends.

Hogging the Conversation

Some of your most enjoyable and fulfilling conversations take place with your friends.

When you talk with one person, you should be speaking approximately one-half of the time. When another person joins the conversation, your share of the conversation is reduced to one-third of the talking. As more and more peo-

ple join a conversation, the amount you should talk is reduced proportionately. Follow these rules unless you are certain that everyone wants you to carry more than your share of the conversation. If so, stay on the lookout for signs of boredom. Relinquish the spotlight if someone is trying to interrupt you, leaves the group, yawns, or starts looking away. Don't make it a habit to conduct monologues when conversing with people.

Too Many *I*'s

"*I* went on an interesting trip. *I* had a great time. *I* flew on the Concorde. *I* went to London. *I* saw the Queen. *I* cruised on the Thames. *I* can go on forever." Avoid nonstop monologues full of *I*'s, like this one. Interrupt your *I*'s with a steady stream of *you*'s so that your conversations are shared experiences.

Gossiping

> Conversations between Adam and Eve must have been difficult at times because they had nobody to talk about.
> **Agnes Repplier**

Finding conversation today shouldn't be difficult, with a population of more than four billion people on earth, and there is no shortage of people to talk about. Most of people's casual conversation does seem to be about friends or acquaintances. When a conversation reveals personal or sensational facts, it becomes gossip. Gossip is slanderous and should be avoided. Stick to the facts when you talk about friends and acquaintances; information and gossip are not the same. Which of the following comments about people would you consider gossip?

1. "The Fishers are going to Florida this winter."
2. "Dave is living very high for his salary."
3. "Jane is redecorating her house."
4. "Bob is going to get fired if he continues to drink on the job."
5. "Pat really flirts with her boss."

Statements **2.**, **4.**, and **5.** are gossip. When you take part in a conversation, keep in mind how George Eliot described gossip in the novel *Daniel Deronda*: "Gossip is a sort of smoke that comes from the dirty tobacco-pipes of those who diffuse it: it proves nothing but the bad taste of the smoker." When you are with an individual or group of people who are gossiping, speak out firmly against it or excuse yourself from the conversation.

Stating Your Point

People are busy. Everyone is always running out of time. Your friends want to listen to what you have to say, but they don't have all day. Don't waste their time by not getting your point across quickly. Avoid rambling on and on. Don't use ten words when five would clearly do. A few details add interest, but too many overshadow your point. Read the following statements. Which one quickly comes to the point?

1. "When you come home from work today, which I imagine will be around 5 o'clock, before you drive the carpool to pick up your children, or go shopping if you decide to; would you go over to our house and take the dog out for a walk?"
2. "Before you drive the carpool to pick up your children or do anything else, could you possibly walk our dog?"
3. "Would you walk our dog when you get home today?"

The third statement quickly states the point: the dog needed to be walked. In the first statement, 47 words were used to try to make the point. Twenty words were used to make the point in the second conversation, but only 10 words were used in the third conversation.

Make a one-minute tape recording in which you make a point about one of the following topics:

1. income tax
2. pollution
3. government spending

After listening to your recording, repeat the activity and see how many seconds you can cut off by shortening your statement. This activity can be repeated several times. See if you can make your point in 20 seconds or less.

Encouraging Conversation

Sports teams appreciate the loud cheers of their fans. The cheers may encourage the teams to win games. In order for your conversations with friends to be winners, you need to become a cheerleader who urges everyone to participate. Encourage nonactive members by sending the conversation their way. Address open-ended questions to them. Avoid asking questions that can be answered with a single word. Which questions below would you use to get someone to join in a conversation?

1. "Do you enjoy skiing?"
2. "How did you find such a great resort?"
3. "What do you think about the devaluation of the dollar?"
4. "Did you watch the launching of the space shuttle?"
5. "Could you explain how you completed that difficult job on time?"

Questions 2., 3., and 5. encourage more conversation than questions 1. and 4. because more than a *yes* or *no* is required to answer them.

Interrupting

Except for emergency situations, don't interrupt people when they are talking. Wait your turn to express your opinions about what is being said. There is no polite way to interrupt. People don't really need your help to finish their sentences and stories or to deliver the punch line of a joke that is being told.

Listening

Have you ever taken the time to think of the number of people you listen to every day? The following list includes only some of the people you probably listen to. How many names can you add to the list?

1. spouse
2. children
3. friends
4. radio announcers
5. boss
6. teacher
7. cashier
8. parents

People listen for different reasons. Some listen to be polite. Others listen to learn. Many listen because, as Edgar Watson Howe put it, "No man would listen to you talk if he didn't know it was his turn next." It is a skill to be a good listener. Good listeners are popular people, and they often acquire valuable knowledge.

If you can answer *yes* to the questions below, you are probably a good listener.

An important part of speaking with family and friends is developing good listening skills.

1. Do you look at the speaker?
2. Does your face show signs of interest?
3. Is your body posture good?
4. Do you ignore distractions?
5. Do you rarely have to ask people to repeat what they have said?
6. Do you notice expressions and gestures?
7. Do you notice the speaker's pitch and tone of voice?
8. Do you remember words and phrases that the speaker stresses?
9. Do you recognize the speaker's emotions?

Test your listening skills now. Begin by turning on a tape recorder. Then close your eyes for a minute or so and listen to the sounds around you. How many sounds did you hear? Play the tape back and check if you missed any sounds.

Words trigger different responses in people. Even though several people hear the same words, they may not have the same responses, resulting in communication problems. Think of one-word responses to the following words. Then read the list to family members or friends. Find out if their responses are the same as yours.

exciting disaster rewarding
haunting relaxing challenging

Speaking to Friends of All Ages

Someone does not have to be your exact age in order to be your friend. It does not matter whether your friends are 7 or 70 years old; you can have interesting and rewarding conversations with them. People have more in common than they imagine. To talk with people of any age, you need to have an open outlook on life and be able to accept different viewpoints.

Speaking to Children

Babies can be won over easily with games of peek-a-boo. Let little children come to you. Ask them to show you a favorite toy or book. It can become a topic of conversation. You can find another possible topic of conversation by observing the clothing a child is wearing. Many children wear T-shirts that indicate their interests. Even 3-year-olds know all about the heroes on their chests.

Children in school have interesting opinions. They study far more than the 3 R's. Try finding out their opinions on such topics as pollution, elections, space, and acid rain. Their knowledge may surprise you. You will also find that specific questions generate more conversation than general questions. Avoid questions such as, "Do you like school?," and "Do you have a hobby?" Overused questions like these are conversation killers. Instead, try asking a specific question, like, "How much time do you spend each day doing homework?" which can serve as a conversational springboard to a discussion on the value of doing homework.

Speaking to Teen-agers

Children's opinions are interesting. Teen-agers' opinions are fascinating. One caution—remember that there are topics other than sex, drugs, and drinking to discuss with a teen-ager. These topics are overused. They also can put the teen-ager on the defensive and put a damper on further conversation. With teen-agers, as with children, specific questions are better conversation openers than general questions.

Speak differently to people of different ages. Tailor your conversations to fit their particular needs and interests.

Speaking to the Elderly

Speaking to the elderly is just the same as speaking to people your age, unless the passage of time has brought profound changes in their personalities. If this is the case, you may share wonderful conversations with older people by talking more about the past than the present. You can ask about how they dressed, what they did for entertainment, and what transportation was available in their youth. Such conversations with older people can be quite informative.

When you are speaking to an older person, look for signs of hearing difficulties. You may need to speak louder. Persons with high-pitched voices may need to lower their pitch to be heard more easily.

Pleasant Conversations

To have pleasant conversations with people of all ages, you need to find topics that you can share with each person. People of all ages can always share their enthusiasms with each other. They can usually find joint concerns. Enthusiasms and concerns both make excellent topics of conversation. Read the following list of topics, and decide how you could discuss each topic with a 7-year-old friend, a teen-ager, and a 70-year-old friend.

1. stamp collecting
2. enjoyable books
3. the Fourth of July
4. an interesting pet

Speaking at Social Events

There are many times in your personal life in which you need to speak. You need to introduce yourself and to introduce others on countless occasions. You need to offer special words on light-hearted and serious occasions, like weddings, graduations, and funerals. You need to engage in small talk at parties and other social gatherings. There is much that you need to know about what to say on different occasions.

Introductions

Almost everyone must make introductions from time to time. Once the rules for making introductions were extremely strict, and it was very important to introduce Miss Nobody to Mrs. Somebody. Today, these rules are more relaxed, but certain guidelines are still generally followed.

Introducing People

Traditionally, introductions have been made in a certain order, which is shown in this chart:

Introduce a:	*To a:*
man	woman
younger person	older person
stranger	relative
new friend	old friend
less-known person	well-known person

Try your hand at introducing people according to the above rules. Whom would you introduce to whom in each of these groups?

1. Jimmy Connors and Chris Evert Lloyd
2. Joe Namath and John Q. Public
3. Michael Jackson and Johnny Carson
4. mailman and Aunt Edith

You would introduce Jimmy to Chris, John to Joe, Michael to Johnny, and the mailman to Aunt Edith.

What to Say.   Once you have learned the mechanics of whom to introduce to whom, you are ready to fill in the missing words. Study these introductions. Which ones would you use for casual occasions? Which are more appropriate for formal occasions?

1. "Martha Jones, I would like to introduce Harold Smith."
2. "Martha Jones, this is Harold Smith."
3. "Martha Jones, may I introduce Harold Smith?"
4. "Martha Jones, have you ever met Harold Smith?"
5. "Martha Jones, do you know Harold Smith?"
6. "Martha Jones, it gives me great pleasure to introduce Harold Smith."

Introductions 2., 4., and 5. are casual. If you like, you can leave out all the words in an introduction and simply say: "Martha Jones, Harold Smith."

Forgetting Names.   The etiquette rules for making introductions can apply only if you know the persons' names. If, however, your mind draws a blank and you forget one of the names, the best thing to do is ask the person his or her name and then proceed with the introduction.

Adding Information.   You cannot just introduce people. You must tell something about each person to help them begin a conversation. After introducing Harold Smith to

Martha Jones you might say, "Martha is quite a tennis player. She won the club tournament last week."

Introducing Yourself

There are occasions when you want to talk to someone, and no one is available to perform the introduction. When this happens to you, take a deep breath to help yourself relax, walk up to the person, and smile. Next, say hello and tell your name. Then, if you have some common bond with the person, mention it as a conversation starter. You might say, "Didn't you go to City College?," or "Haven't I seen you at the library?" Otherwise, if you are complete strangers, it is best to make some type of comment about the occasion.

Special Occasions

People have to attend weddings, graduations, and funerals. At each of these occasions, there are special words and comments that are usually expected. In fact, it is part of the ritual of attending these events.

Weddings

As you walk through the receiving line, you tell the bride how beautiful she looks, and you congratulate the groom. You tell their parents what a lovely wedding it was and

Receiving lines at wedding receptions call for brief, formal conversation.

make similar comments to the attendants. The secret of doing this effectively is to personalize your remarks in some way—for example:

> "Your niece was an adorable flower girl."
> "Suzy and Joe are such a lovely couple."
> "I've never seen you look happier."

Keep your comments brief. Receiving lines must move as quickly as possible. Introduce yourself to the people who do not know you. You can also add appropriate information about yourself, like, "Suzy's family lives next door to us," or "I work with Joe."

At the reception, you will find it easy to talk with the other guests about the wedding service and the newly married couple. The mood of your conversation should be positive.

Graduations

You will want to congratulate graduates on completing their course of study. Stress how proud you are of their achievement. Dwell on the student's accomplishments by saying things like:

> "It will be a long time before Central High has another athlete like you."
>
> "What will the debate team do next year without you?"
>
> "Making Phi Beta Kappa is quite an outstanding achievement."

Funerals

You need to pay condolences to the immediate family of a person who has died. The best thing to say is, "I'm so sorry," or something similar. If you find yourself unable to speak, let the family know your feelings with a hug or by holding their hands tightly. You are better to remain silent than to say some of the unacceptable things that are commonly heard at funerals, such as:

> "You're so young you can have another child."
> "Bob would not want you to stay a widow for long."
> "Your mother would never have wanted you to grieve."

Parties and Other Events

After you have met someone at a social gathering, you want to break the conversational ice. You need to have a ready supply of small talk available to do this. The weather is probably one of the most used ice breakers. It isn't a bad choice if you go beyond such clichés as, "What do you think of the weather?," or "Nice weather." You can use the weather as a stepping stone to other topics; for example, "With such nice weather we can begin to think about . . .

> planting flowers."
> dusting off our golf clubs."
> plowing the vegetable garden."

You need to keep sending and receiving messages until you find a topic that interests everyone participating in the conversation. A good clue that helps you do this is what you learn about people when they are introduced.

If you find it a problem to make small talk, prepare yourself before a gathering. Try to find or think about what topics you could use. Read newspapers and weekly news magazines, watch current events shows, and look at local TV to find interesting topics. Then, before the occasion, you should frame open-ended questions in your mind that could be used as ice breakers. Which of the following questions would really start you talking?

> "Why can't the government cut spending?"
> "What do you think our next adventure in outer space will be?"
> "Would you ever try sky diving?"

To start enjoying yourself at social gatherings, you are going to have to learn to make small talk. At first, it may be difficult. But skill in making small talk can be developed. Study what people who have mastered this skill are saying. Then jump in and try your own skills.

The Party Hosts

If you have laryngitis, you probably should cancel any party that you are giving because the speech duties of the host and hostess are considerable. First, you must greet each guest warmly. Then, if possible, try to introduce all of your guests to each other. Be sure to tell the guests something about each other so they will have starters for their conversations. You might say, "Margaret Dalton, this is David Collins who works with me in accounting." Think about how you would introduce your boss to your mother-in-law and your wife to your old school pal.

Once everyone has arrived, you must circulate from

group to group, keeping the conversations rolling. This is where the topics that you researched for small talk can be put to good use. What topics from today's paper or yesterday's news on TV could you use to keep conversations rolling at a party? Try to think of a humorous story you could share with others to enliven a party conversation.

Don't neglect the shy guests. Join the person standing or sitting alone. You can pull him or her into a group. Or you can talk with this person for a few minutes until other people join you. Then you can graciously slip away, knowing that this shy guest is now part of a group.

During dinner and after dinner, the responsibility for keeping the conversation going remains with you. You should think of yourself as the host or hostess of a talk show, which is what you really are. When the guests begin to leave, say good-bye to each one. If all the guests leave at once, station yourself at the door for this duty. Let your guests leave when they say they must leave. Don't insist that they stay longer by saying, "It's too early," or something similar.

The Party Guests

As a guest, you have certain speech responsibilities. You come prepared with small talk, and you use the secrets of conversation that you have mastered. You introduce yourself to other people if it is necessary. You do your share to keep the conversation rolling at the gathering. You do not ask doctors, lawyers, and other professionals for their advice. You do not get into loud verbal battles over controversial topics with other guests. You look at the people who are talking instead of searching for other people to talk to. You look like you are having a good time, even if you are fighting the flu or your child is flunking chemistry. And finally, before you leave, thank your hosts by making a specific compliment about the party. Don't say, "It was a great party." Instead say, "Your slides of Mexico were fascinating," "I adored the nachos," or "It was lovely to meet Señora Gomez."

Social Speechmaking

For many people, it is just as difficult to make small talk at a social gathering as to make a formal speech at work or before a group. You will never get in the social swim until

Don't hog the conversation at parties. Speak your fair share and allow others to participate.

you start plunging into conversations. If you find large gatherings frightening, begin by talking to one or more neighbors at these functions.

Speak Well with People You Know

Nothing is more rewarding than learning to communicate successfully with family, friends, and acquaintances. It is a skill that can be learned. There are many books that can provide you with additional help to master specific skills, like holding family councils, talking with individual family members, and problem solving. Some day, however, you have to get beyond reading books and begin communicating with people. Start with your family, for they are probably the most important group with which you will ever communicate.

SPEAKING ON THE

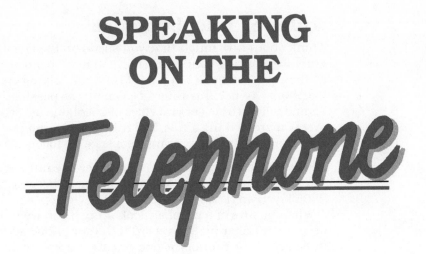

Shortly after the astronauts arrived on the moon, they received a telephone call from the President of the United States. It's getting to be very difficult to imagine where you would have to go to be out of the range of a telephone call. The new cordless phones make it possible to wander around your house or yard while talking on the telephone. It is possible to make calls from your car.

The telephone has become indispensable for most Americans. It has also become a tyrant that interrupts dinners, baths, and conversations. Its ring forces people to stop what they are doing and answer it. The story goes that Alexander Graham Bell once joked that he grew to dislike the telephone because its ringing interrupted his work.

Most Americans conduct a love-hate relationship with the telephone. It quickly puts people in touch with their families and friends. It's a great business tool. And there is no substitute for the telephone when help is needed in a hurry. On the other hand, numbers are often busy, canned music is played on hold, and telephone calls at 3 o'clock in the morning are usually wrong numbers. Yet, even though it can be an instrument of annoyance, few people would really like to do without the telephone. This section is about how to use it effectively.

Rules of Telephone Use

Think about how much time you spend on the telephone every day. During your entire life, you may spend as much as the equivalent of a full year of time just talking on the telephone. To use this time as efficiently as possible, you should follow these general rules of telephone use whenever you are making a call. The rules are very simple, but you'd be surprised how many people fail to follow them.

Be Sure of the Number. It is easy to reverse numbers. The telephone number 345-2806 can easily become 354-2806 if you aren't being careful.

When unsure of a number, look it up. If you wish to keep the number handy, record it in your phone/address directory. If the number is one you are unlikely to use often, underline it in the telephone book so that you can find it easily, should you need it again.

Dial Correctly. Always wait until you hear the dial tone before you start to dial a number. Otherwise, you may reach a wrong number or no number at all. If you are using a rotary dial, always turn the dial until your finger reaches the finger stop. Then, remove your finger and let the dial return to its normal position without forcing or slowing it. Failure to do this may result in a wrong number. If you are using a touch-tone dial, push down each button firmly. Push only one button at a time. After you dial a number on a touch-tone phone, do not touch any buttons on the telephone, or you may be cut off. Should

When making a phone call, remember that the person you're calling may not be in the same mood as yourself.

Plan your phone calls by making a list of the things you'd like to talk about.

your finger happen to slip while you are dialing a number, always hang up and start over.

Plan Your Calls.   Before you make a call, think about whom you want to talk to, what the purpose of your call is, and what you want to say.

Time Your Calls.   Make your calls at times when the people you want to talk to are likely to be available. Think about time differences when you are calling long distance. After all, 8 o'clock in the morning in New York is only 5 o'clock in the morning in Los Angeles.

Answer Promptly.   Answer a phone as quickly as possible. If you are phoning, give people at least one minute to answer the phone. This is approximately 10 rings.

Handle Wrong Numbers Politely.   If you reach a wrong number, apologize before you hang up.

Use the Telephone Book.   In all local telephone directories, the first few pages are devoted to helpful information. You can find out how to contact the business office, how to connect and disconnect phones, where to pay your bill, how to make long distance calls, and much more. Take the time to study these pages.

Your Telephone Voice

The telephone company is always advising people to put a smile in their voices. It is good advice, since only your voice conveys your image when you are talking on the phone. Your listeners do not have the additional clues usually provided by your facial expressions or gestures. Look at the list of descriptive words below. Which ones would you choose to complete the sentence: "When I talk on the telephone, I give an image of being . . ."

young	helpful	talkative	businesslike
friendly	angry	pleasant	argumentative
efficient	bored	abrupt	impatient
insincere	obnoxious	confused	relaxed
lively	patient	kind	inconsiderate

Think of the image you want to give when you speak on the phone. Then work on creating that image. One way to do this is by looking in a mirror as you talk on the phone. If you look tired, your voice will sound that way. If you look animated, your voice will sound lively. Watch your posture, too. Your best tones will be produced when you are sitting or standing up straight and have a good supply of air to speak with.

To develop an effective telephone voice, you will have to speak clearly and distinctly. It helps if you get in the habit of not holding the mouthpiece more than one-and-one-half inches from your lips. Always try to speak directly into it. You do not have to shout. Just speak in a normal tone of voice. Be sure to speak at a moderate rate, neither too fast nor too slow. Make it a rule never to eat or chew gum when you are speaking on the phone. You simply cannot do these things quietly. Think of what it sounds like when you eat potato chips or celery. Make your voice paint an accurate picture of you by using it skillfully.

Personal Calls

Consider personal telephone calls to be just like conversations with people you know. The same skills are used to make both kinds of conversations successful. Of course, the same faults will ruin the effectiveness of either conversation. You must be especially careful not to talk too long or too much on the telephone. When you are making or answering a personal call, follow the basic telephone courtesies that make these conversations more enjoyable for both participants.

Making Personal Calls

Be courteous by not making personal telephone calls at times when people are probably eating or sleeping. As soon as someone answers the telephone, you should identify yourself. Never expect others to identify you by your voice. The easiest and simplest identification is, "Hello, this is (your name)." Be less formal only when you are calling your immediate family.

If the person you want to talk to does not answer the phone, politely request to speak to that person. You might say "Hello, this is (your name). May I speak to Larry, please?" Should this person not be at home, leave a message. It is a good idea to repeat your name again, unless you know the person who is taking the message. When a machine answers the telephone instead of a person, state your name and the purpose of your call. Leave your number, too, if the person doesn't know it.

When your call does not have a specific purpose except for a lengthy chat with the other person, you should ask

Sit up straight and put a smile in your voice when you speak on the telephone.

immediately if it is convenient for the other person to talk to you. Although many people like long chats, you should always warn people of your intentions, in case they do not have the time or are not interested in a long visit on the telephone. If you ever find that all your calls are taking hours, you can limit the time you spend on the phone by setting a timer and stopping your phone conversations when it rings.

Long-distance calls can be expensive. Imagine that you were calling long-distance to your home to explain one of the problems below. Could you do it in one minute?

1. You lost your traveler's checks and need the numbers.
2. Your luggage was stolen.
3. You missed your flight to New York City.

Answering Personal Calls

The most practical way to answer your home phone is with "Hello." You can make your "Hello" sound warm and friendly by stretching out the *o*. Say, "Hello" and "Hel-loooooooooo." Note the difference. "Hello" is a good way to answer because it does not reveal your identity. The caller should identify himself or herself first. If a caller asks you to identify yourself, you should reply, "Who is calling, please?"

Whatever you do, do not let your children answer the telephone until they are capable of carrying on a conversation. If you do, your callers may find they are reduced to saying such things as, "Is your mommy or daddy there?," and "Could you ask your mommy or daddy to please come to the phone?"

If the person for whom a call is intended is not at home or is unable to come to the phone, you should ask if you can take a message. It is always a good idea to repeat a message to make sure that it is correct. If the caller does not provide sufficient information, ask for facts that you think are important. Do be prepared to take messages at every phone in your home. In most homes, it is practical to have a pen or pencil permanently attached to the phone so that nobody can walk away with it.

If you have a call-waiting service, you should always ask your first caller if he or she minds being put on hold. Don't just say, "I have to answer the other line," and put the person on hold. Many people dislike being put on hold.

You may have a machine that answers the telephone. Your message should tell what number has been reached, explain that no one can answer the phone, and ask the caller to leave a message. When you record your message, smile, so that it will be warm and pleasant. You might want to say, "Hello, you have reached area code (245) 689-2345. I am sorry that no one is able to answer the phone at this time. If you would care to leave a message, please do so after the beep. Thank you."

Business Calls

At times, making a business call is like playing a game. It seems like you are moving across a game board, surmounting obstacle after obstacle to reach your goal. You

Your telephone conversations with businesses should be organized and brief.

find yourself switched from office to office. You may spend five to ten minutes listening to music between conversations. And then there are the times when you are disconnected before you have accomplished your goal. There are telephone techniques that people making and receiving business calls can use to make their calls more efficient. If both parties use these techniques, then business calls can become easier for you to make and more pleasant for you to receive.

Think about your experiences in calling businesses. How often do you practice the following techniques:

	Always	Sometimes	Never
1. Write down what I want to say before making a call, especially names and model numbers.			
2. Identify myself properly before asking to speak to someone.			
3. Leave a message if I cannot speak to somebody.			

If you jot down notes, you will have the facts you need at your fingertips. By identifying yourself, you stop the "Who's calling, please?" questions. Leaving a message lets someone contact you at his or her convenience.

Making Business Calls

So much of people's communication with businesses is now done on the phone. Plan your business calls before you make them. When the phone is answered at a business, give your name and either identify yourself, or state your business, or say to whom you want to speak. Make sure that you give the complete name of the person you are calling because some companies may have hundreds of Dick's and Jane's. Project a businesslike image during your business calls by following these practices:

1. Be brief.
2. Avoid making personal remarks.
3. Don't talk with others while you are speaking on the telephone.

4. Avoid slang and confusing technical language.
5. Get to the point quickly.
6. Stay calm. Don't insult people or argue with them.

Study the following business conversation. Notice how ineffective it was because so many of the above rules were violated.

Secretary: Romer's Plumbing Service.
Caller: Hello. Your so-called plumber was just out here repairing a leak, and now I have a Johnstown flood.
Secretary: Who is calling please?
Caller: An irate customer, Les Stone.
Secretary: Can you tell me what the problem is exactly, Mr. Stone?
Caller: My carpet is sopping wet. Oh, Ida, where did you buy the carpet? O.K., lady, I'm back.
Secretary: Could you be more specific?
Caller: Well, it looks like the plumber did a simply awful job. Are you sure he's really a plumber? The kitchen drainpipe that he put together is just gushing out water.
Secretary: I'll send out a plumber right away, Mr. Stone. In the meantime, I suggest that you shut off the water supply to the house.
Caller: Thanks for nothing.

The plumber might have arrived five minutes sooner if Mr. Stone had identified himself, given his address and phone number, and stated the problem as soon as the secretary answered the phone. When you make a business call, you must do your share to speed up the transaction.

Many businesses have automatic answering services that allow you approximately one minute to leave your message. If you were going on a trip, could you leave proper messages for the following situations within that time? Tape your messages and see.

1. A reservation for the dog at the kennel
2. Stopping the daily and Sunday papers for a week
3. Canceling an appointment at the dentist's

Listen to your recorded messages to make sure that you included all of the facts.

Answering business calls requires politeness, efficiency, and understanding.

Answering Business Calls

Whenever you answer a phone call at work, you are representing your company. You are the first impression that the caller receives of the company. Handling a phone call is not always a simple task. Callers can be rude, touchy, angry, shy, and hostile. No matter what the caller is like, you must remain polite, sympathetic, helpful, understanding, and efficient. You can accomplish these tasks by using the following techniques when you answer business calls:

1. Answer the phone as quickly as possible. Try for the first ring.
2. Identify yourself and the company, or your department, or your boss if you are a secretary. ("Lowell Desk Company, Clyde Andrews.")
3. Know how to operate the telephone system in your business. Transfer calls smoothly.
4. Take messages accurately. Be sure to include names, phone numbers, dates, and time.
5. Close your calls politely. Let the person who called hang up before you do.

Emergency Calls

Your father just passed out. Your daughter fell out of a tree and cannot move. Someone is trying to break into your house. These are emergency situations. An emergency requires immediate help. Follow these steps in making an emergency call:

Dial the Emergency Number.   If the emergency is a life-and-death situation, dial 911 if your community has this emergency number. If not, dial the appropriate number or 0. In non-life-threatening situations, dial the number that is appropriate for the emergency. You will find these numbers in the front of your phone book. You may wish to write them on an index card and post them next to your telephone. When the emergency is a fire in your home, leave your home and dial the emergency call from a nearby telephone.

State the Emergency.   When you dial 911, an operator will come on the line. Tell the operator exactly what the emergency is. The operator will say, "I'm going to connect you with the (police, fire, rescue squad, or ambulance), so stay on the line." When the appropriate agency answers, restate what the emergency is. Then give your address. At this point, the operator will dispatch help. Stay on the line to give more details, and tell your name.

The emergency help will arrive sooner if you give the message calmly and clearly. Take several deep breaths to calm yourself down before making an emergency call. You must manage to tell the nature of the emergency and the address to receive help promptly.

Everyone in your home should know how to make an emergency phone call. Children as young as 2½ years can be taught to dial 0. By 5 years of age, a child will also be able to state the emergency and his or her address.

Other Calls for Help

If you have other serious problems, help is just a phone call away. There are local and national hotlines that provide help 24 hours a day for suicide prevention, poisonings, child abuse, drug problems, and many other problems. If you can't find the number you need, call local or toll-free information.

If you need help, use your telephone to get it immediately. Don't always worry about what you are going to say. The people that answer these lines are trained to gather the information that they need to help you. If you have questions, they will answer them. If you just want to talk, they will talk as long as you like.

Selling by phone is an up-and-coming method of buying and selling goods and services.

Telephone Selling

During the 1970's, the telephone emerged as a powerful sales tool. Salespersons discovered that using the phone would save them time, money, and energy. They began to use it to expand their territories. They found that the telephone put them only a dial away from prospective customers anywhere in the world. They also learned that they could contact a far greater number of customers by telephone than in face-to-face meetings. Even including lunch and coffee breaks, some salespersons found that they could contact more than 100 prospective customers in a day. Today, there are few salespersons who do not use the phone in some way.

Salespersons are currently using the telephone to sell such diverse items as stocks, new carpets, vacation homes, children's books, cemetery plots, aluminum siding, and insurance. What products or services have salespersons tried to sell you over the phone in the last year? No matter what they were, part of the reason you bought or did not buy was probably because of the salesperson's speech. There are two basic requirements that all successful telephone salespersons must meet, whether they are selling cars or light bulbs. They must know how to deliver and how to organize their telephone speeches.

The Delivery

Delivering a sales speech on the telephone is not like delivering any other speech. Telephone salespersons have only one weapon—their voices. To use their voices to their advantage, they must banish all speech faults. Very few successful salespersons have harsh or very high-pitched voices. Few mumble or mispronounce words. Few speak in a monotone. The first rule that telephone salespersons must follow is to speak so that their prospective customers can understand them. This means that they must have sufficient volume so that they can be heard. It also means that they don't have to speak so loudly that they are in danger of breaking eardrums. To ensure that people can understand them, most salespersons have to slow their rate of speed. Then, to add interest to their speech, salespersons need to vary the rate and volume.

Even if telephone salespersons speak perfectly, they will not make many sales unless they can transmit their enthusiasm for their product or service to the customer. Their voice must convey the message that they truly believe in the product or service. What products or services do you use that you could show genuine enthusiasm for?

Successful telephone salespersons come in all sizes and shapes. What they share is a good self-image. They are ready to meet the public. Quite often, the secret of their self-confidence is that they have taken the time to groom themselves for a face-to-face presentation before they dial the first number. When people feel good about how they look, it shows in their voices.

There is one thing that telephone sales speeches and other speeches have in common, and that is the need for preparation. Telephone salespersons start their preparation by learning as much as they can about what they are selling. Not only does this help them to believe in what they are selling, it also prepares them to answer questions and objections. Some major telephone sales operations teach their callers about the product before the callers learn what they are supposed to say.

Once telephone callers are acquainted with what they are selling, they must rehearse what they are going to say. Most companies supply their salespersons with recommended scripts for their conversations. If they are reading from a script, they must mark the words and phrases that they will emphasize and the places where they will pause. Read this paragraph aloud, then reread it aloud two more times. Note how practice helps your delivery. Salespersons can never stop refining their speeches. Yet at the same time, they must be careful not to let their speeches sound canned.

The Organization

You are probably familiar with the organization of telephone sales presentations. The salesperson first tries to capture your attention. Then you are told about the product or service, and finally you are asked to buy. Whether a speech is from a script or created by a salesperson, a sales presentation has these three parts. Each part is equally important because people can hang up at any time.

Opener

Salespersons must capture your attention in the first 30 seconds. After saying hello and identifying themselves, they frequently ask a question like one of these:

1. "Were your cleaning bills over $50 last year?"
2. "Have you ever wanted to own a boat?"
3. "Can you afford to put your children through Harvard University?"
4. "Are you tired of mowing your lawn?"
5. "Do you know what a kiwi is?"

Do any of these questions intrigue you? Would you listen to the rest of the sales presentation after hearing one of them? If you would, the opener was successful.

Information

Once telephone salespersons have their feet in the door with a successful opener, they begin to tell about the product or service. In the typical three- to four-minute presentation, salespersons cannot mention more than four selling points. The best point must be mentioned first, to hold the prospective customer's interest.

Closer

This is where the salesperson asks for the order. Some ask directly for the order. Others ask things like, "Would you like the large size or the economy size?" Successful salespersons consider objections at this point as interest in buying and answer the objections confidently. The unsuccessful salespersons think of objections as refusals to buy, and they lose sales.

Phone-Answering Services

Phone-answering services are available to answer calls for doctors, sales representatives, small businesses, and anyone else who wants their services. They also make wake-up calls and calls to check on the sick or elderly.

Working for a phone-answering service is an interesting job that is never boring. Hysterical mothers of infant children may have to be calmed down so their calls can be relayed to doctors at 2 o'clock in the morning. Plumbers and electricians may have to be contacted for emergency services. The hardest task is to convince callers to leave messages instead of making repeated calls to the answering service, asking for a certain business or individual. Apparently, many people do not understand the function of an answering service.

Everyone Uses Telephones

Making phone calls is a favorite pastime of people from teen-agers to U.S. Presidents. Many people have been surprised to receive a call from Ronald Reagan to learn what their views are. It is his favorite way to keep in touch with what people are thinking. People who have spoken to him describe his telephone manner as one that quickly puts them at ease.

If you think that you are not using the phone much in your home, keep a log of the calls you make and receive in a day. You will probably be surprised by the amount of time that is spent on the phone in your home as well as the variety of the calls. It seems like people can use the phone today to do just about anything. In Cincinnati, Ohio, people who have received speeding tickets and want to plead innocent just pick up the phone and call the court and say, "not guilty." A time for their trial is then set up over the phone.

The telephone is here to stay as a communication tool. Each day, new uses for the telephone seem to appear. The telephone has become an essential tool for communication in today's world. Few households do not have telephones. Most businesses have telephones. There is some evidence to show that you can solve complex problems and process information just as effectively on the telephone as you can in person. In fact, for some types of business negotiations, telephone communication has been shown to be more effective than face-to-face communication.

Index